Following
the Drum

Following the Drum

Women at the Valley Forge Encampment

Sunny wishes from Valley Forge!
Nancy K. Loane

Nancy K. Loane

POTOMAC BOOKS, INC.
WASHINGTON, D.C.

Library of Congress Cataloging-in-Publication Data
Loane, Nancy K., 1943–
  Following the drum : women at the Valley Forge encampment / Nancy K. Loane.
  — 1st ed.
      p. cm.
  Includes bibliographical references and index.
  ISBN 978-1-59797-385-4 (alk. paper)
  1. Valley Forge (Pa.)—History—18th century. 2. Washington, George, 1732–1799—
Headquarters—Pennsylvania—Valley Forge. 3. United States—History—Revolution,
1775–1783—Women. 4. United States—History—Revolution, 1775–1783—
Participation, Female. 5. Women—Pennsylvania—Valley Forge—History—18th
century. 6. Women—Pennsylvania—Valley Forge—Biography. 7. Women—United
States—Biography. I. Title.
  E234.L63 2008
  973.3'341082—dc22

                                                                        2008044817

Printed in the United States of America on acid-free paper that meets the American
National Standards Institute Z39-48 Standard.

Potomac Books, Inc.
22841 Quicksilver Drive
Dulles, Virginia 20166

First Edition

10 9 8 7 6 5 4 3 2

"A Tribute to Mom"
Where are the ribbons, the statues, the steeds,
Proclaiming that she has lived?
That beauty—named woman—once
Walked this earth, expressing
Goodness in all that she did?
With a passion for justice,
And love as our song,
Let us rise in a tribute.
Let the shadows be gone.
Bev Feldman

Contents

Preface

I have answered many visitor questions over the past decade in my work as a seasonal ranger and costumed interpretive volunteer at Valley Forge National Historical Park.

"Is this where Washington crossed the river?" is a popular query. (The short answer is no.) "Where is the battleground?" is often asked. (There was no battle; Valley Forge was a six-month encampment.) Some visitors mistakenly think that the battle of Gettysburg came immediately after the 1777–78 winter of Valley Forge. Others—those more savvy and historically aware—quickly remove their caps before stepping respectfully over the threshold of Washington's Headquarters, General and Mrs. George Washington's home for much of the Valley Forge period.

Our visitors all have a vague idea of what happened at Valley Forge. Most speak in hushed tones of hutted soldiers, tattered uniforms, scanty rations, and disease. Some even know of the great Valley Forge successes—of Baron von Steuben's new training manual and superb organizational skills, of Gen. Nathanael Greene's achievements with the quartermaster's department, of the soldiers' perseverance and grit and determination, of General Washington's achievement in keeping the army together.

But who speaks about the hundreds of women who came to camp?

Or the ladies?

Or the women who traveled during the Revolution with Washington's military family?

This part of the Valley Forge story has never been told. And so it has been, for me, both an obligation and a privilege to research and write *Following the Drum: Women at the Valley Forge Encampment*.

I am grateful for the help I have received along the way.

Joseph Lee Boyle, retired historian at Valley Forge National Historical Park, piled books and folders and manuscripts before me at the Horace Willcox Memorial Library and even now responds to my many questions. The staff and administration of Valley Forge National Historical Park, especially Dona McDermott, archivist, and Barbara Pollarine, assistant superintendent, have been exceedingly generous. Janice McDermott, Cindy Neel, Steve Rector, Ajena Rogers, Kimberly Szewczyk, and the other interpretive rangers have been helpful and encouraging.

I am indebted to Maria Roberts, who judiciously and kindly read every word of the manuscript, and to the Meeting House Writers, who got me started. And a big "huzzah!" to Kathy King, Mike Bertram, Patty Torres, Terral Johnston, and Sandy Momyer.

Both John Nagy and John U. Rees offered their guidance and thoughtfully shared their knowledge of history.

I am thankful to those who gave permission to use material in the book: the University of Georgia Press, the University of North Carolina Press, the University of South Carolina Press, the Pierpont Morgan Library, the Mount Vernon Ladies' Association of the Union, Eastern National, Morristown National Historical Park, Valley Forge National Historical Park, Joseph Lee Boyle, John U. Rees, the Chester County Historical Society, the Historical Society of Montgomery County, the Phoenixville Area Historical Society, and Bev Feldman.

Sincere thanks to those who gave permission for use of the illustrations in *Following the Drum*: Vassar College; Independence National Historical Park; C. Herbert Fry; Valley Forge National Historical Park; the French and Pickering Creeks Conservation Trust; Laura Kostyk; Telfair Museum of Art of Savannah, Georgia; the Massachusetts Historical Society; and Michael J. Ticcino.

Potomac Books, Inc., has been wonderful, and Elizabeth Demers, senior editor, and Julie Kimmel, production editor, especially so.

Throughout this long adventure, I have been emboldened by friends, our sons J. B. and Brad and their wives, and my two sisters, Bev Feldman and Marj Babiak and their families.

Special gratitude goes to Tom, my husband, who has been beside me, every step of the way.

NANCY K. LOANE
VALLEY FORGE, PA

1

Setting the Stage

The War, Army, and Community

The arrival of Gen. George Washington's troops on Friday, December 19, 1777, quickly transformed a bucolic southeastern Pennsylvania farming region into a sprawling, noisy, smelly hut city. For the ensuing six months of the Valley Forge encampment, Elizabeth Stephens, along with her family and other farm neighbors, were bombarded with the sight, sounds, and stench of thousands of Continental Army soldiers, officers, camp women, horses, and livestock. This was not the first time Elizabeth Stephens's life had been disrupted by an army camped in the neighborhood. Just three months earlier, British and Hessian troops had raided and burned the forge in the valley (the Valley Forge), destroyed other nearby buildings, camped on the surrounding lands, and then played cat and mouse with Washington's troops. The Redcoats eventually outsmarted Washington, crossed the Schuylkill River at Fatland Ford, fought the rebel American army at Germantown, and marched victorious into Philadelphia. The British Army occupied that city for nine months, and then, after an engagement with Washington's army at Monmouth, moved on to New York. Peace was not declared until five years later.

Gen. George Washington had faced down years of frustration to reach the winter of 1777–78, the third encampment of the American Revolution. The war was not universally popular in the self-proclaimed United States of America. About one-third of the population of almost three million was for independence. These were the Patriots or Whigs—or rebels, as the British called them. About one-third of the population—the Loyalists, or Tories—remained true to the British crown. The remaining one-third of the populace was neutral or vacillated between supporting the British and supporting the Americans—depending, perhaps, on which army was currently camped out on their lands. Some families in the Valley Forge area supported Washington. Others remained loyal to the king.

The divisiveness of the American populace dismayed Gen. Louis Le Beque de Presle Duportail, who had come from France to serve in the Continental Army as chief engineer. "There is a hundred times more enthusiasm for this revolution in a single café in Paris," Duportail wrote, "than in all the united colonies."[1] No doubt a despairing General Washington sometimes shared Duportail's frustration.

The American Revolution as most know it began on April 19, 1775, with the firing of a "shot heard around the world." At the time, not everyone agreed on the goals of the confrontation. Some Americans fought for freedom from taxes or for respect from the British. Others would accept nothing less than independence. Officially, the Revolution began when the Second Continental Congress formally adopted the Declaration of Independence in Philadelphia on July 4, 1776. (Most signed the document on August 2, 1776.) Both the British and the Americans had anticipated a quick resolution of the conflict, but the war dragged on for years.

Although the British Army under Gen. Charles Cornwallis surrendered to American forces at Yorktown, Virginia, on Friday, October 19, 1781, sporadic fighting continued, especially in the south. The Treaty of Paris was signed on Wednesday, September 3, 1783. But ships sailed at the whim of seas and winds, so it took some time for any document, no matter how important, to reach America. It was not until Tuesday, December 23, 1783, that Washington resigned his commission and, finally, turned toward home. The warrior arrived at Mount Vernon on Christmas Eve.

Once the American Revolution began, tranquil American farms, such as the Stephenses' and the other twenty or so other farms in the Valley Forge area, became campgrounds and battlefields, studded with hundreds, even thousands, of British Redcoats, Hessian troops, American soldiers, and state militia. Once-thriving, now-occupied American cities became fetid stinkpots. Philadelphia, the most sophisticated, populated city on the continent, had a population of just under thirty thousand before the British took over in September 1777 and claimed it as their winter quarters.[2] At Valley Forge, the Continental Army quickly constructed housing and an infrastructure for about fourteen thousand soldiers, about half the population of the largest city in the land. Suddenly, dramatically, with Washington's army in residence, the quiet Valley Forge area exploded into one of the largest cities on the continent.

Washington had chosen the Valley Forge site because it was only about eighteen miles from the British in Philadelphia and was strategically located between the enemy and Congress, which had fled from Philadelphia to York, Pennsylvania. To support the troops at the 1777–78 encampment, trees were felled for miles around, huts constructed, "vault" trenches dug (where the soldiers relieved themselves), camp hospitals built, cooking facilities established, and fortifications thrown up. And this gargantuan effort had to be completed quickly. Winter had arrived. Although the camp fortifications were never finished, within a month soldiers were hutted and senior officers had moved into neighboring homes. An enormous task had been completed quickly and well. "This Log-City," declared Ebenezer Crosby, an army surgeon, "part of which is as regular as Philadelphia, affords much better quarters than you would imagine, if you consider the materials, season, & hurry with which it was built."[3] "We have got our Huts to be very comfortable," Surgeon Albigence Waldo wrote on January 6, "and feel ourselves happy in them."[4] "Our men have got all comfortably covered in their Huts," Tench Tilghman, one of Washington's aides, wrote from Valley Forge on January 18, 1778, "and better quarters are not in the World, I mean as to warmth and I believe will turn out so as to health."[5]

But Washington's army overwhelmed the Stephens family, as it did the region's other farm families. It was impossible to escape the soldiers' demanding presence. While small boys may have delighted in watching the soldiers' maneuvers and teenage girls perhaps strained to glimpse the officers in their uniforms, the farmers despaired of the army tramping over fields, ripping down fences, and, sometimes, snatching up livestock and food. As for Elizabeth Stephens and the other local women, they gaped in astonishment at the hundreds of unkempt women and children who traveled with the army. And sometimes they marveled when catching a glimpse of the fine ladies who came to camp.

Perhaps Elizabeth Stephens watched the four hundred or so women with the army trudge into camp with the baggage on December 19, 1777.[6] Some of these destitute army women were "on the strength," which means that, in exchange for working as a seamstress, laundress, cook, or nurse, the army provided the women with food, shelter, and sometimes cash and clothing. Many, perhaps most, of them were married to the soldiers. Some women had children with them. The most famous camp woman of the American Revolution, Mary Hays—known today as Molly Pitcher—

followed her husband to the Valley Forge winter encampment. Some women at Valley Forge were common whores, and this group, in spite of Washington's orders, had become "numerous" by spring. Washington did not think much of the women with the army; he once commanded every woman to leave camp, no matter what her contribution or marital state. And his orders of August 4, 1777, thundered, "The multitude of women in particular, especially those who are pregnant or have children, are a clog upon every movement."[7]

General Washington's unfavorable attitude toward the common camp women did not extend to all women at the Valley Forge encampment. Throughout the Revolution, Washington traveled with a "military family" comprising gentlemen who faithfully served as his secretaries, aides-de-camp, and officers of his guard. Washington's household help—including cooks, a laundress, a housekeeper—traveled *with* this military family, although they were not included *in* it. Although the women with this select family were also poor and of the "common sort" (that is, lower class), they had more status than other camp women. After all, they directly served the commander in chief. Washington depended on the assistance of the women with his military family; indeed, he needed them. The general even declared himself to be "entirely destitute, & put to much inconvenience" when his housekeeper abruptly left.[8]

The general also regarded with favor the "ladies" at camp, and especially the lady whom he addressed as "My dearest," Martha Washington. Unlike many other women with the army, Martha traveled only to the winter encampments. Martha Washington, Catharine Greene, Lucy Knox, Rebekah Biddle, Alice Shippen, and Lady Stirling, all wives of officers, all came to camp to share the Valley Forge winter with their husbands. In class-conscious eighteenth-century America, these women were referred to as "ladies." Firmly entrenched in America's upper class, the ladies had worn stays since they were babies and had been drilled since childhood in the finer points of etiquette. The ladies had not traveled to Valley Forge to earn money for themselves and their families, as many of the common camp women did. Some also came to camp because it offered them a safe haven. Others braved the winter roads to demonstrate support for their husbands and the cause of freedom. Some came for their own pleasure, for, surprisingly, the Valley Forge encampment had some bright spots. At camp the officers staged theater productions, "elegant" dinners were served at headquarters, and there was at least one artist present. All this meant that the winter of 1777–78 could be a lively and entertaining place for a lady.

Elizabeth Stephens was not a lady. She, like the other farm wives in the area, did not share in camp frivolity. She did, however, experience the staggering impact that the encampment had on the Valley Forge area. When the Continental Army marched in, the rural community around Valley Forge segued, literally overnight, into an international metropolis. Officers from at least ten countries presented themselves at camp. Soldiers from each of the thirteen self-proclaimed states were there. Camp activity focused on the Isaac Potts House, just down the road from the Stephenses' farmhouse. (Both houses are open to visitors today.) The Potts House became the Continental Army's headquarters, home to Washington's military family, and the residence of the general himself. For four months, it was also the residence of Washington's wife.

For the private soldier, the Valley Forge winter was another bleak and dreary encampment, yet another period of deprivation and misery. While at Valley Forge, Washington wrote repeatedly to Congress and to the would-be independent states, imploring them for assistance. The situation at camp was so dire four days after arriving at Valley Forge that Washington was convinced "beyond a doubt" that "unless some great and capital change suddenly takes place . . . this Army must inevitably be reduced to one or other of these three things: Starve, dissolve, or disperse."[9] Two days later, on Christmas, Maj. Gen. Johann de Kalb observed, "It is certain that half the army are half naked, and almost the whole army go barefoot."[10] In February, Alexander Scammell, the adjutant general, found it a "most melancholy scene" to see "Men destitute of Clothing, who had risked their Lives like brave fellows, having large Arrearages of pay due to them and prodigiously pinched at times for provisions."[11] Fortunately, camp conditions improved in the spring.

Elizabeth Stephens's family, like the other families in the area, did not need to read these letters to know the army was desperate for food and clothing. One look from any farmhouse window revealed the poorly clad, hungry army camped in the fields. A knock on the door could mean the army's foraging detail, which traveled as far as New Jersey and Delaware, had come to call. Because the hungry soldiers threatened the very existence of those in the area, some families hid their livestock and food from army soldiers searching for sustenance. But foraging was imperative; the army was hungry. Ravenous camp soldiers chanted, "No meat, no soldier" more than once during the winter of 1777–78.

At least one soldier, however, recalled that he "fared much better than I had ever done in the army before, or ever did afterwards" during the months of the Valley Forge encampment. Pvt. Joseph Plumb Martin, who had drawn foraging detail miles away from camp, remembered eating "very good provisions" that Valley Forge winter and "generally enough of them."[12] Martin also found "the inhabitants [of Pennsylvania] were remarkably kind to us. . . . [We could] take what we would from their barns, mills, corncribs, or stalls." The stables, however, were a different matter. The women, Martin wrote, wanted the "ponies" left in the barn so they could attend church.[13] Or so they told him.

Hundreds of soldiers' huts sprouted from the fields of the Stephenses' farm and the other twenty or so farms located within the Valley Forge encampment area. The Continental Army also planted fortifications (redoubts and redans, designed by the French engineers who had been recruited by Benjamin Franklin) on the acreage.[14] Under the direction of Baron Friedrich Wilhelm Augustus von Steuben, who had also been recruited by Franklin in Paris, soldiers executed military drills in corn and wheat fields. Because the army was camped on the fields, winter and spring planting was impossible that year; this brought on more economic hardship for the farm families.

While the soldiers camped in the farmers' fields, some officers stayed in the farmers' houses. During the Revolutionary War it was common practice for the officers and military families of both armies, when on campaign or during an encampment, to move in with a local family. Farm wives who had hosted the British officers in September now "welcomed" the Continental Army officers to their homes. Washington ordered his officers to give the farmers rent money—or at least to promise it.

Elizabeth and David Stephens and their family hosted Gen. James Varnum, who commanded two regiments of Rhode Island and two regiments of Connecticut soldiers, until Varnum's hut was completed in mid-April. Varnum was not an easy guest; Thomas Rodney wrote of him in 1781, "General Varnum of Rhode Island is a man of about thirty, of florid habit; he has read some little in books, is fond of Speaking and Spouting out every thing that his reading has furnished him with whether apt or not to the purpose."[15] True to form, on February 12, 1778, about two months after the army settled into Valley Forge, Varnum, noting that "Duty obliges me to speak without Reserve," offered his opinion that the Valley Forge encampment site was unacceptable and the army should immediately leave camp and remove to "places where they can be supplied."[16] Instead the army stayed put.

General Varnum did not find Elizabeth and David Stephens's home a happy one. Elizabeth Evans had married David Stephens about 1747. The bride was a Baptist; the groom a Quaker. In 1758 David was read out of meeting (that is, the Quaker congregation) because he was "married to a woman of a different persuasion . . . and since had become a frequenter of taverns and places of diversion . . . too often overcome with strong liquors and refuses to make any acknowledgement."[17] A 1761 codicil to the will of Eleanor Evans, Elizabeth Stephens's mother, states, "David taketh no care for her [Elizabeth Stephens] support." Eleanor Evans's will further directed that, upon her death, Eleanor's personal goods were to be sold and all proceeds given to her daughter, Elizabeth.[18]

In spite of marital problems, there is no evidence that David and Elizabeth Stephens divorced. They had three children. Although daughter Eleanor had probably already married and moved away, both Abijah and Maurice, their sons, seem to have been at home during the winter of 1777. The Stephenses' farmhouse would have been crowded and uncomfortable with their military guests.

Varnum and his staff of six probably lived in the two rooms that composed the second floor of the Stephenses' thirty-three-by-twenty-two-foot stone house. It is likely that Elizabeth and David Stephens and the two children were crammed into a small first-floor room of the farmhouse. Besides the house, the Stephens family's modest property included two horses, two cows, a small wood shed for the animals, a smoke house, and a privy.

General Varnum was, of course, not the only officer at Valley Forge to live with a local family. Both Gen. Nathanael Greene and Gen. Clement Biddle, and their wives, resided at Moore Hall. Lord and Lady Stirling, along with their daughter and niece, lived with Rev. William Currie and his family in a house near the Valley Creek. It appears that the Marquis de Lafayette lived with the John Havard family, and Gen. Anthony Wayne stayed with his Quaker cousin, Sarah Walker, in a farmhouse near the encampment. Col. Israel Shreve spent some time at the widow Davis's home and in late January moved to "John Rolands Mill about three miles up the Valley from the forge" to live in a "Good house" with a "Credible

Family."[19] While at Valley Forge, it is said that Capt. Merryman Green of the American Cavalry Unit found the Pritchard family so agreeable that he married Ann, one of the Pritchard daughters, on April 30. An army chaplain, Rev. William Rogers, performed the ceremony.[20]

Lt. Col. William Butler and Lt. John Marshall of the Pennsylvania line stayed at the home of Anne Jones. In January 1778 Butler left an army receipt book in one of the unlocked rooms of Mrs. Jones's home. According to the account, her small son entered the room, snatched up the book, and threw it into the fire. The maid "pulled the Book out of the Fire before it was consumed," but not before, Mrs. Jones wrote, "the greatest Part of the Book [was] Consumed."[21] The army did not learn about this incident until about a year later, in March 1779, when Anne Jones wrote a "To Whom It May Concern" letter on Lieutenant Colonel Butler's behalf, possibly because he was attempting to reconcile his account books.

Although the Continental soldiers occupied the fields and lived in the area homes, the army was not a good neighbor to those who lived near the military camp. On May 27, 1778, James Barry, whose family was obviously much better off than the Stephens household, was robbed of Continental money and hard dollars, a diamond ring, silver spoons, buckles, gold buttons, a sword, and "valuable men's & women's wearing apparel," among other things. It was thought that the thieves belonged to the army, and all officers were implored to make the "strictest enquiry" of their men so that the "villains may be brought to justice." A sizable reward of fifty dollars was offered for bringing the culprits to justice.[22]

Other local families also suffered losses. After the war ended, the estate of William Moore of Moore Hall filed an extensive list of items "lost from American Army." Included are a "handsome new gate with hinges, a fine cow, a doz. Knives & 1 doz. Forks, 2000 oak shingles, a handsome roasting Jack destroyed, large Copper Dutch oven"—the list goes on for three pages. Although several American officers and their wives and the visiting Committee of Congress had all lived with the Moore family at various times during the encampment, their presence did not provide the Moore family immunity from army molestation. William Moore, a vocal Loyalist, was considered a fair target.

Moore Hall, however, had also been a target for the British Army when they occupied the region during the autumn of 1777. Although William Moore supported King George III, the British Army's "forage master came out constantly" for hay. British horses grazed on the Moore's meadows, "destroying the crops that were uncut." Thirty-six acres of corn were pulled up or destroyed. Straw was taken from the barn to make beds for the soldiers. A "stock of Swine" was driven off, "numbers of poultry" destroyed, "fifty Turkeys" taken, "a field of potatoes" eaten by the soldiers. Irate, Moore's estate filed for restitution from both the Americans and the British.[23] There is no record, however, that the family received any compensation for the losses.

Rowland Evans had nearly six hundred bushels of grain taken from his farm "Between the two Armies"; he was unable to pay his rent that year.[24] The Continental soldiers "ruin the Country for miles around wherever we lay," observed Ebenezer David, a chaplain from Rhode Island, on December 22. David had also traveled to nearby Germantown to find that, after the British left, "The ruins of furniture, & Rooms knee deep with feathers from beds was truly affecting." And there was no cow, horse, or sheep to be seen for miles.[25] As Gen. Jedediah Huntington wrote to his father from Valley Forge, "An Army, even a friendly one, if any can be called so, are a dreadful scourge to any People—you cannot conceive what Devastation and Distress mark their Steps."[26]

When the British soldiers came through the Valley Forge area in September 1777, they had destroyed not only William Dewees's forge (the Valley Forge) but also his sawmill, two large stone dwelling houses, a large frame store, and a stone iron house. They also wrecked or carted away from Dewees four feather beds and bedding curtains, two large looking glasses, kitchen furniture, one large silver tankard, and two cream pots. Two cows and forty-four sheep were taken. In the fields, 2,200 bushels of wheat and rye were destroyed. It is not surprising that William Dewees, who had begged the Americans not to store supplies in his buildings, lamented that he had been "nearly ruined by the Enemy." When the Continental Army marched in, Dewees speculated that "the ruins of his buildings are likely to be destroyed by this army."[27]

The William Currie household lost to the British all their cabbages, bacon, cheese, butter, and "a bushel of fine salt," as well as such items as "fine sheets Table linen fine Shirts Shifts headdresses Stockings & a Table Silverspoon." The Curries were also stripped of a cart, wagon, saddles, ropes, and two hundred pounds of Continental money.[28] "An Estimate of Damages Sustained by the British Army," signed by Mary Howel, listed the following losses: one hogshead of whiskey; one hogshead of rum; twenty gallons of gin; thirty-six sheep; one black horse; one hundred bushels of

Indian Corn; butter, cheese, and kitchen furniture; and six thousand rails of fence.[29] Hoping to receive reimbursement, John Havard enumerated an inventory of goods forcefully taken by the British Army in September 1777. His losses, too, were numerous, and included a horse, cow, and bull; six sheep and two pigs; four geese and one turkey; money, eight gowns, silver, fine sheets, coats, jackets, and hats; ten knives, nine forks, and six spoons; wheat, rye, oats, and hay; four hives filled with honey; and sixty heads of cabbage.[30]

Nevertheless, despite suffering losses, deprivation, and the undisciplined Continental Army's soldiers, it seems that the neighborhood women faithfully carried food and clothing to the encampment.[31] Elizabeth Stephens herself, according to local stories, took food and clothing to camp. A Mrs. Henry was one of several women who brought fresh strawberries to headquarters. Elizabeth Ramsay allegedly knitted socks for the soldiers. Mary Worrell Knight, family stories relate, both knitted for the soldiers and brought them food. It is said that two sisters, Martha and Mary Williams, of Charlestown, Chester County, whose father, grandfather, and three brothers served in the Pennsylvania militia, took food and clothing to the soldiers. So did Sarah Walker, Priscilla Stephens, Margaret Beaver (or Beiber), Rosina Kucher Orth, and Elizabeth and Jane Moore.

As generous and well meaning as these local women may have been, however, their offerings were only a symbolic gesture. Realistically their gifts did nothing to alleviate the army's burden. Thousands upon thousands of soldiers and officers, and hundreds of women and children with the army, needed food and supplies day after day, for six months. Several pints of local strawberries, while delicious, were nothing but a proverbial drop in the army's provisions bucket.

There were occasions during the encampment, however, when incidents of a different nature interrupted the misery at Valley Forge. On Thursday, February 5, 1778, Elizabeth Stephens was undoubtedly surprised at the curious sight of a handsome coach, drawn by fine horses and accompanied by a military escort, swaying from side to side as it lumbered along the rutted road. The coach turned toward the stone house that served as headquarters for the Continental Army's commander in chief. The coach stopped by the front door. A short lady, rather plump—eagerly awaited—stepped out.

Lady Martha Washington had arrived for her annual visit. Her burdened husband rejoiced.

2

Martha Washington at Valley Forge

"The Worthy Partner of the Worthiest of Men"

MARTHA WASHINGTON, JUNE 2, 1731–MAY 22, 1802

Martha Washington bounced along for ten days in a dignified, though uncomfortable, carriage to reach her husband at Valley Forge, the third of the eight winter encampments of the American Revolution.

The general's wife had left her Virginia home on Monday, January 26, 1778, with a heavy heart, for Anna Maria "Nancy" Bassett, Martha's sister and "greatest favorite . . . in the world," had died only about a month before.[1] The oldest of eight children, Martha was close to her brothers and sisters, and that autumn of 1777 she had cared for Nancy's two sons at Mount Vernon while they underwent inoculation for smallpox. The "exceedingly good Boys indeed," as their doting aunt described them, had the pox "exceedingly light." After paying the doctor's bill (which Martha thought "very high but I did not say a word—as he carried the children so well though the smallpox"), she sent her nephews home to Eltham.[2] Martha herself had been inoculated against smallpox two years earlier. Her husband would not have permitted her to come to army camp unless she had done so.

Washington had sent for his wife to come to Valley Forge sometime after January 6, for on that date Marie Joseph Paul Yves Roch Gilbert du Motier, the Marquis de Lafayette, wrote from Valley Forge, "General Washington has resolved to send for his wife." Washington was among "several staff officers," Lafayette wrote, who "are having their wives join them at camp." The Marquis found himself "very envious," he confessed to his own teenage wife in France, "not of their wives, but of the happiness that this propinquity brings" the officers.[3]

11

Martha herself was uncertain of her arrival date at Valley Forge. She wrote to Mercy Otis Warren, an intellectual who corresponded with many patriot leaders and published letters, pamphlets, and satirical plays in support of the Revolution, that she "came to this place about the first of February."[4] Gen. Nathanael Greene, however, declared that Mrs. Washington's carriage and entourage arrived at headquarters on Thursday, February 5, in the evening.[5] Two days later, on February 7, Gen. James Varnum wrote that "Lady Washington has Just come in to Camp."[6] On February 10 Washington wrote that his wife had joined him at headquarters. When she did finally reach her husband at Valley Forge, Martha was relieved to find her general to be "very well."[7]

Washington's request for his wife to join him at Valley Forge was not unusual. It was his practice during the Revolution, after settling in at one after another of the eight encampments, to write for her to come to camp. And every year after receiving the request, Martha Washington—although she delighted in being at Mount Vernon with her large extended family and was lonely and anxious when away from Virginia—dutifully packed up her bags, boarded the carriage, and started north. She had never traveled far from home before the Revolution began, but this determined woman covered hundreds of miles during the hostilities to reach her husband. Military affairs kept George Washington away from Mount Vernon for all but about two months of the American Revolution. Lady Washington was away from Mount Vernon for—incredibly, in view of her attachment to home—nearly five years of the eight-and-a-half-year war. Once George Washington accepted the position of commander in chief of the Continental Army, the lady who loved hearth and home frequently left both to join her husband at military camps in Massachusetts, New York, New Jersey, or Pennsylvania.[8]

Although accompanied by servants or slaves, a scarlet-and-white-clad postilion (the rider on the left horse of the leading pair when drawing a carriage), a military escort for at least part of the way, and always a friend and family member or two, Martha Washington found her journeys north long, tedious, cold, uncomfortable, and dangerous. General Washington was ever solicitous and did whatever he could from camp to make his wife's travels easy. But America's eighteenth-century roads consisted mostly of ruts, punctuated by potholes. Rivers and streams had to be forged, somehow. Martha often traveled in snowy, icy weather, on treacherous roadways. Acclamation and festivities greeted Lady Washington as she traveled through the cities and towns, but she still encountered vast stretches of loneliness. And she was not a young woman. Martha Washington celebrated her forty-seventh birthday at Valley Forge. (George Washington celebrated his forty-sixth.)

George Washington Parke Custis, Martha Washington's grandson, wrote about fifty years after the hostilities ended that his grandmother had said "that it had been her fortune to hear the first cannon at the opening, and the last at the closing, of all the campaigns of the Revolutionary war."[9] This statement cannot be taken literally. Although she dutifully supported the Revolution by traveling to all eight winter encampments, Martha was far from the artillery at both the beginning and end of the hostilities. Martha's own letters spell out what her grandson could not say: she did not relish traveling to camp. In a December 22, 1777, letter written before she left for Valley Forge, Martha wrote from Mount Vernon that "the General" would be unable to come home that winter, "but as soon as the army under his command goes into winter quarter he will send for me." Then these plaintive words: "If he does I must go."[10] As she had expected, the general's invitation arrived from Pennsylvania soon after she penned this letter, and on Monday, January 26, 1778, Martha and her entourage left her Virginia home for Valley Forge.

Washington had sent Col. Richard Kidder Meade, an aide-de-camp, to escort Martha on the last leg of her trip into camp. Colonel Meade spent two days and twenty dollars (for beer, suppers, breakfasts, dinners, horses, lodging, and servants) waiting at the Susquehanna ferry dock for his charge.[11] To prepare for Martha's visit, Washington had his private baggage, including bed, plates, and dishes, brought forward from New-town, Pennsylvania, where it had been stored during the campaign.

Headquarters at Valley Forge was the small stone Isaac Potts House, located by the confluence of the Valley Creek and the Schuylkill River. The house had two rooms downstairs, three up, and a detached kitchen, as well as a full basement and an attic. When she arrived, Martha found the house crammed with her husband's military family and the servants who supported Washington and this family. It made for tight quarters, indeed. General Washington, in fact, described the Valley Forge encampment as a "dreary kind of a place, and uncomfortably provided."[12] Martha was similarly uncomplimentary about her temporary winter home; she wrote that she and the general lived in a "very small" apartment."[13]

But all this really mattered little, for at Valley Forge Martha was again with the general, and that's what she really cared about.

LIFE AT VALLEY FORGE

Martha came to camp to be a comfort to her husband, the commander in chief of the Continental Army. General Washington, a serious, determined, focused warrior, needed her to ease his mind. And she delighted in being with him. The Washingtons' marriage lasted almost forty years, and the couple doted on each other. Based on what others wrote in the eighteenth century, at Valley Forge Martha slipped into her familiar, comfortable roles of running the household, acting as hostess, socializing with the ladies and officers, and participating in ceremonial functions. There is nothing from those with her at camp, however, indicating that Martha informally visited among the soldiers at camp, or even that she patched and knit for the men. (The appendix, titled "Making the Myth of Martha Washington," traces the development of today's commonly held, though erroneous, notion of Martha Washington visiting among the private soldiers at Valley Forge.)

Martha had been thoroughly trained by her mother, Frances Dandridge, to be a capable and efficient household manager. Like other girls in the middle and upper tier of Virginia plantation families, she also received instruction in needlework, art, music, and dancing. (Martha's erratic spelling patterns, however, testify that proper spelling was never stressed.) On May 15, 1750, when she was almost nineteen, Martha Dandridge married Daniel Parke Custis. She married very well, for Custis's family, among the elite of Virginia planters, owned about eighteen thousand acres and hundreds of slaves. Custis was also twenty years older than Martha—but this was not unusual for the times.

When Custis died—suddenly, on July 5, 1757, without a will—Martha and the two surviving Custis children, Martha "Patcy" Parke Custis and John "Jacky" Parke Custis, each inherited a third of the vast Custis estate, as the law of the times required. (Martha and Daniel had had four children, but their first two died young.) With the death of her husband, it also became Martha's responsibility to direct the slaves, lands, and "the Administration of his Estate & management of his Affairs of all sorts." As Martha felt the estate would be kept together "for some time" and thought it "proper to continue his Account in the same manner as if he was living," the widow Custis continued to do business with the London factors (purchasing agents) her husband had used.[14] (Wealthy American families of the time procured every imaginable item from England, as it was thought European goods were superior to those made in America. London factors, or agents, facilitated the purchase and shipping of the goods.) Martha Custis's letters to her London factors, including Robert Cary and Company and John Hanbury and Company, concerned both procurement of necessities and sales of the plantation's crops. They also demonstrate Martha's assertiveness, determination, and abundance of common sense—all qualities that would be useful to her throughout the long Revolutionary War.

A 1758 letter to the London firm of Robert Cary and Company, for example, requests "One Genteel suite of cloths for my self to be grave but not Extravagent [sic] nor to be mourning." She also sent a nightgown to be dyed a "fashanable couler fitt [sic] for me to ware [wear]." Martha had not been happy with the way her nightgown had been dyed the previous year—it was "very badly done"—and wrote Robert Cary and Company to do better with this one. Her letter goes on to list page after page of items she considered necessary for the children and herself. The words "fine," "best," "handsome," and "very handsome" appear often on her list.[15] Martha Custis was, after all, a very wealthy woman.

But because she was also responsible for a vast plantation, Mrs. Custis had to be mindful of more than clothes, perfumed powder, nightgowns, and "pickles of all sorts." Martha wrote several times to the London factors about the prices she wanted for her tobacco crop, again demonstrating her common sense and assertiveness. In August 1757 she wrote her tobacco was "extremely good" and wanted it sold at a "good Price."[16] On December 20, 1757, the plantation shipped "very good" tobacco to London; this would also, Martha hoped, be sold for "a good Price."[17] Tobacco shipped from the Custis farms in June 1758 was considered "very fine," and for this Martha wanted "an uncommon Price," especially since tobacco had now become, Martha felt, "very scarce."[18]

According to the laws of the day, after the widow Custis married George Washington (on January 6, 1759), her one-third portion of the Custis fortune now belonged to him. Colonel Washington married very well, for his wife's wealth and connections propelled him to the highest tier of Virginia landed gentry. After the marriage, Washington also acted as the custodian and loving guardian of Martha's children, Patcy (then three) and Jacky (five), and scrupulously managed the children's financial affairs. As Mrs. Washington, Martha moved to her new husband's home, Mount Vernon, and gave careful attention to that growing, vibrant plantation, just as she had to White House, the Custis plantation. And, although they were hundreds of miles away from home during the American Revolution, the hearts of both George and Martha Washington remained at Mount Vernon throughout the war. General Washington, while commanding his troops during the Revolution, sent Lund Washington, the manager of his plantation, a steady stream of detailed instructions for enlarging the mansion house during the war. Martha Washington inquired after the servants, slaves, and family members when away from Virginia.

As Mrs. Washington was a hands-on household manager at Mount Vernon, undoubtedly she also directed the households when she was present at the various encampment headquarters. In fact, soon after she arrived at Valley Forge, Patrick McGuire, the household steward who was responsible for the male servants, was fired. He was not replaced while Mrs. Washington remained in camp. Food purchased for "his Excellency and the General officers" at Valley Forge required Martha Washington's proverbial stamp of approval, too. In early March 1778 an urgent appeal went out from headquarters for "a few good Gammons" (smoked or cured hams). They were to be procured "as cheap as you can" and forwarded "as soon as possible." And, tellingly, the request continues, "Wish they may arrive before Lady Washington leaves Camp and meet her approbation."[19]

At Valley Forge, Mrs. Washington assumed the role of hostess at headquarters. She also socialized with other wives of the senior officers. Years after the encampment, Pierre DuPonceau, an aide to Baron von Steuben, recalled that in the evenings the ladies met at each other's quarters for conversation; occasionally they gathered at General Washington's, too. During these social evenings each lady and gentleman present was "called upon in turn for a song" over a dish of tea or coffee. There was little for the ladies and gentlemen of camp to do during the evening gatherings except to talk and sing, as dancing and card playing were prohibited at camp.[20]

General and Mrs. Washington sometimes had guests in for a glass of wine at Valley Forge, or even dinner, which was served in the log cabin built for dining at headquarters. (Martha, who may have suggested this addition, wrote that the hut made quarters "much more tolarable [*sic*] than they were at first."[21]) On December 26 James Allen of Philadelphia, a Loyalist, "rode . . . to headquarters and dined with the Gen'l who was very civil to me; no doubt my visit was unexpected."[22] Charles Willson Peale, now the famous painter but then a member of the Pennsylvania militia, arrived at Valley Forge on February 14, 1778. Befitting his status (years before he had painted portraits of both George and Martha Washington and the two Custis children), the soldier-artist dined with General and Mrs. Washington the day he arrived in camp. In mid-February, Williams Weeks wrote that he took a glass of wine with General Washington and his lady at Valley Forge. When Gen. Charles Lee arrived at camp, he was escorted to headquarters and "entertained with an Elegant Dinner, and the Music Playing the whole time."[23]

Years after the Valley Forge encampment, Pierre DuPonceau, who accompanied Baron von Steuben to headquarters for dinner several times a week, recalled both General and Mrs. Washington at the dining table. The commander impressed DuPonceau as being "grave, yet not severe; affable, without familiarity," with an expression of "calm dignity." DuPonceau could not keep his eyes from Washington's "imposing countenance."[24] Mrs. Washington also impressed Steuben's aide. "I still see her at the head of that table, with her mild but dignified countenance, which often reminded me of the matrons of ancient Rome," he recollected for a "Harvest Home" celebration at Valley Forge fifty years after the encampment. "Grave, yet cheerful, her countenance and her manner reflected the feelings of the hero whose name she gloried to bear."[25]

On April 6 Elizabeth Drinker, Mary Pleasants, Susanna Jones, and Phoebe Pemberton came from Philadelphia to Valley Forge to plead with Washington to release their husbands from jail. The men, all Quakers who had been exiled to western Virginia, had refused to swear a loyalty oath to the United States and were considered dangerous to the Patriot cause. The four Quaker ladies arrived at Valley Forge headquarters at 1:30 p.m., only to find that the commander was not available to speak with them. While waiting, they visited with Mrs. Washington, who was, Mrs. Drinker wrote, "a sociable pretty kind of Woman." After Washington spoke with the visitors, he invited them to dinner, served at headquarters at 3:00 p.m. At least fifteen officers were at the table with General and Mrs. Washington. Mrs. Drinker found the dinner to be "elegant," but also "soon over," and afterward the ladies then "went with ye General's Wife up to her Chamber, and saw no more of him."[26]

During her audience with Washington, Elizabeth Drinker may well have related the problems that she faced in Philadelphia without male protection. In occupied Philadelphia, British officers considered it their right and privilege to stay in the city's private homes. Mrs. Drinker and her sister, however, had expected to be excused from housing British officers. They, after all, were two ladies living alone.

So Drinker was dismayed when, on December 29, 1777, British major Cramond arrived at her front door and made arrangements to move in. The occupation initially went well, for a few days later Mrs. Drinker wrote in her diary that Major Cramond had "now become one of our family, appears to be a thoughtful, sober young man." His servant also appeared to be "sober and orderly."[27] Soon, however, Cramond moved his horses, cows, sheep, and turkeys into the stable, collected an entourage of three aides and three servants, claimed the two front parlors, upstairs bedroom, stable, and part of the kitchen as his own, and began hosting raucous dinner parties. The provoked hostess could do little but complain—silently, in her diary.

An officer in residence meant, at best, protection for the house and the family. As Drinker discovered, an officer in residence could also mean that the owner would be relegated to a small portion of her own home. Some women were ousted from their homes altogether. Others were resigned to watch helplessly as the officer and his entourage destroyed the place. Sally Logan Fisher, who was eight months pregnant, was stranded in Philadelphia when her husband, like Elizabeth Drinker's, was exiled to western Virginia. "I feel forlorn & desolate," Mrs. Fisher wrote from Philadelphia, "& the World appears like a dreary Desert, almost without any visible protecting Hand to guard us from the ravenous Wolves & Lions that prowl about for prey."[28]

At Valley Forge headquarters, Mrs. Drinker, her friends, and General Lee were fortunate, for not every dinner there could be described as "elegant." The fare seems to have been often much simpler. DuPonceau, reminiscing many years later, recollects eating only "a scanty piece of meat, with some hard bread and a few potatoes" at Washington's dining table. Dessert was, he remembered, "a plate of hickory nuts."[29] But it must be noted that while General and Mrs. Washington and those gathered around the table were munching hickory nuts for dessert, the camp soldiers were eating food far more mundane and monotonous. In December Dr. Albigence Waldo groused that he dined on only fire cake and water for dinner and supper. And after they had eaten, the troops retired to log huts, said by Lafayette to be "little shanties that are scarcely gayer than dungeon cells."[30]

Because, as mentioned previously, Elizabeth Stephens and other women in the neighborhood sometimes brought food to headquarters, Isaac and Hannah, Washington's cooks, at times had delicacies to put on the table. In early 1778 the general also received cheese and pickled oysters, spoils from the capture of British ships. Lord Stirling, one of Washington's generals, delivered more oysters to the commander in chief on March 27. A large delivery of food for a feast (fowls, partridges, onions, potatoes, cabbages, turnips, parsnips, eggs, veal) was received at the kitchen at headquarters before the general's forty-sixth birthday in February. And this was not unusual, for Caleb Gibbs's *Expense Report* from the Valley Forge period records page after page of such items as fowls, butter, eggs, veal, potatoes, parsnips, apples, cabbages, partridges, and turkeys sent to headquarters throughout the six-month encampment.[31] The food came from the local farms and was paid for from Washington's accounts. And not to be forgotten were those "few good" hams requiring Martha Washington's approval that were ordered in March.

The request for superior food supplies for Washington's table was not limited to the Valley Forge encampment. The following year, "very good hams," a rump, and "sirloin best beef" as well as a "hind Quarter Mutton" were ordered for the commander's table. A request from West Point began, "A word to the wise [as the saying is] is fully sufficient," and then went on to state that the general was "destitute of Loaf sugar, Cheese, Coffee, Chocolates, &c, &c." Furthermore, "If a quarter Cask of Claret or good port Wine could be forwarded . . . it would not be amiss." In 1780, from the Morristown encampment, an order went out for beer for headquarters—a large quantity was needed—and it was to be sent immediately. A "barrel of Cranberries" was also much wanted, as well as a half pound of nutmeg, two loaves of sugar, some candles, and a coffee mill. On December 6, 1780, Mrs. Washington asked for "thirty or forty pounds of currents and six pounds of citron procured and sent to head quarters as soon as possible."[32] While the army was facing down a difficult winter at the New Windsor,

New York, encampment, it seems that Mrs. Washington was supervising the baking of the holiday fruitcakes.

PORTRAITS, PLAYS, PRAYERS, CELEBRATIONS

For the soldiers, Valley Forge was a place of deprivation—of shoddy shoes, meager food, and sparse clothing. But at headquarters some elegant meals were being served, and at the officers' quarters ladies and gentlemen gathered in the evenings over a dish of tea or coffee to raise their voices in song. At Valley Forge, officers and their ladies also sat to have their portraits painted.

Charles Willson Peale painted a miniature of Washington and presented it to Mrs. Washington at camp on February 16, 1778. His charge was his usual "56 Dollars."[33] Peale made several other miniatures of Washington that Valley Forge winter; miniatures that John Laurens, one of Washington's aides, called "successful attempts to produce the General's likeness."[34] When not on militia duty, Peale also sought out commissions from other officers and their ladies. Gen. Nathanael Greene, Col. Clement Biddle, Gen. Henry Knox, Lord Stirling, Col. Henry Procter, and at least fifteen other officers, plus some ladies, all took leave from their camp activities to be captured on canvas by Captain Peale.[35]

On May 11 Martha Washington and her husband attended the camp production of Joseph Addison's *Cato*, one of the general's favorite plays. Cato was a Roman statesman, soldier, and author who stood up to the mighty Greek empire; Washington identified with the man. The tragedy was performed by the staff officers for a "very numerous and splendid audience," which also included Lady and Lord Stirling and their daughter Kitty, Mrs. Nathanael Greene, and many officers. William Bradford Jr. wrote to his sister that he found the performance "admirable" and the scenery "in Taste."[36] There is, however, no record of what either General or Mrs. Washington thought of the production.

But Congress's opinion of such frivolity is known. In October 1778, the autumn after the Valley Forge encampment, Congress decided that theatrical entertainments had the "fatal tendency to divert the minds of the people from a due attention to the means necessary for the defense of their country." Congress further determined that "any person holding an office under the United States, who shall act, promote, encourage or attend such plays, shall be deemed unworthy to hold such office and shall be accordingly dismissed."[37] No officer wanted to risk his honor and dismissal from the service, and camp theater productions abruptly ended.

May 6 was an exceedingly festive day at Valley Forge, and Mrs. Washington happily participated in the joyous celebration of the formal announcement of the French-American alliance. After receiving official word that France had joined with the Americans against the British, General Washington immediately declared, "It having pleased the Almighty ruler of the Universe propitiously to defend the Cause of the United American-States . . . by raising us up a powerful Friend among the Princes of the Earth to establish our liberty and Independence . . . it becomes us to set apart a day for gratefully acknowledging the divine Goodness and celebrating the Important Event which we owe to his benign Interposition."[38] The day to be set apart was the next day—Wednesday, May 6.

Lady Washington and the others at camp woke to a day that dawned "excessively hot" and a celebration that began with worship services. The soldiers first assembled by brigades at 9:00 a.m. to hear a proclamation of the alliance and sermons by their respective chaplains. Along with other general officers and their wives, the Washingtons attended services with the New Jersey brigade. The preacher was the Revered Mr. Hunter, who delivered up what one observer pronounced to be a "suitable discourse."[39] (This was not the only camp worship service the Washingtons attended. Four days later, they were seen at a service led by a "Mr. Evins.")[40]

The festive May 6 celebration had been carefully staged to show the encampment's thousands of soldiers to best advantage. At 10:30 a.m. cannons signaled the men to be under arms. At 11:00 a.m. the cannons roared out once more, directing the troops to assemble at the Grand Parade. After the commander in chief, accompanied by several principal officers, reviewed the soldiers on the Grand Parade, the cannon spit out thirteen volleys in honor of the thirteen (prospective) states. Thousands of soldiers, lined up with precision, responded with a *feu de joie* (literally, a fire of joy), or running fire, from gleaming muskets. "Long Live the King of France," shouted the men, followed by another round of thirteen blasts from the cannon and the running fire from thousands of muskets. "Long live the friendly European Powers," cried the troops. After a third round of cannon and running fire, the hills echoed with a proud "To the American States." The army put on a grand show, conducted with great judgment and regularity. "Approbation indeed was conspicuous in every countenance," Maj. Joseph Bloomfield wrote in his diary that day, "& universal joy reigned throughout the Camp."[41]

As General Washington and his entourage turned toward headquarters, the camp resounded with spirited, spontaneous "Huzzahs." The commander in chief turned in his saddle again and again to acknowledge the cheers of his men. Later, General and Lady Washington received in the center of a large marquee that had been fashioned from dozens of officers' tents, and the entire company enjoyed a cold collation. Although there is no record of Mrs. Washington's attire on that august day, General Washington, usually so staid and proper, was said to have worn an expression of "uncommon delight and compliance." As might be expected, the officers from France were especially pleased with the American army's grand display of support for the alliance. Not forgotten were the private soldiers, who had "never looked so well, nor is such good order since the beginning of the war."[42] Each soldier received a gill (a quarter pint) of rum. Every prisoner was released from the stockade. It was indeed a day for rejoicing.

Then, as she did at every encampment, Martha headed home before the campaign began. In late May, about a week before she left camp, Martha asked the army's deputy quartermaster for four or five mugs to carry back with her to Mount Vernon. (The requested mugs were Pennsylvania earthenware.) But these were difficult times, and the deputy quartermaster was unable to honor her request. "I have done all in my Power to procure Mrs. Washington the mugs and jugs in the Place & have sent to Lancaster," Col. James Abeel wrote regretfully from Reading to Valley Forge, "but they are to be had at neither Place at any Rate."[43]

Lady Washington set off for Virginia on Monday, June 8, 1778, with a hopeful heart, for now the French had officially joined the battle against the British. Surely, she thought, she would not be asked to any more army encampments! Then, just eleven days later, on June 19, the invigorated and renewed Continental Army marched from the Valley Forge encampment to engage the British at Monmouth. During the battle the American soldiers, who had been smartly trained by General von Steuben at Valley Forge, acquitted themselves with honor. After a fierce contest fought in excessive, exhaustive heat, the British, under the cover of darkness, retired from the field. The Continental Army had learned well the lessons of Valley Forge.

Why did she do it? Why did Lady Washington leave her family and home to join her husband during the American Revolution? To see her husband during the war, Martha Washington had to travel to him. General Washington rarely left the army to come home to her. (Not that he didn't want to. The commander wrote from Valley Forge "that there is not an Officer in the Service of the United States that would return to the sweets of domestic life with more heart felt joy than I should.")[44] But Martha Washington was more than simply a dutiful, even devoted, wife. Lafayette observed that she loved "her husband madly."[45] Gen. Nathanael Greene wrote, "Mrs. Washington is excessive [*sic*] fond of the General and he of her. They are very happy in each other."[46] Of course Mrs. Washington would go any distance to be with, and support, her husband. He need only ask.

And, indeed, he did.

3

Martha Washington at the Other Encampments

A Resolute and Loyal Lady

CAMBRIDGE, MASSACHUSETTS, DECEMBER 1775–APRIL 1776

Martha Washington's activities at the winter encampments before and after Valley Forge give us more insight into this very surprising lady.

Her first invitation to winter camp apparently took Martha by surprise. Hadn't the general promised during the summer of 1775 that he would "return safe to [her] in the fall"?

On June 18, 1775, three days after being elected commander in chief of the Continental Army, Washington wrote his wife from Philadelphia "on a subject which fills me with inexpressible concern." Then he penned the words that would change Martha's world forever: he had accepted command of "the whole army raised for the defense of the American cause." Washington assured Martha, "his dear Patcy," that "so far from seeking this appointment I have used every endeavor in my power to avoid it." (Washington had, however, habitually appeared in military uniform at the Continental Congress meetings.) To Martha, he declared, "I should enjoy more real happiness and felicity in one month with you at home, than I have the most distant prospect of reaping abroad." Nevertheless, Washington had accepted the post because it was, he wrote, "a kind of destiny that has thrown me upon this Service" and "utterly out of my power to refuse this appointment." Washington would soon leave for Boston from Philadelphia; he could not return to Mount Vernon to say good-bye before he traveled north. He realized his new command would distress his wife, so he begged her "to summon your whole fortitude Resolution, and pass your time as agreeably as possible—nothing will give me so much sincere satisfaction as to hear this, and to hear it from your own pen." After stating his wishes for her housing arrangements—she was to do whatever she thought best—the new commander in chief sent greetings to his friends, signed off, and closed with a postscript: "Since writing the above I have received your Letter of the 15th and have got two suits of what I was told was the prettiest Muslin. I wish it may please you." (Was Washington offering a husbandly bribe?) He prudently enclosed his will and noted that he was "not doubting but that I shall return safe to you in the fall."[1]

Washington wrote again from Philadelphia to his Patcy five days later, on June 23, 1775, just "within a few minutes of leaving this City." Declaring, "I could not think of departing from it without dropping you a line," he wrote, "I go fully trusting in that Providence, which has been more bountiful to me than I deserve, & in full confidence of a happy Meeting with you sometime in the Fall." (But no mention this time that he would come to her.) He declared his "unalterable affection for you, which neither time or distance can change" and his best love to Jack and Nelly (Martha's son and daughter-in-law), with regards to the rest of the family. Then he signed the letter "Yr [Your] entire Geo. Washington"—an exceptionally tender and very unusual closing for the eighteenth century.[2]

Autumn was well along when, in October 1775, Martha received the invitation to come north. As he wrote to his brother from Cambridge, Washington saw "no prospect of returning to my Family and Friends this Winter," and so had sent a letter to Martha suggesting that she might join him at headquarters. Recognizing that the season was "far advanced," the general had laid out the difficulties for her and then "left it to her own choice" as to whether or not to travel to camp. Washington had addressed his invitation to Mount Vernon, although he thought Martha to be miles away at her sister's home in New Kent.[3]

And she was. Weeks before, Martha Washington had traveled to Fredericksburg and then on to Eltham, the New Kent County plantation of her favorite sister, Anna Maria Bassett. Lund Washington sent the general's invitation along to her there. Lund also quickly notified Washington that he expected Mrs. Washington "home immediately, as she has often declared she would go to the Camp if you would permit her."[4] But Mrs. Washington did not exactly run for her coach when she arrived back at Mount Vernon. Extensive, proper preparations for the journey had to be made. Martha was also reluctant to leave the security of her home; she had never before traveled so far from the familiar, warm comforts of her beloved Mount Vernon.

The frustrated Lund Washington sent almost weekly progress reports about Mrs. Washington's travel preparations to military headquarters in Cambridge. On November 5 Lund, who wrote to George Washington that it would probably be close to November 20 before Mrs. Washington set off, vowed to "do all I can to get her off sooner if possible."[5] On November 14 Lund wrote that Martha remained at Mount Vernon, which, to his dismay, had now become "crowded" with visitors. That same day Fielding Lewis wrote his brother-in-law General Washington of his concerns that Mrs. Washington would have a "very disagreeable journey" because of the winter weather. Lewis also accurately predicted that the lady would "meet with every assistance" on the road.[6]

Finally, on November 20, a relieved Lund reported that Mrs. Washington had set off for camp. After a torturous carriage ride, Martha and her traveling companions (Jacky Custis and his wife Nelly; Mrs. Horatio Gates; and Washington's nephew, George Lewis) arrived at camp on December 11, 1775. Headquarters was the Vassall House, in Cambridge, later Henry Wadsworth Longfellow's home. The group had been traveling together on the unfamiliar roads for three weeks.

As he would throughout the war, George Washington had done all he could from headquarters to smooth his wife's travels north. He sent an aide, William Hanson Harrison, to meet her carriage in Philadelphia. He wrote to Joseph Reed, then his military secretary, that, as Martha and her companions were "perfect strangers to the road," he "would be much obliged in your particular instructions and advice to her." Then he gave some advice himself: because of its large Loyalist population, the travelers were "by all means" to avoid New York City.[7]

Martha's first journey north was not without incident. The roads were bad and her horses not the best, forcing travel in short stages. The travelers rested awhile in Philadelphia, where Martha stayed at the home of Joseph Reed and his wife. (Reed wrote the general that Mrs. Washington and the two women who accompanied her were "very agreeable ladies. . . . No bad supply, I think, in a cold country where wood is scarce. . . . The face of your camp will be changed.")[8] A ball had been planned in Lady Washington's honor at the New Tavern (now the City Tavern) in Philadelphia, but after a contingent of congressmen called on her suggesting the impropriety of the event while a war was going on, Martha sent her regrets.

Fanfare, unexpected it seems, as well as additional security often greeted the commander in chief's wife as she traveled from town to town toward Cambridge. The *Pennsylvania Post* reported that the light infantry escorted "The Lady of his Excellency General Washington" through Philadelphia.[9] When she left the city on November 27, two companies of light infantry accompanied her carriage. "We were so attended and the gentlemen so kind, that I am . . . under obligations to them that I shall not for get soon," Mrs. Washington wrote of her departure from Philadelphia, "and I left it in as great pomp as if I had been a very great somebody."[10] As she continued north, the Light Horse (cavalry carrying light arms and equipment) and a multitude of prominent ladies and gentlemen came forward to escort her through Elizabethtown, New Jersey. As Martha's entourage and a contingency of Minute Men traveled through Newark, New Jersey, the sounds of festive church bells filled the air.

General Washington ordered Col. George Baylor from camp to escort the carriage to Cambridge headquarters. To adequately prepare for his wife's arrival, the general asked Baylor to notify him the "evening before if convenient" as to when Mrs. Washington would arrive in camp.[11] When Martha finally reached headquarters on December 11, the intrepid traveler herself stoutly declared she had had "a very pleasant journey through New England" and pronounced the countryside "beautyfull" (*sic*). To her delight and great relief, she also found the general to be "very well."

Martha's fortitude and determination were on full display at Cambridge. "To me that never see any thing of war," she wrote on December 30, 1775, "the preparations, are very terable [*sic*] indeed, but I endever [*sic*] to keep my fears to myself as well as I can." Everyone was cheerful and happy at Cambridge, she wrote, although "some days we have a number of cannon and shells from Boston and Bunkers Hill, but it does not seem to surprise any one but me; I confess I shudder every time I hear the sound of a gun." Seeing Charlestown "with only a few chimneys standing in it" and Boston, which contained a "number of very fine Buildings . . . but god knows how long they will stand," tormented her. And the fact that the Boston "warfs" (*sic*) were being pulled up for firewood was also disconcerting.[12]

Despite the presence of her companions, she was lonely. A month after arriving in Cambridge, Martha wrote a long letter to her sister Anna

Maria, grumbling that she believed herself "quite forgot" by her sister and friends. In Martha's view, distance was no excuse for not writing, as "the post comes in very regularly every week." Her letter included the latest health report ("The Gen. myself and Jack are very well") and a bit of family gossip ("Nelly Custis is I hope getting well again, and I beleive [sic] is with child"). (Nelly Custis, her daughter-in-law, had suffered a miscarriage soon before leaving for Cambridge.) Martha also knew something of current military affairs, for she wrote that Gen. Henry Clinton, the British commander in chief, had sailed from Boston Harbor. It was Martha's fervent hope that should Clinton be bound for New York, Gen. Charles Lee, who was already in New York City, "will give him a very warm reception."[13]

At Cambridge, Martha met the literary figure Mercy Otis Warren, who later wrote *The History of the Rise, Progress, and Termination of the American Revolution*, one of the first published histories of the conflict between Britain and its American colonies. Mrs. Warren, recognizing that Mrs. Washington might be in harm's way at Cambridge, invited her to stay at her own home. Martha graciously declined the offer, then turned and invited Mrs. Warren to come to Cambridge, assuring the lady that "every civility" the commander's wife could muster would be extended to her.[14]

The visit took place in April 1777. Mrs. Warren, for one, was pleased, as she wrote to Abigail Adams, "I was received with politeness and respect shown in a first interview among the well bred, and with the ease and cordiality of friendship of a much earlier date. The complacency of her manners," Mrs. Warren continued, "speaks at once of the benevolence of her heart, and her affability, candor and gentleness, qualify her to soften the hours of private life, or to sweeten the cares of the hero, and smooth the rugged pains of war."[15] This was high praise from Mercy Otis Warren, a personage in her own right, and a discriminating one at that.

Lady Washington and her entourage left Cambridge headquarters in April, setting out by the "upper road" through Hartford and New Haven. For security considerations, Washington and his aides traveled a different route—the "lower road" along the coast.[16] Although Jacky Custis had an illness that caused some delay, Martha's traveling party finally met up with Washington in New York City. The couple left together for Philadelphia on May 21, where the general met with Congress. Martha, as planned, underwent inoculation for smallpox after she arrived in Philadelphia. Washington had written in April that he "doubted her resolution," but his wife surprised him and went through with the procedure.[17] The general wrote to both his brother and brother-in-law that Mrs. Washington had the smallpox "favorably," with very few "Pustules." When she had "perfectly" recovered, Washington wrote, she would join him in New York if that promised to be a "fit place for her to remain."[18]

Instead she stayed behind in Philadelphia, and she was in that city when the Continental Congress voted for independence on July 2, 1776. On August 28, 1776, almost two months later, she wrote Anna Maria that she was still in Philadelphia and, in fact, had "Noe [sic] prospects at present of my leveing [sic] it." Anna Maria must have been writing less often, for now Martha says, "I don't hear from you so often as I used to doe [sic] at Cambridge." Mrs. Washington knew about the military action on the Hudson River and uttered an impassioned, "I thank god [sic] we shant want men." But it is peace that was her most fervent desire. "I doe [sic] my Dear sister most relegiously [sic] wish thare [sic] was an End to the matter that we might have the pleasure of meeting again."[19]

Soon after writing this letter, the general's wife left Philadelphia for Virginia and arrived at Mount Vernon in early September. Could Martha have guessed at that time that she would be traveling to seven more encampments?

MORRISTOWN, NEW JERSEY, MARCH–JUNE 1777

The Continental Army staged an unusual campaign in 1776–77, for Washington's soldiers actually fought that winter. Because it was difficult to move the officers and soldiers, artillery, horses, wagons, and camp women through winter's mire, muck, and snow, eighteenth-century armies traditionally camped during the frigid winter months. Washington's famous strike at Trenton on Christmas Day 1776 caught the Hessian soldiers unprepared; few had anticipated Washington's forces attacking in winter.

Several months later, after this unusual winter campaign concluded and he had settled in at the Jacob Arnold Tavern in Morristown, New Jersey, Washington sent for his wife. In preparation for the invitation, Martha and her good friend Mrs. Theodorick Bland, whose husband was with Washington, had already traveled from Mount Vernon to Philadelphia to await the general's instructions to come north. As he had at Valley Forge, Washington sent an aide to escort his lady into camp; Martha arrived at headquarters on March 15. Meanwhile, Mrs. Bland remained in Philadelphia to undergo smallpox inoculation. Unfortunately, she was "for four weeks very ill" under inoculation and left with many facial scars. Finally a "very agreeable Gentleman and Lady" who were passing through Philadelphia on the way to Boston accompanied Martha Bland to camp. She arrived in Morristown in early April.

From Martha Bland, whose husband later commanded the cavalry troops and dabbled in Washington's spy network, we learn about the Morristown of 1777.[20] Mrs. Bland described Morristown as "a very clever little village," located in a beautiful valley beneath several mountains. It had a "consequential look," she wrote, thanks to its "three houses with steeples." In Lady Bland's opinion, however, its residents were not as consequential. Two families, refugees from New York, lived there; otherwise, Mrs. Bland wrote, "it is inhabited by the errentest [?] rustics you ever beheld."

Washington was no rustic; Lady Bland called him "*our* Noble and Agreeable Commander." Personal friends of the Washingtons, Colonel and Mrs. Bland visited headquarters, the lady noted proudly, several times a week by "particular invitation."

The commander in chief, his wife, and some of Washington's aides-de-camp occasionally set out together on horseback parties at Morristown, and Mrs. Bland at times rode along. Mrs. Bland observed at these gatherings that his "Worthy Lady seems to be in perfect felicity when she is by the side of her *Old Man* as she calls him." (This was obviously said in jest; Martha Washington was about eight months older than the general.) It seems that Washington relaxed on these outings. Mrs. Bland was charmed by the man and observed that when he "throws off the Hero—and takes on the chatty agreeable companion—he can be down right impudent sometimes."

Martha Bland also commented on several other aides who rode out on these jaunts: Alexander Hamilton, Tench Tilghman, and Caleb Gibbs, all of whom continued as important members of Washington's military family at Valley Forge. Col. Alexander Hamilton, Lady Bland wrote, was "a sensible Genteel polite young fellow a West Indian." She felt Col. Tench Tilghman (Mrs. Bland spelled the name "Tillman") to be "a modest worthy man . . . who acts in any capacity that is uppermost without fee or reward." The captain of the guard, Caleb Gibbs appeared to her to be "a good natured

Yankee who makes a thousand Blunders in the Yankee style and keeps the Dinner table in constant Laugh."

Lady Washington spent less time in Morristown than she had at Valley Forge; she remained in town only from March until the start of the campaign in mid-June. Although Joseph Reed again invited her to stay in his Philadelphia home on her way to Mount Vernon, Mrs. Washington chose instead to honor the earlier invitation of Charles Pettit, assistant quartermaster of the Continental Army. She remained with Pettit for three or four days, and her only extant letter from this Morristown encampment is to Joseph Reed confirming housing arrangements for her Philadelphia stay. While she was in the city, the Assembly of Pennsylvania voted to honor General Washington by purchasing a replacement for the worn out coach that Mrs. Washington had used to travel to the encampments. They planned to "present the same to the Honorable Mrs. Washington . . . as a small testimony of the sense the Assembly have of his [Washington's] great and important services to the American States."[21]

Martha Washington arrived at Mount Vernon in late June 1777 and spent summer, autumn, and Christmas with her family. On January 26, 1778, she left her home to join her husband at winter camp at Valley Forge, Pennsylvania.

MIDDLEBROOK, NEW JERSEY, DECEMBER 1778–JUNE 1779

Lady Washington had five months to rest up after returning from Valley Forge before she set out again. On November 2, 1778, Martha confessed to her brother Bartholomew Dandridge that she was "very uneasy," as she had "some reason to expect that I shall take another trip to the northward. The pore [sic] General is not likely to come to see us from what I can hear." Her letter continued, "I shall write to you to inform you and my friends—if I am so happy to stay at home."[22] Martha did not stay at home that winter, for soon the anticipated letter arrived and she and her entourage set out to meet the general, who was in camp near Middlebrook, New Jersey. Martha's planned visit to her ailing mother had to be postponed, once again.

On November 11 Washington wrote of his plans for his wife's journey north. The springs on Martha's carriage had broken—his stepfather suggested that Jacky Custis had been negligent in attending to them—and

Washington assigned Col. John Mitchell, deputy quartermaster, to send a special messenger with new springs to meet his wife along the road to Philadelphia. Washington thought Martha may have already started out to Philadelphia on his recommended route: Bladensburg, Maryland, to Baltimore, to the lower ferry of Susquehanna, to the head of Elk (Elkton, Maryland), to Christiana, to Wilmington and finally to Philadelphia. (This route roughly follows the modern I-95 through Maryland and Delaware to Philadelphia.) Washington directed that his wife wait in Philadelphia for the carriage to be repaired; he would write for her there when his own quarters were, as he phrased it, "fixed up." Colonel Mitchell had offered his Philadelphia home to Lady Washington, but this kind invitation was declined as the commander felt "the trouble of such a visitor (for more than a day or two) being too much for a private family." Instead, Mitchell was to find good public lodgings for Mrs. Washington in the city. Her carriage horses were to be sent to the public stables, this being "most convenient."[23]

After a jarring ride on those broken springs, Martha Washington arrived in Philadelphia by December 12, for on that date she attended a splendid ball at the New Tavern given by the French in honor of the "principal ladies and gentlemen of Philadelphia." Lady Washington was the guest of honor; other luminaries included the governor of Pennsylvania and his lady and His Excellency the minister of France. The ballroom, both inside and out, was decorated with all manner of "ingenious devices and mottoes, signifying the present happy alliance between the court of Versailles and the United States." The evening was spent agreeably, and "every heart seems to exult in safety, freedom, and independence."[24]

But it seems that on this august occasion not every man behaved as a gentleman. Gen. Nathanael Greene wrote that Gen. Charles Lee did the unthinkable at the assembly: he "affronted Mrs. Washington." Unable to let this slight go unchallenged, Col. John Laurens challenged Lee to a duel. Lee and Laurens did come to a duel on December 23, but it is not certain that the duel was forced over the affront to Lady Washington. Whether Laurens and Lee fought over Lady Washington's honor or for some other reason, Greene wrote, "I cannot tell."[25]

Martha Washington arrived in camp at Middlebrook by early January, for the commander wrote on January 2, 1779, that she was in good health and with him in the Wallace House (now presumably "fixed up").

Conditions at the Middlebrook encampment were an improvement over those of the Valley Forge encampment the previous year. "The American troops are again in Hutts; but in a more agreeable and fertile country than they were last winter at Valley forge," Washington wrote on March 8 to the Marquis de Lafayette. In fact, Washington believed that the men were "better clad and more healthy than they have ever been since the formation of the Army."[26] From Martha's perspective, too, things were going well, for on March 19, 1779 (she mistakenly dated the letter "1778"), Mrs. Washington wrote to her son and daughter-in-law that she and the general were well and that everything was quiet at camp. Everyone, however, was most anxious to learn about how affairs were going in the south. On a more personal nature, Martha had not heard from the family for two posts, and this annoyed her. "If you doe [sic] not write to me," she pouted to Jacky and Nelly, "I will not write to you again or till I get letters from you." She also feared that her friends had forgotten her.[27] It is obvious that Martha Washington relished and required frequent letters from her family and friends at home.

The New-Jersey Gazette reported that Gen. Henry Knox and the artillery corps officers staged a "very elegant entertainment and display of fireworks" on February 18 to celebrate the signing of the French Alliance. (The French Alliance had first been celebrated at the Valley Forge encampment in May 1778.) General and Mrs. Washington, Mrs. Knox, and Mrs. Greene—all ladies who had been at Valley Forge—as well as other ladies and gentleman from miles around the camp were part of the festivities and ball. Other individuals, described as a "a vast concourse of spectators from every part of the Jerseys," looked on.[28] General Washington opened the ball, but the Pennsylvania Packet reported that he did not seem to enjoy himself much. "When this man unbends from his station, and its weighty functions," the Packet recorded, "he is even then like a philosopher, who mixes with the amusements of the world, that he may teach it what is right, or turn its trifles into instruction."[29] But Washington certainly unbent at a little frisk given in early March by General and Mrs. Greene at their quarters. After opening the festivities with the rotund Lucy Knox, the commander danced for "upwards of three hours" with Mrs. Nathanael Greene, a beguiling sparkler, "without once sitting down."[30]

On May 2 the army was paraded and reviewed by the French minister, Monsieur Gerard, and Don Juan de Miralles, described as "a gentleman of distinction from Spain." Mrs. Washington, Mrs. Greene, and Mrs. Knox, as well as a few other ladies, drove up in their carriages to witness the field maneuvers of the soldiers and marvel at the precision firing of the artillery and muskets. The display impressed James Thacher, a surgeon with the Continental Army, who recorded in his journal that the whole was performed with "marked regularity and precision, as to reflect great honor on the character of our army." Washington impressed Thacher, also. We cannot but "pride ourselves," Thacher wrote, on the "conspicuous figure exhibited by our commander-in-chief." The general displayed a remarkable stature, "and being a good horseman . . . displays a lofty carriage, and benign dignity of demeanor." Not unexpectedly, Thacher thought his commander far more majestic and dignified than either Monsieur Gerard or the Don Juan.

On May 14 one brigade of the army was paraded for General Washington and some visiting Indian chiefs. Thacher wrote that Washington "deems it good policy to pay attention to this tribe in the wilderness" so to convince them of the Continental Army's strength and discipline. In the review, Washington, accompanied by William Lee, his faithful servant, rode up on a beautiful gray steed. The "savages" appearance, meanwhile, was "beyond description ludicrous," Thacher penned. Their horses were "the meanest kind," some had no saddles, and occasionally old lines doubled as bridles. The chiefs looked "equally farcical," Thacher wrote, with painted faces, jewels dangling from ears and nose, tufts of hair sprouting from their heads, and dirty blankets thrown over their shoulders flapping in the wind. "In short," Thacher concluded in his journal, "they exhibited a novel and truly disgusting spectacle."[31]

Thacher does not say Lady Washington was at the event. Benson J. Lossing's *Mary and Martha: The Mother and Wife of Washington* (1886), however, contains a letter allegedly written by Mrs. Washington to her daughter-in-law that can only describe the May 14 review. Lady Washington, according to this letter, found the inspection the "funniest, at the same time most ridiculous review of the soldiers I ever heard of." The general and his servant William, the letter says, as well as "a lot of mounted savages" reviewed the army. "Some of the Indians were fairly fine-looking," Martha supposedly wrote, "but most of them appeared worse than Falstaff's gang. And such horses and trappings! The General says it was done to keep the Indians friendly toward us. They appeared like cutthroats all."[32]

This is a colorful, vivid letter, but did Martha Washington write it from the Middlebrook encampment? Did she write it at all? The tone and construction of the letter is very different from Mrs. Washington's usual proper style. There are no spelling errors. It is no surprise that that original has never been located. In all probability, this is one of Benson J. Lossing's fanciful nineteenth-century constructions, this time based on Thacher's journal. (See the appendix for more information on Benson J. Lossing.)

On May 31, just a few days later, Catharine Greene and Martha Washington left camp together to visit friends in Morristown. Then Catharine departed from Morristown to return home to Rhode Island, while Martha returned to the encampment. She finally left Middlebrook for good around the middle of June. (The general later wrote, "Mrs. Washington, according to custom, *marched home* [emphasis in original] when the Campaign was about to open"—a rare and delightful sample of the commander's dry sense of humor, or perhaps a charming slip of his quill pen.)[33] On June 15 Lady Washington, accompanied by twenty or so military officers, traveled from Easton, Pennsylvania, to Bethlehem, Pennsylvania. She stopped in Bethlehem long enough to visit places of interest and to attend a worship service that evening. In her honor, Brother Ettwein conducted the service in English, rather than his customary German. She left Bethlehem for home the next day.[34]

Gen. Nathanael Greene shared breakfast with General Washington on July 8 and learned from him that Mrs. Washington had arrived at Mount Vernon. Greene also observed this about his commander: "Poor man he appears oppressed with cares and wants some gentle hand free from deceit to soothe his cares."[35] And that is why, five months later, Martha Washington was back at military camp.

MORRISTOWN, NEW JERSEY, DECEMBER 1779–JUNE 1780

Martha had written her husband that she wanted to get to headquarters "before the Roads get bad & weather severe" and avoid the difficult winter conditions she had endured traveling to Valley Forge and Middlebrook. So Washington, in mid-October, wrote Col. John Mitchell to "hire lodgings in some genteel (but not a common boarding) house in Philadelphia" for her.[36] Mrs. Washington had many friends in that city, and it would be easy and pleasant for her to occupy herself there until the general sent for her to come to camp.

Mitchell sprang into action and found lodgings in one of the largest homes in town, Clarke Hall, locally famous for its gardens and view of the Delaware River. Mrs. Washington would have the "handsome front Parlour, a good bed chamber, kitchen & Rooms for Servants." Mitchell would meet Mrs. Washington on the approach road, have the wood laid in when she arrived at her lodging place, and have available "some of the best Tea, Sugar, Coffee &ca. for her." Mitchell also pledged that Mrs. Mitchell would do everything possible to make Lady Washington's stay pleasant and agreeable. And if anything else was needed or desired, the general was assured that Col. John Mitchell was at his command.[37]

Washington replied to Mitchell from West Point on November 6. He planned to write Mrs. Washington "by next Post" to come to Clarke Hall and remain there until he would know "where my own quarters will be and remove her to them." Washington also acknowledged, "At present I am totally in the dark respecting this matter." "Of Mrs. Mitchell's kind attentions," Washington wrote, "I am sure she [Mrs. Washington] will have no cause to complain—I am sure also she will hold them in grateful remembrance."[38] But things did not work out as planned. Although Mrs. Washington had wanted to travel before the winter set in, and Washington had said on November 6 that he would write to her immediately, she did not arrive in Philadelphia until December 21. Ten days later, she finally joined her husband in Morristown.

Why the delay? It was the weather. The winter of 1779–80 was extremely harsh—far more grim than that of the Valley Forge encampment. The skies dropped copious amounts of snow, the winds howled long and hard, and icy conditions prevailed. Under these circumstances, it was difficult for Martha to leave her family and comfortable Mount Vernon for a long, cold, miserable carriage ride. To prepare for the journey, Martha's coachmen, anticipating hazardous road conditions, hitched up seven horses for the carriage. Nevertheless, Martha still endured many harrowing days in a clumsy coach that bounced and jerked along the perilous roads. By the time she reached Philadelphia on December 21, the Delaware River had frozen solid. After celebrating Christmas in the city, Lady Washington left for camp on December 27. Capt. Caleb Gibbs met her in Princeton and escorted her to Morristown. Four days after leaving Philadelphia, Lady

Washington arrived at winter camp. New Year's Eve 1779 found General and Mrs. Washington by the fireside at Morristown headquarters.

The home of the widow Theodosia Ford had been chosen as army headquarters for the 1779–80 Morristown encampment. It was well known to Washington, for his guards had occupied the Ford Mansion during the 1776–77 Morristown encampment. Washington and his military family settled in on December 1, occupying two rooms on the lower floor, all of the upper floor, and the kitchen, cellar, and stable. It was a large house, but still too small for Mrs. Ford, her four children, Washington's military family, General and Mrs. Washington, and the Ford and Washington servants. "Eighteen [servants] belonging to my family and all Mrs. Fords are crowded together in her Kitchen," Washington wrote that Morristown winter, "and scarce one of them able to speak for the colds they have caught."[39] To ease living conditions, the general, as he had at Valley Forge, called for some construction work; in this case a log kitchen and office were built beside the mansion. Washington also restored the well, replastered two rooms above the stairs, and had a stable built.

Today little is known about Martha Washington's activities during her nine-month stay at Morristown. She did go to several dinner parties with her husband, including one at Col. Clement Biddle's hut in April. Other guests included General Greene, Colonels Tilghman and Stewart, Captain Gibbs, George Olney and his wife, Miss Elizabeth Schuyler, and numerous other gentlemen and ladies. Later Elizabeth Schuyler, the daughter of Gen. Philip Schuyler, sent Lady Washington a pair of "very pretty" cuffs that she had made. The gift prompted Mrs. Washington to reciprocate with, as she phrased it, "some nice powder," which Martha Washington hoped would be found "acceptable."[40]

On June 7 Washington left Morristown to deal with the British in Connecticut. Martha Washington remained at the Ford Mansion. Capt. John Steele, an unmarried nineteen-year-old, was temporarily placed in charge of Martha Washington's guards. The lady enchanted him; he dubbed her "the most amiable woman upon earth." In a letter to his brother, Steele writes about the general's wife: "I am at present enjoying myself incomparably well in the family of Mrs. Washington, whose guard I have had the honour to command, since the absence of the General and the rest of the family, which is now six or seven days. I am happy in the importance of my charge as well as in the presence of the most amiable woman upon earth, whose character should I attempt to describe I could not do justice to, but will only say I think it unexceptionable."

The captain had to be alert on his watch, as it was rumored that the enemy was poised to attack the Ford Mansion. But the guards were well prepared, Steele wrote, and, besides, they were assisted by four members of Congress who had rushed over to headquarters with their muskets and bayonets at the ready to protect the commander in chief's wife. Although the British attack never came, the gentlemen of Congress lingered on. They dined with the command nearly every day, consuming rations, Steele recalled, that "considerably overbalance all their service done as volunteers." The congressmen, Steele noted with dismay, also drank copious amounts of wine.[41]

The army left the Morristown area on June 23. Martha Washington had departed a few days earlier, as she and her entourage arrived in Philadelphia on June 21. While she was in the city, John Mitchell purchased a new chariot for her, which, he wrote to the general, "I believe will please your lady."[42] On June 29 Martha and numerous other ladies and gentlemen spent several enjoyable hours floating down the Delaware River on barges. In honor of her visit, the wharves and decks along the river banks had been decorated with yards and yards of bunting. In Philadelphia she again settled in at the now-familiar home of Esther and Joseph Reed, who was now president of the Supreme Executive Council of Pennsylvania. After spending several weeks with the Reed family, Martha Washington left the city in early July. But "her company gave us so sincere a pleasure," Reed wrote Washington, "that we could not but regret that it was so short."[43]

Through her conversations at the Reed home, Mrs. Washington may have influenced the beginnings of the Association, one of the earliest women's groups in America. (She may also have contributed $20,000 to the effort.) Founded in 1780 by Esther Reed, the organization was planned and administered by upper-class ladies, although donations were solicited and accepted from men and women of every social class. The Association raised money for the army by going door to door—scandalous behavior for eighteenth-century ladies.

Although the Association's financial campaign was successful, not everyone approved of the solicitation methods. Anne Rawle Clifford of Philadelphia, a Loyalist, wrote that those asking for money "were so importunate that people were obliged to give them something to get rid of them." Mrs. Clifford leaves us a vivid picture of the women purposefully going about their mission. They "paraded about the streets . . . some carrying ink stands," she wrote, "nor did they let the meanest ale house escape. The gentlemen were also honoured with their visits. Bob Wharton declared he was never so teased in his life. They reminded him of the extreme rudeness of refusing anything to the fair sex; but he was inexorable and pleaded want of money, and the heavy taxes, so at length they left him, after threatening to hand his name down to posterity with infamy."[44]

The Pennsylvania ladies raised $300,000 in paper money. Other states also raised significant funds, and in a few months the men of Washington's army received more than two thousand completed shirts. Not that this was what the ladies had planned. The goal had been to give each American soldier two hard dollars spending money. Washington, however, nixed this idea, fearing his soldiers would buy liquor with the cash and so cause troop "irregularities and disorders."[45] The ladies bowed to the wishes of the illustrious commander in chief, found their needles and thread, and dutifully stitched up shirts for the shabby Continental soldiers, each personalized with the name of the seamstress who had made it.

General Washington was appreciative of the ladies' efforts. "Amidst all the distresses and sufferings of the Army," Washington wrote to Sarah Bache, Benjamin Franklin's daughter, who took over leadership of the Association after Mrs. Reed died, "it must be a consolation to our Virtuous Country Women that they have never been accused of with holding their most zealous efforts to support the cause we are engaged in."[46] Just a month later Washington wrote, "The spirit that animated the members of it [the Association] entitles them to an equal place with any who have preceded them in the walk of female patriotism."[47]

While this fund-raising was going on, Martha arrived back at Mount Vernon, perhaps in her new chariot, about the middle of July 1780. She was exhausted from her travels to Morristown and Philadelphia. "I got home on fryday [sic] and find myself so much fatigue [sic] with my ride," she wrote in a July 18 letter to her brother-in-law, "that I shall not be able to come down to see you this summer." In spite of her exhaustion, however, the resolute woman was already making plans for her next journey north. Because she had "suffered so much last winter by going late" to camp, she had "determined to go early in the fall before the Frost set in." Camp conditions at Morristown also worried her. "There was not much pleasure thar [sic]," she wrote, "the distress of the army and other difficultys [sic] th'o I did not know the cause." And most important to her—"The pore [sic] Gen. was so unhappy that it distressed me exceedingly."[48]

NEW WINDSOR, NEW YORK, DECEMBER 1780–JUNE 1781

Because of the traitor Benedict Arnold—denounced by Washington as being guilty "of the greatest Meanness imaginable"—Martha Washington was, once again, unable to leave in early fall for winter camp.[49] Arnold's plot to surrender West Point was uncovered in late September 1780. His stunning betrayal and subsequent defection to the British galvanized Washington and the entire Continental Army. No one initially knew the extent of Arnold's diabolical plot. Had plans been drawn to capture other strongholds besides West Point? Had plans been laid to capture General Washington? Or, perhaps, Mrs. Washington?

The officers and soldiers of the Continental Army were in an uproar over Arnold's treason. Uncertain about what would happen next, the soldiers at West Point were "convulsed," as one recorded, and "stood almost day and night upon our arms, for I suppose three days at least." The heightened alert continued until "a beloved father, a beloved Washington visited and passed personally among the encampments at West Point."[50] The popular Maj. John Andre's role in the affair, along with his subsequent execution, also jolted the officers and men on both sides of the conflict. All this ruckus kept Washington busy, and he did not call for his lady to come north until late November. So much for Mrs. Washington's plan to travel to camp "before the Frost sets in."

That year Martha reached Philadelphia on November 30, 1780, and stayed, yet again, at Joseph Reed's home. The Marquis of Chastellux, a French officer who was also visiting there, remembered her as a woman of "about forty or forty-five, rather plump, but fresh and with an agreeable face."[51] (Martha was actually forty-nine at the time.) Because the winter season was fast approaching and the commander had already settled in at camp, she did not linger in Philadelphia. The day after she arrived in the city, Lady Washington, accompanied by James Duane, crossed the Delaware to Trenton. Martha's destination this year was the small William Ellison House in New Windsor, New York. Washington did not think too much of the place, writing frankly to Lafayette that he felt headquarters offered "very confined Quarters . . . little better than those of Valley Forge."[52]

From the Marquis de Chastellux comes one of the few firsthand accounts of Mrs. Washington's activities at New Windsor. On December 20 the Marquis, who had come to camp to see General Washington, met up with the commander and Mrs. Washington in their carriage. The couple was on their way to pay a social call to Martha's friend Lucy Knox, who was staying about three miles from the military headquarters. (General and Mrs. Knox and their little daughter had wintered at Valley Forge.) Although a carriage ride with his wife must have been a welcome break in Washington's usual military routine, when the general saw Chastellux he immediately offered to return to headquarters. The Marquis refused this offer, so Washington had an aide, Col. David Humphreys, accompany Chastellux back to army headquarters. Just a half hour later, Washington himself appeared back at camp. Chastellux noted of the evening, "Dinner was excellent; tea succeeded dinner, and conversation succeeded tea, and lasted until supper."[53]

The day after Christmas, Martha Washington wrote from New Windsor to Charles Willson Peale, the artist who had been at the Valley Forge encampment, asking him to set three miniatures he had painted for her in 1772 and 1776 in "Braceletts [sic] to wear round the wrists." The small portraits (of daughter Patcy, son Jacky, and herself) were to be set exactly alike, to be made all the same size, and were to be made up "neat and plain." If Peale had no glass crystals, she would "beg" him to get some, and quickly, as she was "very anxious" for her new adornments. Martha also asked that the diamonds surrounding one of the pictures be removed and set in a hair pin.

Peale replied on January 16, assuring her he had indeed "begged" the jeweler to "take the utmost pains" to set the miniatures neatly. He had no crystals, but glass had been molded to cover the paintings, "which, I hope, will not be inferior to those made abroad." Peale even went beyond what Mrs. Washington had directed. He had small loopholes made so the settings could also be used as lockets. "The additional expense," he promised his wealthy customer, would be "inconsiderable."[54]

While the Washingtons were at New Windsor, the British were making mischief at Mount Vernon. When British ships sailed up the Potomac in

April, Lund Washington met the enemy at the plantation dock and offered refreshments. He reasoned that in placating the British he could save the house and plantation from destruction. The conciliatory action may have protected the property, but it earned Lund the wrath of Washington. On learning of his manager's actions, the general sent a sharp letter of reprimand. "To go on board their [the British] vessels," Washington wrote, "carry them refreshments, commune with a parcel of plundering scoundrels, and request a favour, by asking the surrender of my Negroes, was exceedingly ill-judged." The politically astute Washington went on to write that he feared Lund's action would have unhappy consequences and would become a subject of, as the general put it, "animadversion."[55]

Toward the end of May, Martha Washington became seriously ill with severe abdominal pain, biliousness, and jaundice—all symptoms of gall bladder disease. "The news of Mrs. Washington's illness has filled Mrs. Boudinot and myself with the most alarming fears," wrote Gen. Elias Boudinot to Washington on June 28. "We earnestly pray God for the restoration of her health."[56] But mail delivery was neither speedy nor reliable during those Revolutionary times, and when Boudinot, who had also been at the Valley Forge encampment, penned this letter Martha had already recovered sufficiently to board her carriage for the journey south to Mount Vernon.

General Washington had noted his wife's illness, as well as the difficulty in securing medical supplies for her, in separate letters to Jacky Custis and Lund Washington. Both of these letters, as well as two others in the packet, had been intercepted and delivered to the British commander Gen. Henry Clinton. When Mrs. Martha Mortier, widow of a British Army paymaster and General Clinton's confidante, learned of Mrs. Washington's illness, she took it upon herself to personally assist in Mrs. Washington's recovery. Mrs. Mortier wrote Washington that she had taken "the liberty to send her [Mrs. Washington] such as this place [New York City] affords, by means of a flag of truce . . . and begs leave to offer Mrs. W: any other Assistance her situation may require." Included among the items Mrs. Mortier thought necessary for Mrs. Washington's recovery were two dozen pineapples, two hundred limes, boxes of lemons, oranges, and sweetmeats, a keg of tarmarinds (medicinal seed from *tamarindus indica*), two dozen capillaire (to prepare a syrup from maiden hair fern), two dozen orgeat (used to prepare a syrup made from barley, almonds, and orange flower water), and two pounds of Hyson (Chinese green) tea.[57] Such was the state of eighteenth-century medicine.

Mrs. Mortier may have been well-intentioned. Or, she may have been trying to trap General Washington into accepting ministrations from the British. Either way, her efforts were promptly rebuffed. Not only did Washington receive the letter late—on June 21, after Martha had already recovered—but the commander in chief did not want anyone, whether Patriot or Loyalist, American or British, to accuse either he or his wife of accepting favors from the enemy. He promptly ordered nothing to be landed under Mrs. Mortier's flag. All fruits, tea, and the other items were to be returned. A courteous third-person note, dated June 21, 1781, accompanied the gifts back to Mrs. Mortier: "Gen. Washington presents his compliments to Mrs. Mortier and thanks her for her very polite attention to Mrs. Washington, who has so perfectly recovered as to be able to set out for Virginia in a day or two. This being the case, Gen. Washington hopes Mrs. Mortier will excuse his returning the several articles which she in so kind a manner sent up by Flag, assuring her at the same time that he shall ever entertain a grateful sense of this mark of her benevolence."[58]

With the army ready to begin the summer campaign, and now sufficiently recovered to travel—even without Mrs. Mortier's offerings—Lady Washington once more was assisted into her coach. She started for home on June 25. She traveled with her husband to Peekskill, New York, then south to Philadelphia, arriving on June 30. That very day Lady Washington's coachman returned the brown horse to the public stable that had been borrowed for her journey.

Another winter encampment was over. Lady Washington would have been delighted to know there were only two more to go.

GEORGE WASHINGTON AT MOUNT VERNON

Just a few months later, something happened to Martha Washington that had never happened before during the war—General Washington traveled to her, at Mount Vernon.

The "rebellion"—as the British first thought of it—had persisted for years. By 1781 the campaign had shifted from north to south, with the British in firm control of Savannah, Georgia, and Charlestown, South Carolina. American finances, always shaky, had collapsed completely. Enriched and encouraged by the French ground and naval support, Washington planned a major campaign against Gen. Charles Cornwallis at Yorktown, Virginia. On his way to the field, Washington, accompanied by several of his officers, detoured to Mount Vernon. He arrived on September 9, 1781, to joy and acclamation, for this was the first time in over six years that the general had been back to his plantation. Then, just three days later, the commander in chief of the Continental Army left for battle.

Jacky Custis was the last of Mrs. Washington's four children. (Two children had died young; seventeen-year-old Patcy died of an epileptic seizure on June 19, 1773.) Although Jacky had accompanied his mother to the Cambridge winter encampment, he had never participated with his stepfather in a campaign. Now Jacky asked to serve as a kind of aide to General Washington for the pending Yorktown action, and the offer was accepted. Addressing Martha Washington as "My Dear & Honored Madam," Jacky, a good and dutiful son, wrote his mother from the "Camp Before York," on October 12, just days before the important battle. The letter contained news about his health (he was feeling much better) and the health of General Washington ("tho in constant Fatigue looks very well"). Jacky had stopped to visit Bartholomew Dandridge, Martha's brother, on the way to the battle. His uncle, Jacky wrote, "has suffered very much by the Enemy," but was "in good health" and would welcome a visit from Martha. Jacky also reported about the slaves who had left Mount Vernon during the war. Although he had made "every possible Enquiry," Jacky wrote, he had not seen any of them. The mortality rate among slaves who had left the plantations for the army was "really incredible," Jacky believed, and he feared that "most who left us are not existing." Jacky, with his own eyes, "had seen numbers [of slaves] lying dead in the Woods, and many so exhausted that they cannot walk." Jacky signed his letter with these words: "I am dear Madam with the sincerest affection Your very dutiful son J.P.Custis."[59] This is the last letter Martha received from her son.

With help from the French, the siege of Yorktown was a resounding victory for the Continental Army. Although Cornwallis surrendered one-third of the British Army to the "rebels," the triumph did not bring an immediate end to hostilities. New York was still in British hands. Fighting—often fierce fighting—continued in the south for two more years. And the victory at Yorktown was bittersweet personally for the Washingtons. Even as they rejoiced in a great military victory, George and Martha mourned a great personal loss. Jacky Custis had contracted "putrid fever which he caught in camp," as Gen. George Weedon described it, and died November 5, 1781, at Eltham, the home of his uncle, Burwell Bassett.[60] After funeral services, his bereaved mother and stepfather left Eltham for the sanctuary of Mount Vernon. The general later wrote of his wife, "Poor Mrs. Washington . . . has met with a most severe stroke in the loss of her amiable Son, and only Child Mr. Custis."[61]

Although Washington and Jacky had had some difficult times together when Jacky was growing up, Washington cared deeply for Martha's son. "The general was uncommonly affected at his death," Chastellux noted, "insomuch that many of his friends imagined they perceived some change in his equanimity of temper, subsequent to that event. It is certain that they [Washington and Jacky] were upon terms of the most affectionate and manly friendship."[62]

Much as he loved and needed the comfort of his own hearth and home, Washington, as commander in chief of the Continental Army, could not remain in Mount Vernon indefinitely. When he left Mount Vernon on November 20, he took the heart of his home—his grieving Martha—with him. The couple and their entourage reached Baltimore on November 23 and Philadelphia on the twenty-sixth. A month later they celebrated Christmas at the Philadelphia home of Mr. and Mrs. Robert Morris.

NEWBURGH, NEW YORK, MARCH 31–JULY 10, 1782

General and Mrs. Washington did not leave Philadelphia until March 22, 1782. They arrived at the Newburgh encampment on March 31. As would be expected, an official military escort, this time an officer, sergeant, and twelve dragoons, met the general and his wife along the road to escort them into camp. Hasbrouck House, headquarters for the Newburgh encampment that year and the year following, is still standing (and open for visitors) today.

Martha would have been pleased that her travels to the encampment were not difficult that year. Not only did her husband accompany her to headquarters, but they traveled in late March, when the roads and weather were not as treacherous as in winter. Rather than spending the winter and spring months with her husband, as was usual when she came to an encampment, in 1782 she spent spring and part of the summer at headquarters. She left Newburgh on July 10, two days before the general left camp. After leaving New York State, the general and his wife met in Philadelphia on July 14, where they remained for ten days. On July 24 Washington headed north to return to the Newburgh headquarters, and Martha started south to Mount Vernon. Undoubtedly she traveled to Mount Vernon with a lighter heart, for she had heard rumors of a completed peace treaty between Britain and the United States. She so wanted the war over!

As did her husband. An unusually candid letter written by Washington on June 15, 1782, from Newburgh shows just how much he yearned for home. "I pant for retirement," the commander wrote. "I can truly say that the first wish of my Soul is to return speedily into the bosom of that Country which gave me my birth and in the sweet enjoyment of domestic pleasures and the Company of a few friends to end my days in quiet when I shall be called from this Stage."[63] This was a man who wanted to be with his friends and wife—at Mount Vernon. He had to settle for writing.

One of the three letters that have been found from George Washington to Martha was written in October from Newburgh. This was not a personal letter, but rather a few words scrawled on a letter of introduction carried by James Brown, should Mr. Brown travel near Mount Vernon. "My dearest," Washington wrote, "If this should ever reach your hands it will be presented by Mr Brown . . . from whom I have received civilities. . . . As he has thoughts of going into Virginia I recommend him to your notice & attention." Then the general ended with a closing that sounds restrained today: "I am most sincerely & affectionately—Yrs Geo. Washington."

But Brown, whose Providence, Rhode Island, merchant father supplied the army with tent cloth and munitions, did not travel as far south as Mount Vernon that year. In December 1786, when Brown finally reached Mount Vernon, he wrote a glowing report of his visit. "The immortal Man and his very kind & hospitable Lady were there," Brown wrote, "and the attention I recd while there from all the family made an impression so strong and so agreeable, that it never can be erased from the Tablet of Memory."[64]

THE EIGHTH (AND FINAL) WINTER ENCAMPMENT, NEWBURGH, NEW YORK, AND ROCKY HILL, NEW JERSEY, DECEMBER 1782–OCTOBER 3, 1783

Just four months after returning to Mount Vernon, Martha started north in her carriage for what would be her longest wartime absence from home.

As Washington was "despairing of seeing my home this winter," he planned to write to his wife around October 17 about, as he phrased it, "her annual visit."[65] Although he had expected Martha to set out for camp on November 14, she did not enter her carriage until November 20. Dr. David Stuart—who later married the widow of Martha's son, Jacky—accompanied Lady Washington to Newburgh. They arrived at headquarters, the familiar Hasbrouck House, ten days after setting out, on November 30. This would be Martha's eighth, and, as she had hoped, final journey north during the Revolution.

On December 5 the Marquis de Chastellux arrived at Newburgh to confer with the commander. Chastellux's journal gives some idea of conditions at headquarters, which he approached on roads that were "very bad." When he finally found Hasbrouck House, he deemed it "neither spacious nor convenient." The family parlor, oddly constructed with seven doors and only one window, had been converted into the dining room. The small room that Washington used as the parlor became, with the addition of a camp bed, Chastellux's sleeping chamber. During the day the bed was folded up, and, as Chastellux wrote, "my chamber became the sitting room for the whole afternoon; for American manners do not admit of a bed in a room in which company is received, especially when there are women." Chastellux noted that supper was served at nine in the evening, breakfast at ten in the morning.

Chastellux left headquarters on December 7. The ride took him past rows and rows of what he called "log-houses" (soldiers' huts) that, he noticed, were not quite finished. Each hut was built with two rooms, and "each inhabited by eight soldiers when full, which commonly mean five or six men in actual fact." Chastellux learned, to his surprise, that no nails were used in the construction of the huts, "which would render the work tedious and difficult were not the Americans very expert in working with wood."[66]

A few things are known about Martha Washington's activities at Hasbrouck House. She requested, and received, a pair of shoes. She asked her husband to have six yards of fine muslin, fifty-four inches wide, sent up to camp. She requested three yards of black silk to repair some old black gowns. And, accompanied by Mrs. Knox and some other ladies, Mrs. Washington attended the celebration of the French Alliance.

The first celebration of the French Alliance had taken place at Valley Forge five years earlier. At Newburgh, as he had at Valley Forge, Washington pardoned "all military prisoners now in confinement" to commemorate America's friendship with the French. This happened on February 6, 1783. Then on February 7, according to Lossing's *Mary and Martha*, Martha Washington wrote from Newburgh that a group of prisoners—"over fifty soldiers, thinly clad, and with pale but happy faces"—came to her door at Hasbrouck House. Martha was touched; the letter says her eyes filled with tears as she gave the leader money to share with the other pardoned prisoners. Lossing continues that she "bade them 'go, and sin no more.' The poor fellow kissed my hand and said 'God bless Lady Washington.' Poor Fellows!"[67]

This touching letter depicts Martha Washington interacting directly with the soldiers. The incident, however, is found only in Lossing's book. The original letter has never been found. Most surprising, Lossing writes that Martha addressed the letter to her sister, Anna Maria Bassett, who, of course, had died years ago, just before Martha left for the Valley Forge encampment. It is likely that it depicts an incident in Martha Washington's life—and an image of Martha Washington interacting with the common soldiers—that never occurred.

At Newburgh, Martha did make a hairnet for General Knox and had it delivered to Knox at West Point. She also helped out the busy aides by copying a few letters of the extensive army correspondence. It was routine for Washington's aides to make several copies of any letter or order that went out from headquarters. But that spring Martha Washington did an unusual thing—she copied out two of the letters herself: one dated March 31, 1783, from the general to Alexander Hamilton, and the second, also to Hamilton, dated April 22, 1783.

On April 15, George Bennet, an Englishman, arrived at headquarters at Newburgh, then wrote about his visit to his mother. After Bennet arrived, the general invited him ("with great affability") to share a glass of wine and then to dinner—an "honour which I could never have expected & would by no means decline." At the dining table, Washington placed Bennet by the left hand of Lady Washington; the commander sat on her right. About fifteen officers were also at the table. Everyone sat on camp stools. "The dinner was good," Bennet wrote, "but everything was quite plain." About his dining companion, Mrs. Washington, Bennet wrote, "Mrs. W.

was as plain, easy, and affable as he was, & one would have thought from the familiarity which prevailed there, that he saw a respectable private gentleman dining at the Head of his own Family."[68]

George Washington and his wife devoutly wished for the British to evacuate New York and the war to be over. Indeed, on June 18 the commander wrote that he looked forward to the end of public life with "great solicitude" and "with heart felt satisfaction that in the Walks of private life my Mind may enjoy that relaxation and repose of which it stands much in need."[69]

And, to prepare for private life in Virginia, Washington started to shop. He asked David Rittenhouse to grind him lenses for spectacles. He ordered "superfine Buff Cloth (not of the yellow kind)" for a vest coat, breeches, and coat facing. He purchased six strong hair trunks with good clasps and locks to transport his books and papers to Mount Vernon. He ordered two pipes (large casks) of old Madeira wine. Table cloths were wanted, as well as napkins, sheeting, linen, check cloth, and twelve bed blankets of the best quality. (Later the general wrote that his wife would inspect the linen when she arrived in Philadelphia, "that she may please herself in the quality.")[70] Two hundred "ordinary blankets" were required for Washington's slaves. He also asked that a good house joiner (carpenter) be purchased for him at Philadelphia "at a price not exceeding Thirty pds" (pounds) from among the Irish indentured servants recently come into port. The servant was to be sent directly to Mount Vernon.[71]

June 18 found Mrs. Washington away from camp on a little jaunt with Governor and Mrs. Clinton. In mid-July Washington left Newburgh on army business, leaving the guards to care for Mrs. Washington. The general was gone from camp for nineteen days—and traveled more than 750 miles—finally returning to Newburgh on August 6. During August Mrs. Washington was "exceedingly unwell" but recovered enough toward the end of the month to travel with her husband to a home near Princeton, New Jersey.

This time headquarters was established at "Rocky Hill," about four miles north of Princeton, on August 24. After arriving at Rocky Hill, Mrs. Washington had a "severe return" with what her husband called "the Cholic," but by September 11 she was, Washington felt, "as well as usual."[72] Then, just a few weeks later, Mrs. Washington, the commander's guard, two of the aides, and many of the servants were stricken with an ailment that was both mysterious and debilitating. After recovering, Martha visited Philadelphia, where she walked in on her husband having his face plastered for a life mask. The sculptor, Joseph Wright, had just "oiled my features over," Washington related to a visitor, "and placing me flat upon my back upon a cot, proceeded to daub my face with the plaster. Whilst [I was] in this ludicrous attitude, Mrs. Washington [then visiting at Rocky Hill] entered the room; and seeing my face thus overspread with the plaster, involuntarily exclaimed [in alarm]. Her cry excited in me a disposition to smile, which gave my mouth a slight twist . . . that is now observable in the busts which Wright afterward made."[73]

This excitement over, Mrs. Washington left for Mount Vernon on October 3, anxious to get home before the weather ruined the roads. Washington declared himself ready to head for home also, and would do so, "as soon as the Definitive Treaty arrives" or the city of New York, he continued with a touch of sarcasm, "is evacuated by our Newly acquired Friends," the British.[74] The general accompanied his wife from Rocky Hill as far as Trenton, and she continued on to Philadelphia, where she stayed for several days with Mr. and Mrs. Robert Morris. She purchased some furniture and other items for Mount Vernon in Philadelphia, and perhaps determined the quality of the linen that the general had ordered.

Then Martha climbed into her carriage, waved good-bye to the city and her friends, and, finally, started for hearth, home, and family at Mount Vernon. She was going home for good, or so she thought.

As Martha bumped along in her carriage, she could not have helped reflecting on the sad bereavements that had affected her life during the long, long Revolutionary War. Her son John Parke Custis, the last of her four children, had died soon after the great American victory at Yorktown. Jacky and Eleanor Custis's first child—and Martha's first grandchild—died shortly after birth, in the autumn of 1775. Martha's brother, Thomas, died in 1776. Mrs. Washington lost her favorite sister, Anna Maria Bassett, soon before she left for the Valley Forge encampment.

The family had also grown during the war. On August 21, 1776, Jacky and Eleanor Custis had another daughter, Elizabeth Parke Custis. The relieved Jacky's jubilant letter to his "dearest Mamma" described the baby as "fine a Healthy, fat Baby as ever was born."[75] Martha "Patty" Parke Custis, Jacky and Eleanor Custis's next daughter, was born at Mount Vernon on December 31, 1777. On March 31, 1779, Martha Washington became a grandmother again with the birth of Eleanor Parke Custis—known as Nelly by the family. George Washington Parke Custis (called Washy, Wash, or even Tub or Tubby by the family) was born on April 31, 1781. After Jacky Custis's death, George and Martha Washington brought little Nelly and Wash to live with them at Mount Vernon.

GENERAL WASHINGTON COMES HOME

While his wife was preparing Mount Vernon for his arrival, General Washington was preparing for his departure from military service. On December 4, 1783, he bid an emotional farewell to the officers of the army at Faunces Tavern in New York City. (Lt. Col. Benjamin Tallmadge, who attended the event, wrote, "Such a scene of sorrow and weeping, I had never before witnessed.")[76] After embracing each officer present at the tavern, Washington raised his hand in a final farewell and left the room. He boarded his barge, already packed with his belongings and gifts for Martha, Nelly, and Wash, and set off across the Hudson to Elizabeth, New Jersey.

Washington traveled through New Brunswick and Trenton to Philadelphia, where he was again hosted by Robert Morris. The general stayed at "The Hills," known today as Lemon Hill, the larger of the two Morris properties, and he spent days with Morris, the "Financier of the Revolution," attempting to settle his financial accounts. Washington refused pay for his services as commander in chief but had requested reimbursement for such things as equipment, travel, official entertaining, and personal necessities during the war. He calculated his expenses to be $160,074, which, when audited, was found to be very slightly less (eighty-nine ninetieths of one dollar) than what he was actually owed.[77] Washington also requested reimbursement of $27,665.30 for Mrs. Washington's traveling expenses to and from his winter quarters.

Washington was feted by every assembly, on any occasion, while he remained in Philadelphia. Robert Morris put it this way: "We are much employed here," he wrote, "in showing the most affectionate marks of our strong attachment to the Commander in Chief."[78] While in the city, Washington gave speeches to such groups as the General Assembly of Pennsylvania and the American Philosophical Society. As he had at Valley Forge, he sat for a portrait by Charles Willson Peale. He acquired another pair of spectacles from David Rittenhouse, who refused payment. Washington finally left Philadelphia on December 16.

Washington's farewell journey took him through Baltimore to Annapolis, where Congress—or what there was of it at Annapolis—had made elaborate, formal plans for Washington's address. Washington himself had given careful thought to the occasion and its significance. But before he addressed the delegates, he stopped to write one final letter—his last "while I continue in the service of my Country." It was to Baron von Steuben, commending Steuben for his "faithful and meritorious Service."[79] Steuben, at the Valley Forge encampment, had transformed the Continental Army into a powerful fighting force.

Then, on December 23, 1783, at twelve noon, to an audience convulsed with emotion, Washington acknowledged that he was retiring from "the great theater of Action." He bid "an Affectionate farewell to this August body under whose orders I have so long acted," returned his commission, and declared he was taking "leave of all the employments of public life."[80]

And so this "great and good man" retired from military life. After delivering his farewell speech, Washington bid good-bye to each member of Congress, walked out the door, mounted his horse, and rode toward his beloved Martha, who had remained in Mount Vernon. Although John Turnbull's monumental *The Resignation of Gen. Washington, 23 December 1783*, painted in 1824, depicts Lady Washington at the farewell event, there is no evidence from the time that she traveled to Annapolis. (Turnbull also painted in James Madison, who was not there either.) Benson J. Lossing, too, errs when he writes in *The Pictorial Field-Book of the Revolution* (1860), "When the whole business [of the resignation] was closed, Washington and his lady set out for Mount Vernon."[81]

Martha Washington greeted her husband with a joyful heart and open arms on Christmas Eve 1783. She had everything in readiness at Mount Vernon for her warrior, who, she believed, would remain with her in Virginia forever.

Instead, in 1789, General Washington became President Washington, and Martha again packed her bags, climbed up into her carriage, and followed him north.

4

Catharine Greene and Lucy Knox

The Ladies Come to Valley Forge

Many picture the Valley Forge encampment crowded with sick, shivering, hungry soldiers dressed in tattered uniforms. Less well-known is that for some the winter encampment of 1777–78 was a place of enjoyment. Several senior officers, General Washington among them, invited their wives to join them at camp. These eighteenth-century women of privilege were called and regarded as "ladies." And at least one lady, Catharine Greene, had herself a fine time at camp.

How many ladies came to camp the winter of 1777–78? Although there is no definitive answer, there are a few clues. Maj. Gen. Johann de Kalb wrote, "Fifteen hundred persons sat down to the tables, which were spread in the open air," at a grand banquet to celebrate the French Alliance on May 6, 1778, at camp. "All the officers with their ladies, and the prominent people of the neighborhood were invited."[1] Joseph Addison's *Cato* was performed in mid-May before "a very numerous & splendid audience."[2] That winter Charles Willson Peale painted portraits of about fifty officers and their ladies.[3] Pierre S. DuPonceau, an aide to General von Steuben, spent memorable evenings making music with Mrs. Washington, Mrs. Greene, Lady Stirling, Lady Kitty Alexander, Miss Nancy Brown, Mrs. Rebekah Biddle, and, as he wrote, some other gentlemen and ladies he could not "recollect."[4]

And herein lies the problem. There were ladies at Valley Forge who will never be "recollected." Undoubtedly the "very numerous & splendid audience" that enjoyed an evening of *Cato* included ladies whose names will never be known to us.

Some ladies were invited to camp but refused the invitation. Col. Israel Shreve promised his wife, Mary "Polley" Shreve, a "Genteel Place" to stay if she came to the Valley Forge encampment. (The "Genteel Place" was a private bedroom—scarce in the eighteenth century—in a farmhouse.)[5] Gen. Elias Boudinot, commissary general of prisoners, attempted to lure his wife, Hannah, to camp by writing her that Mrs. Washington "often speaks of you, always asks after you and wishes you with her." Martha Washington was lonely at Valley Forge, Boudinot wrote, and "almost a Mope, for want of a female Companion."[6] William Bradford Jr. tried to beguile his sister, Rachel, to visit by promising a trip to the camp theater. And, he wrote, "The maneuvering of the Army is in itself a sight that would Charm you."[7] But neither the promise of good lodgings, nor the theater, nor army maneuvers, nor even Lady Washington's company was enough to tempt Polley Shreve, Hannah Boudinot, or Rachel Bradford Boudinot to come to Valley Forge. They all remained in their own homes, far from the encampment.

Perhaps these ladies stayed home because of their children. And, with the men off to war, some ladies had family farms or businesses to run. The road to camp was long, cold, and dangerous. Not many ladies, even in the best of circumstances, would be willing to undertake the forbidding journey. Some wives did not have the carriage, horses, or necessary finances to travel during the war. Others were simply not interested in traveling to Valley Forge that winter. Although camp was only eight miles distant from her home at "Waynesboro," Polly Wayne, for example, would not join her husband Gen. Anthony Wayne at camp. Nor did "Mad Anthony" travel home to her.

Some officers' wives did not come to camp because their husbands went to them. A huge number of officers—almost six hundred—resigned their commissions at Valley Forge. Many more attempted to do so, but their resignations were not accepted. Albigence Waldo, an army surgeon, wrote that one day after Christmas "fifty officers in General Greene's division resigned their commissions." They resigned not because of the difficult conditions they were facing at camp but because their families were "so much Neglected at home on Account of Provisions."[8] At an earlier encampment Lt. David Perry asked permission to leave the army because his wife had broken both her arms falling from a horse and needed him home to care for the "small and helpless children."[9] Soon after he made the request, Lieutenant Perry was on his way home.

As for the ladies who did come to Valley Forge, information is less available and reliable than one would like. There are letters, journals, and diaries of the period. But, like the tales of Martha Washington's activities at camp, there are also fanciful stories about what the other officers' wives did at Valley Forge. Elizabeth Ellet's *The Women of the American Revolution*, for example, has Rebekah Biddle and the Marquis de Lafayette reminiscing fifty years after the encampment about the masses of pigeons captured, cooked, and eaten at Valley Forge.[10] But there is no evidence for this. Nor, as is alleged in some accounts, does any eighteenth-century primary source record any officer's lady informally visiting among the soldiers at the Valley Forge encampment.

Yet even a peek into the lives of the remarkable ladies who traveled to the encampment broadens our knowledge of eighteenth-century gentry—and enriches our understanding of that extraordinary winter at Valley Forge.

MRS. NATHANAEL GREENE: CATHARINE "CATY" LITTLEFIELD GREENE, DECEMBER 17, 1753–SEPTEMBER 2, 1814

Gen. Nathanael Greene, who was appointed quartermaster general of the Continental Army at Valley Forge, was one of Washington's best and most trusted officers. Not only did Washington have a close professional relationship with Greene, but personal connections also developed between the Greene and Washington families. Caty and Nathanael Greene named their first son George Washington Greene and their first daughter Martha Washington Greene. After Nathanael Greene died, George Washington offered to see to his namesake's education. (Instead, Caty sent her son off to France to be educated by the Marquis de Lafayette.) When Caty wanted to join her husband in the south during the war, Washington wrote Greene that he would "strew the way over with flowers."[11] Cornelia Greene, the Greenes' second daughter, lived with the Washingtons for a time during the presidential years. After being elected president, Washington visited the Greenes' South Carolina plantation when he traveled throughout the country. And of course, as has been noted, Washington danced for three hours straight with Catharine Greene at the Middlebrook encampment.

Independent, intelligent, and determined, Catharine Littlefield Greene was quite a lady—and a woman who enjoyed the company of men. Caty was also a beauty. Twenty-four years old when she came to Valley Forge— and twelve years younger than her husband—she was remembered for having "glossy black hair" and "brilliant violet eyes." Her "clear-cut features, transparent complexion, and exquisitely molded hands and feet," all "united to make her lovely."[12] Caty also possessed fine manners, a "retentive memory, lively imagination, and great fluency of speech," which made her "one of the most brilliant and entertaining of women."[13] Such a lady wanted to flirt, to flaunt, to be admired. Caty Greene relished the excitement and adventure of army camp, and once, much to her husband's surprise—and chagrin—even showed up at a military camp uninvited.

Nathanael Greene adored his "Angel." "I long to be with you again," Greene wrote to Caty in a tender July 1777 letter. "The soft delights, the sweet pleasures of social endearments I felt at our meeting still dances round my heart, makes me anxiously wish their continuance, but fate, cruel fate, cuts the thread." (In this same letter, Greene wrote that he wanted everybody to love Caty as he did, "only to a less degree.")[14] And then, in November 1777 he wrote, "I wish the campaign was over that I might come and partake of your diversions but we must first give Mr How a twiging and then for a joyous winter of pleasant Folly."[15] ("Mr How" was Gen. William Howe, commander of the British Army, and Caty and Nathanael Greene would spend their "joyous winter of pleasant Folly" at Valley Forge.)

In anticipation of the 1777–78 winter encampment, Caty Greene had left Rhode Island months earlier—in June. The two Greene children (little George and Martha, called Patty by her family) remained behind in Rhode Island with one of Nathanael Greene's five brothers. After visiting for months at the New Jersey estate of friends, Caty arrived at Valley Forge on January 6, 1778. She was one of the first ladies to come to camp.

At Valley Forge, General Greene and his lady lived in a log hut for several months, an arrangement that originally pleased Greene. "After a most fatiguing campaign," he wrote to a brother, lodging in a log hut was "a sweet life" indeed.[16] But all was not well for his wife. Caty was so sick on February 26, Greene wrote, that she was unable to sit up. On March 7 General Greene wrote, "Mrs. Greene . . . has been very ill for about a fortnight with a fever, but is getting better."[17] Two days later Greene reported that Caty remained very sick. What Greene does not say in any letter (few did in those days) was that his wife was pregnant once again.

Apparently, however, Caty roused herself when eighteen-year-old Pierre DuPonceau visited the Greenes at their hut in early March. DuPonceau never writes that Caty showed signs of illness when he came to call. In fact, the lady was, to his teenage eyes, a "handsome, elegant & accomplished woman." DuPonceau does say that, on March 5, the two of them chattered away in French, and the very next day he sent her eight volumes of French comedy. DuPonceau later recalled that because Mrs. Greene "understood and spoke the French language, and was well versed in French literature," the officers from France enjoyed visiting at her home.[18]

Near the end of March General Greene and his wife relocated. Greene eventually found life in a cabin "very inconvenient" to carry on the business of the quartermaster's department,[19] so the couple moved several miles down the road to stately Moore Hall, a large home owned by William Moore, a Loyalist. The Moore family remained in residence throughout the Valley Forge encampment. (Moore Hall remains as a private home today.)

Nathanael Greene had reluctantly accepted the appointment of quartermaster general of the army in February. While he reorganized and improved the quartermaster's department at Valley Forge, his wife entertained, visited with the other ladies, read those eight volumes of French comedy, sat for her portrait, and accepted gifts. Charles Willson Peale's diary records that he began miniatures of General and Mrs. Greene on March 28; he completed Lady Greene's portrait on April 5.[20] On March 16 General Greene wrote to Col. James Abeel, the assistant quartermaster, saying that his wife was "much obliged to you for the Coffee Mill." (Abeel had also sent along an inkstand and wax for General Greene, which necessitated a request from Greene for "some good paper.")[21] Also on March 16, General Greene, on behalf of his wife, sent Gen. William Smallwood a note thanking him for the Hyson tea that he had sent the Greenes. The tea had been taken from the *Symetry*, a British brig captured by the Americans.[22]

Caty Greene also participated in the encampment's May 6 celebration of the French formally aligning with the Americans against the British. Mrs. Washington, Lady Stirling, Kitty Stirling, and some other ladies were present, "amongst whom good humor and the graces were contending for pre-eminence," reported the *New York Journal*.[22] As noted before, Lady Greene was also in attendance at the May 11 camp production of *Cato.*

Three months after Catharine Greene came to camp, plans were put in motion for her departure. On April 12 Elihue Greene wrote to his brother Nathanael, "I hear Sister Caty is Coming home. Tell her that we Shall be very glad to See her and will make her as happy as we can while she is from you."[23] Nathanael's cousin Griffin Greene was also eager to be of assistance, writing to Nathanael, also on April 12, that, once Caty arrived back in Rhode Island, should she call on him, he would be pleased to be "at her command."[24] Maj. Samuel Ward of Rhode Island, who was at Valley Forge, had been approached to accompany Caty back to Rhode Island. Cousin Caty, Ward wrote to his new bride in Rhode Island on April 28, intended to leave camp "in a few Days."[25]

But Mrs. Greene delayed her departure again and again. In spring the camp took on a festive air, just as Caty liked it. Finally, on May 25, after the French Alliance had been celebrated and *Cato* had been enjoyed, Caty started home. Soon before she left, as a token of their esteem, the Greenes presented a large punch bowl to General Washington. It had been ordered through the assistant quartermaster and was delivered to them on May 12.

"Poor girl," Nathanael Greene wrote about Caty after she had left camp. "She is constantly separated, either from her husband or children, and sometimes from both."[26] That same day he also sent his cousin Griffin the news that Mrs. Greene had left Valley Forge, adding, "You will see her situation and condition and I hope accommodate her accordingly. I shall be much obliged to you and brother Jacob to endeavor to render her as happy as circumstances will admit."[27] This was Nathanael Greene's delicate way of communicating that his wife was pregnant with their third—as he had once phrased it—"little pledge of mutual affection."[28]

CATHARINE GREENE IN RHODE ISLAND

"I hope you got home safe," Nathanael Greene penned plaintively to Caty a month after she left Valley Forge for Rhode Island. Although he had written to her several times, General Greene had not heard a word from his wife for weeks after she left camp. Perhaps, Greene speculated, Caty's letters had been confiscated and opened "by some impudent scoundrel." After Caty left camp, General Greene had, he reported, remained busy at Valley Forge "in the usual style, Writing, Scolding, Eating and Drinking." But he missed his wife. He no longer had "Mrs. Greene to retire to spend an agreeable hour with."

And, Greene assured Caty, others missed her, too. The Moore family "all enquire after you with great affection and respect, and I believe with a degree of sincerity." Mrs. Washington and the other ladies at camp, Greene wrote, asked about Caty daily. Even Mrs. Henry Knox, who had arrived at camp two days after Catharine Greene left, "professes great regard for you and often inquires how and where you are . . . she really seems sincere." Col. John Cox and Mr. Charles Pettit (two of General Greene's business partners) desired "their most respectful compliments." And Mr. Lebrune, Greene wrote, "wants to see Mrs. Greene very much, "as he "thinks he loves her very well."[29] Catharine Greene made quite an impression wherever she went.

Caty had arrived home safely. After picking up little George and Martha, who had been shunted to Nathanael's brother Elihue at Potowomut, Rhode Island, Caty traveled to her own home in Coventry. Finding it too remote for her taste, she moved to Westerly, a farmhouse near the Connecticut border that was also owned by her husband. She was surprised to find herself "extremely pleased with my situation here. The house is pleasantly situated. . . . We have fine fish and in abundance good butter milk." Caty was pleased with the social scene, too—always of importance to her. The "finest circle of ladies I have seen for a long time" had called on her, and she had received two invitations to dine. (She had been able to accept only one of the invitations, however, because of the torrential rains.) Caty was stepping out, in spite of the admonitions of a local blacksmith who had observed her condition and, Caty wrote, informed her in no uncertain terms that "home was the proper place for women—that he thought I had better be spinning than riding about."[30] But Caty was not to be deterred; she was an independent woman and did exactly what she pleased. No man was going to tell her what to do.

Although Caty started well, she quickly became anxious and unhappy at Westerly. A July 8, 1778, letter to her husband tells of her poor health, her fears and jealousies, and her desire to have the protection of her husband and even the army nearby. When General Greene finally wrote that he was coming to Rhode Island, Caty and the children rushed from Westerly to Coventry to meet him.

General Greene had been home only twice in three years. This was his first time he could hold his small daughter Martha in his arms. This was the first time in months that he and little George would play together.

But there was a war on. Family time together in Coventry would be brief. Thinking a change of scenery would be helpful to his wife, Nathanael took Caty and baby Martha to East Greenwich so Caty could visit at the home of her Aunt Catharine, where she had been raised. Then all too soon General Greene, with the family carriage horse, returned to army camp.

The change of scenery did little to ease Caty's discontent. Before long she wrote to her husband that she wanted to return to her own home and son in Coventry. "Would to God that it was in my power to give peace to your bosom, which I fear, is like a troubled ocean," General Greene wrote back in frustration.[31] But soon the Greenes' horse, accompanied by a servant, dutifully arrived from camp, and Caty and little Martha set out for Coventry.

Soon afterward, Nathanael Greene, accompanied by his troops, himself returned to Coventry. The Greenes' home became headquarters for the general and his military aides; his soldiers pitched their tents in rows in the yard. But they did not stay long. Within a few days General Greene and his troops were ordered back to New York. Caty was heartbroken.

Greene wrote General Washington on September 16 asking permission to return to his wife, as he expected Caty to be "put to bed any day." Caty was "very desirous of my stay," Greene wrote, "and as she has set her Heart so much upon it I could wish to gratify her for fear of some disagreeable consequence as women sometimes under such circumstances receive great injury by being disappointed."[32] Washington gave his permission, but Greene did not arrive home in time for the birth. While hastening back to Coventry, he met a servant on the road who reported that Caty "had been in travail two Days." The Greenes' second daughter had been born September 23, leaving "Mrs. Greene in bed very ill."[33] The baby was born at least a month premature. Caty named the tiny child Cornelia Lott Greene, after the Abraham Lotts, with whom Catharine Greene had stayed in New Jersey the year before.

The new baby's arrival elicited some good-natured ribbing from Greene's friends in the field. General Weedon, who had also been at Valley Forge, displayed his mathematical skills by pointing out that the addition to the Greene family was "the Effect of her [Caty's] Visit to Valley Forge." Weedon "would have given my Hat, and I have but one," he continued, "if it had been a boy, he no doubt would have cut a figure in the profession of Arms as he might with propriety have said he was on Picket before he was born."[34] Gen. James Varnum, too, sent "best compliments" and wrote that his wife would have liked to visit Caty but could not hire a good dressmaker "to put her in decent Attire."[35] William Moore, with whom the Greenes had stayed while at the Valley Forge encampment, also sent along a note of congratulations on the birth of the Greenes' little daughter. And, Moore wrote, he had heard Caty's baby girl was "very Beautiful."[36]

LADY GREENE AT THE OTHER ENCAMPMENTS
MIDDLEBROOK, NEW JERSEY, 1778–79

Two months after the birth of Cornelia, Caty received a letter saying that her husband was "impatient" to see his "Angel" and that her presence at winter camp (that year at Middlebrook, New Jersey) would "greatly contribute" to his happiness. Furthermore, Greene wrote, Gen. George Washington had also "enquired very particularly after you." As long as the weather was not too cold, Greene asked Caty to bring their son George, almost three, with her from Rhode Island to camp.[37]

Accompanied by little George and Nathanael's aide, Caty set out from Rhode Island on November 26. After a "most disagreeable and distressing journey," her coach arrived at the Middlebrook, New Jersey, encampment on December 21, 1778. Greene wrote that his son, George, stood the journey "finely." Caty, however, "was somewhat impaired in coming."[38]

But once safely at Middlebrook, Catharine Greene had some marvelous times. She visited with friends in Trenton and Philadelphia. She attended a gala "entertainment" on February 18 to, once again, celebrate the French Alliance. The Greenes gave at least two parties themselves, including the one where Caty danced for hours with the commander in chief. Toward the end of March, two friends arrived at camp to stay with Caty.

Caty's personal maid left sometime during the Middlebrook encampment. On February 28, General Greene wrote to Colonel Abeel, assistant quartermaster, saying that he would be very obliged if Abeel would find a maid for Mrs. Greene. Greene was especially interested in having Abeel "buy a good Negro Girl that has been in a Gentlemans family."[39] Abeel promised to do everything that he could to "procure a good honest Girl for her," but he wanted Greene to know that, with the war on, the task would be difficult.[40] On March 2 Abeel again wrote saying it was "Impossible to Get a good Wench as they are very Scarce."[41] Colonel Abeel persisted, however, and he did eventually locate a maid for Catharine Greene, but whether she was a free woman is unknown.

As another campaign was about to open, Caty, her son George, and her entourage left New Jersey for Rhode Island near the end of May.

MORRISTOWN, NEW JERSEY, 1779–80

Catharine Greene did not remain in Rhode Island for long. Six months later, on November 15, she appeared at army camp at West Point—a visit that flabbergasted her husband. Although friends and relatives had tried to keep her at home, she had been, as a friend wrote Nathanael Greene, "Obstinately bent" on joining him.[42] Greene had not expected his wife to travel to camp that November because the winds and snow were ferocious that year—and Caty was almost seven months pregnant.

Soon after Caty's unexpected appearance at West Point, arrangements were made for her to travel with George and Deborah Olney to more comfortable accommodations in Morristown, New Jersey. General and Mrs. Greene eventually took quarters at the Jacob Arnold Tavern on Morristown's village green. On December 3 her husband wrote, "Mrs. Greene is in pretty good health, as comfortably situated as could be expected in Camp."[43]

But she did require some items, and Greene ordered them in: a cap, a pair of cuffs, two ostrich feathers, a lady's pocketbook, some cloth, some silk. Caty also requested new teacups, and "paste board" or "whale bone" used "to make a bonnet upon."[44] About the middle of December, Greene also ordered a quarter cask of port or Madeira wine "as Mrs. Greene has none to drink, and expects to be sick [in childbirth] in a short time."[45] The Greenes' fourth child and second son, Nathanael Ray, was born on January 31, 1780, at Morristown.

In early June, with the campaign imminent, Caty and baby Nathanael Ray left camp for Rhode Island. General Greene had purchased a carriage, one previously owned by a Tory, for the journey. Although the carriage had not been used for some time, Greene thought it to be "nearly as good as new." (George Washington had once considered purchasing this same carriage but declined when told it was "Old fashioned and uncouth.")[46] In preparation for the trip to Rhode Island, General Greene asked his wife to have the Tory crest on the carriage door painted over. She was also to pack her husband's things in chests and trunks. The Greenes had borrowed bedding from Benedict Arnold, and now Caty was directed to return it to Peggy Arnold. General Greene also advised Caty to "take such of the Servants home with you as you please but let me know which will be your choice."[47] Finally, on June 11, with everything in place, Catharine Greene and her four-month-old son set out from Morristown for Rhode Island.

A month after his wife's departure from Morristown, General Greene penned a familiar complaint: "Not a line have I received from you since you left Morris. I beg you write at every post, and by every express." He also needed Caty to do some things for him. Greene required black and white feathers for his hat, as "the General officers being directed to wear them by way of distinction." Because of the "shattered condition of my shirts," he urged her to forward new ones as soon as she could. And because Caty had procrastinated in painting over the crest of the new carriage, General Greene implored her to "get the carriage painted with family Arms, [as the] present Arms are Tory arms."[48]

LATER ENCAMPMENTS

Benedict Arnold, who had commanded West Point, "fled to the enemy," as Nathanael Greene put it, in late September 1780.[49] Consequently, Greene wrote to Washington asking for command of West Point. After he received the appointment, however, he quickly decided that it would not suit after all. "The situation is not much to my liking," he wrote to his wife just two days after receiving the post, "there being little prospect of glory or comfort." Nevertheless, Greene invited Caty to join him at West Point, writing that if she thought she could find happiness in "this dreary situation with me, I shall be happy to receive you in my Arms."[50]

But the couple did not meet at West Point. Even before his wife had completed preparations to go to New York, General Greene, on October 15, received orders to march south. He had been named commander of the southern army. Greene also knew full well that his wife would be exceedingly distressed by the appointment.

And she was. Indeed, Caty was distraught even *thinking* about her husband going south: Mrs. Greene is "much Alarmed for fear you Should go to the Southward," was how Jacob Greene had expressed it earlier to his brother.[51] Although General Greene had requested the position, his letter telling his wife the news reads, "What I have been dreading has come to pass. . . . This is so foreign to my wishes that I am distressed exceedingly."[52]

(Washington had also penned a disclaimer to his own wife—"I have used every endeavor in my power to avoid this appointment"—when informing Martha that he had been appointed commander in chief of the Continental Army.)

Nathanael Greene was desperate to see Caty before he left to take command of the southern troops. Thinking she had already left Rhode Island to join him at West Point (she had not), he begged Caty to "come forward as fast as the state of the roads, the condition of your health, and the circumstances of the weather will permit."[53] When he realized he would not see his beloved angel before heading south, Greene poured out his heart to her: "I am rendered unhappy beyond expression that fatal necessity obliges me to take my leave of you in this way. . . . My longing eyes looked for you in all directions, and I felt my heart leap for joy at the sound of every carriage. O Caty, how much I suffer. . . . Could I have seen you it would have given my bosom great relief. . . . How or when I shall return God only knows. . . . I wish you all the happiness your situation can admit."[54]

With her husband far away in the south, Catharine Greene was again left on her own. Accordingly she set off to meet and flirt with the French officers stationed at Newport. Col. Claude Blanchard, chief commissary of the Newport garrison, was one of these officers; so was Captain Haake of the Royal Deux-Ponts. Caty was so charming that both officers pledged to visit her at her Coventry home at the first opportunity. But she and her four children were unprepared for company, for Blanchard's journal entry describes Caty as an "amiable, genteel, and rather pretty lady" but one with "no bread in the house." Since company was present, Blanchard continued, "some was hastily made; it was of meal and water mixed together, which was toasted at the fire; small slices were served up to us. It is not much for a Frenchman. . . . Mrs. Greene's house is situated upon a barren piece of land. . . . There is not a single fruit tree, not even a cabbage. . . . In the evening she invited [two ladies] to her house and we danced; I was in boots and rather tired; besides the English dances are rather complicated, so I acquitted myself badly. But these ladies were complaisant."[55] It is easy to see that, for Caty, who loved the life of fun and frivolity, military camp was so much more exciting than living with four little children on a "barren piece" of Rhode Island soil.

SOUTHERN CAMPAIGN

Catharine Greene had wanted to hurry south to her husband, but his letters did not encourage this. "You have no idea of the distress and misery that prevails in this quarter," Greene wrote.[56] "Indeed you are infinitely better off at home."[57] Nevertheless, soon after learning of Cornwallis's surrender at Yorktown, the resolute Catharine Littlefield Greene packed up and started south, accompanied part way by a former aide of her husband's, her son George, and a female companion. Lady Greene arrived in Philadelphia by November 22, 1781, and lingered in the city almost two months, finally leaving in late January. Caty left six-year-old George Washington Greene under the care of Charles Pettit, a business associate of her husband's. Pettit promised to see to the education of the "young shaver," as his father had once referred to him.

The Washingtons, who were mourning the sudden death of John Parke Custis, were also in Philadelphia, and Caty visited with them in the city. Seeing Caty's determination to continue her travels south, George Washington wrote ahead to Nathanael Greene to reassure him that Caty was in excellent health and high spirits and that he would assist her in her travels. The general also encouraged Caty and her entourage to rest at his Virginia plantation before continuing on to South Carolina. The group did visit at Mount Vernon, where Lucy Knox, in Mrs. Washington's absence, served as hostess.

On her way from Mount Vernon, Caty stopped in Fredericksburg, Virginia, arriving there on February 4. To honor her, and to celebrate George Washington's birthday, the gentlemen of the city invited Caty to a February 8 ball at the local coffeehouse. The *Maryland Gazette* put it this way: "Though Mrs. Greene was anxious to prosecute her journey to the southward, [she] suffered herself to be prevailed upon to stay." Caty was one of about 120 "brilliants" who attended the ball, and she would have loved every minute of it. Nevertheless, on February 13, Caty and her attendants left Fredericksburg—"much to the regret of all who were honoured with her acquaintance"—and continued south.[58]

Once on the road again they endured "a most disagreeable ride indeed," as Maj. Ichabod Burnet described it to Nathanael Greene. "The difficulties and hardships arising from the badness of the accommodations and the excessive deep roads," Burnet continued, "exceed anything I had an idea of." But even Burnet, a "notorious grouch," sang the praises of his companion. "Everything has been undergone with cheerfulness and fortitude by Mrs. Greene who appears to be much less affected than could be expected."[59] Finally, in early April 1782, months after setting out from Rhode Island, the exhausted travelers approached Nathanael Greene's camp near Charlestown, South Carolina. "I will venture to say there is no mortal more happy in a wife than myself," Greene had once written to Caty. "I can assure you with great truth that I never enjoyed a moment's rational and refined happiness until I had the good fortune to be united to you."[60] The reunion was undoubtedly joyful, as Caty and Nathanael Greene had exchanged only letters for the previous two years.

Although she had traveled a great distance to be with her husband, Caty did not remain with him for long. When the stifling summer heat and illnesses overcame several of his aides, Greene sent them to Kiawah Island, which was held by the British. Caty, who served as a companion and kind of nurse, accompanied the invalids, camp surgeon, cook, and others to the island. Caty's doting Nathanael had sent her to Kiawah to escape the fever, as he feared there were some "disagreeable symptoms hovering about her" that, he hoped, "would disappear upon a change of air, diet, and exercise."[61] After several weeks of abundance on Kiawah Island, the party, healthy and rejuvenated, returned to the mainland.

The British finally evacuated Charlestown on December 14, 1782. Greene had selected his friend Gen. Anthony Wayne to lead the first American soldiers into the city. Around three in the afternoon, Greene rode into the city on horseback accompanied by his officers, the governor of South Carolina, and other officials. And then came Caty in her phaeton, accompanied by several ladies of distinction. The common citizens of the area trailed behind.

It was a time of triumph for Caty. Her outfit had been carefully chosen to show her to best advantage. One of Greene's aides once wrote that she was "determined to appear in uniform with her husband, and therefore prefers deep blue with yellow buttons and buff facings." To complete the look, she sought a pair of "very small" gold epaulets. "Mrs. Greene has so much of the spirit of the military about her," gushed the aide.[62]

With the British Army gone, Charlestown underwent a transformation. Even the name of the city changed: Charlestown became Charleston—it sounded more American. Catharine Greene, wife of the commander of the southern forces, occupied the top rung of society's ladder. One would expect Caty to be happy. General Greene wrote to a relative that his wife was "much esteemed by both the army and the people, as well as loved and admired by her husband." But happiness eluded her. Her husband thought it was because "her absent children are a great deduction. A divided family leaves a blank in the heart that often causes a flowing tear, and yet she cannot think of returning (to Rhode Island) without her husband."[63]

So she promoted something she loved—a ball. In spite of her husband's objections, Charlestonians of the right sort danced the night away in a hall festooned with magnolia leaves and paper flowers. Catharine Greene herself had done much of the decorating. On the night of the Victory Ball, General Greene led his lady out to the dance floor for the opening number, then relinquished her to General Wayne for an evening of minuets played by the army band. Caty Greene had herself a wonderful time.

But things did not remain wonderful for long. There were some good times: the Greenes made a triumphal journey into Savannah, which, like Charleston, had been freed of the enemy. But then John Banks, who had purchased clothing and food for the southern army with notes signed by Greene, was found to be dishonest. The courts demanded payments from Greene, who had some land but no ready cash. To pay off his creditors, Nathanael Greene was forced to borrow from, among others, Robert Morris and the Marquis de Lafayette. And, as the army still had to be kept together, even more money and supplies were needed.

Then, in April 1783, came the news that everyone had been waiting for. A preliminary peace treaty had been signed in Paris. Because there were no funds to allow the soldiers more than partial pay, and no ships arrived until early summer to take the frustrated soldiers home, many men simply left camp and started walking. Caty, pregnant once more, wanted to go home, too.

Her husband, ever sympathetic and accommodating, put Caty on the first transport ship to Philadelphia. Col. Thaddeus Kosciusko, who had assisted Caty in decorating for the Victory Ball, and a lady chaperone served as traveling companions. Once in Philadelphia, Caty attended, among other festivities, an extravagant party in a home along the Schuylkill River. Next Caty went on a wild spending spree, purchasing gown after gown (all in the newest fashion), a phaeton, a chariot, and two horses. She charged

$1,400.00 to her husband's company, which, unbeknown to her, tottered on bankruptcy. Her husband's business partner, irate, wrote Greene that the bill had been paid, but he expected early repayment. General Greene, however, had no money to pay.

Caty left Philadelphia, scooped up her son George at Princeton, and drove north to Rhode Island. Nathanael's brother Jacob had been caring for the three other children, but the reunion with her little ones was bittersweet. Possession of the house in Coventry where the children had been staying now belonged to Jacob and his family through a financial settlement. Undaunted, Caty turned her back on Coventry and purchased—on credit—a home for the family in Newport.

LATER YEARS

It was a joyous day when Nathanael arrived in Newport to join Caty and their family—George now seven, Martha age six, Cornelia five, and little Nathanael three. The children had not seen either parent for years. Soon Caty bore a third daughter, Louisa, so there were now five children to care for. But Nathanael Greene's investment stocks were close to worthless. The family's shipping business had declined precipitously. Greene had been given acreage confiscated from the Tories of Georgia and the Carolinas, but these plantations were held as security against debts accrued in supplying the army in Charleston. "I am not anxious to be rich," her husband wrote Caty from Georgia, while checking on the advisability of moving the family to the Mulberry Grove estate, "but wish to be independent. . . . To have a decent income is much to be wished; but to be free from debt more so. I never owned so much property as now, and yet never felt so poor."[64] And Caty was pregnant once again.

The baby, named Catharine, developed whooping cough and died in her mother's arms. Caty, who was already distraught from the loss of this infant daughter, became completely unhinged when she learned she was pregnant once again. It was now Nathanael's responsibility to care for the five surviving children. He also engaged a nurse to care for his wife.

Greene soon realized that the children would need additional supervision and some formal education. He contemplated sending them away to school, but instead approached Phineas Miller to tutor the children. The twenty-one-year-old Yale graduate turned down a more lucrative offer and agreed to the Greenes' terms. In exchange for three pounds per month with room and board, he would tutor the five children, assemble

General Greene's war papers, and relocate with the family to Georgia. The schoolmaster also found that he enjoyed spending time with Caty.

In October 1785, although Caty was far from well, the Greenes set sail for Georgia. Their servants had been sent ahead to prepare Mulberry Grove, on the Savannah River, for the new owners.

The estate—consisting of the main house, out buildings, an unkempt garden, and vast marshy lands—had been uninhabited for years. But both Nathanael and Caty were determined to make Mulberry Grove succeed. By the spring of 1786, almost two hundred acres were planted with rice and corn. "The house is large and the garden extensive and elegant," Nathanael wrote. "The Trees shrubs and flowers are numerous and beautiful. There is a great variety of fruit Trees which add both to the pleasures of sight and taste."[65] But they did not have a new baby. Caty had taken a nasty fall in the kitchen, bringing on premature labor. The baby died a short time after birth.

And soon Nathanael Greene himself was dead. Greene suffered sunstroke, was bled by two different doctors, and died on June 19, 1786, at the age of forty-four. He left his beloved Caty, a widow at thirty-two, with five children. Greene's death also left his survivors with extensive debts and acres of property. Because of low property values, however, the land had little value and would not be sufficient to pay off Greene's creditors even if sold. Caty's best hope for immediate survival was to make a financial success of the Mulberry Grove plantation. She appointed Phineas Miller, the children's former tutor, to the task.

CATY AFTER NATHANAEL'S DEATH

Caty's long-term financial success would depend on recouping the thousands of dollars the government owed Nathanael for equipping the army during the southern campaign. On April 27, 1792, Congress indemnified the estate of General Greene for 8,688 pounds, six shillings sterling. That same day, President Washington sent a message to Congress saying that he "approved and signed" the act.[66] Thirty-eight-year-old Caty was beyond jubilant. "I . . . feel as saucy as you please—not only because I am independent, but because I have gained a complete triumph over some of my friends who did not wish me success—and others who doubted my judgment in managing the business. . . . They are now as mute as mice—Not a word dare they utter. . . . O how sweet is revenge!"[67]

Also sweet was the marriage of Catharine Littlefield Greene and Phineas Miller, who had pledged themselves to each other years before. They wed in a private ceremony on May 31, 1796, that was attended only by President and Mrs. Washington and a few friends.

Their business dealings were not as successful as the marriage. To raise capital for Eli Whitney's cotton gin, in which they had invested heavily, the Millers poured money into a Georgia land development scheme—the Yazoo Company. The shares were signed by Caty and secured by her property. When the Yazoo scheme collapsed, so did the fortune. Although the Millers' attempted to sell Mulberry Grove for living expenses, there were no buyers, and the plantation was sold at auction in August 1800. But by this time Caty and Phineas had already fled Mulberry Grove and begun a new life on Cumberland Island, Georgia, where Nathanael Greene had been given property years before. By 1803 Dungeness, a vast five-story mansion begun by Nathanael, was complete.

Daughter Cornelia later described Dungeness as a "superb pile." With its thick walls constructed of "tabby" (made from oyster shells), the place was considered to be indestructible. The grounds were gorgeous; the hospitality superb. Henry Knox came to Dungeness, and Cornelia recalled that he taught her to ride there. Henry "Light Horse Harry" Lee, who had also been at the Valley Forge encampment, died at Dungeness in 1818 after having spent several years in the Caribbean combating an unknown illness. Caty invited inventor Eli Whitney to Dungeness, too. According to Cornelia, Whitney's cotton gin was perfected in Dungeness' living room. "Madam . . . you have perfected my invention!" Whitney is to have said with delight when Caty, placing a clothes brush against the teeth of a saw, eliminated the clogs in Whitney's prototype cotton gin.[68]

There was more rejoicing when Whitney brought the joyful news that the South Carolina legislature had purchased patent rights to the cotton gin. And soon, under Phineas Miller's direction, Dungeness became self-sufficient and began to bring in a handsome cash income.

But again the joy could not be sustained. On December 7, 1803, Phineas Miller died at the age of thirty-nine of blood poisoning. Hired to tutor the Greene children, Miller had found himself besotted with their mother, and eventually married her. He had also partnered with Eli Whitney in the invention of the cotton gin. Miller is buried in an unmarked grave on the grounds of Dungeness plantation.

Catharine Greene Miller was fifty when her second husband died. She spent her remaining eleven years shuttling back and forth between Cumberland Island and the northeast, where she attempted to help untangle Eli Whitney's complicated patent appeal. Congress also finally appropriated funds to assist those who had lost money in the Yazoo scandal, a move that gave Caty relief from her creditors.

But she did not live to see the money. After suffering raging fever for a week, Caty died on September 2, 1814, at Dungeness on Cumberland Island, and is buried there. She was almost sixty-one years old.

Catharine Littlefield Greene Miller was first the wife of a prominent Revolutionary War general and then, when Gen. Nathanael Greene died, the wife of Phineas Miller, the partner of Eli Whitney. Whitney's invention, the cotton gin, transformed the south. This lively, intelligent woman of the "glossy black hair" attracted many men, including Whitney. Catharine Greene corresponded with such luminaries as Gen. James Varnum, Gen. Henry Knox, Gen. Anthony Wayne, and Edward Rutledge, a signer of the Declaration of Independence. Twice in May 1791, while on his southern tour, President George Washington stopped at Mulberry Grove to visit General Greene's widow. Even a man of the cloth extolled her special attributes. "Where ever Mrs. Greene is," wrote Rev. John Murray in 1780, "she will diffuse happiness all around her."[69]

Although Catharine Greene Miller was known at the time as a beauty, no definitive portrait of her from the period exists today. The miniature that Charles Willson Peale painted of her at Valley Forge is lost. The only extant portrait of Catharine Greene, painted in her later years, was never completed.

CHILDREN OF NATHANAEL AND CATHARINE GREENE
Catharine Greene's concerns, it has been said, "rarely centered on her children."[70] Isaac Briggs, a Georgia politician who called on Catharine and Nathanael Greene at their home in 1786 believed this, too—until he visited with the lady. Briggs wrote that people said Catharine Greene "had no more gravity than an air Balloon . . . that she had no more affection or regard for her children than if they were no human creatures & consequently paid no manner of attention to their education; that she cared for nothing but flirting, rattling and riding about." But after visiting with Caty, Briggs gave her high marks for motherhood and everything else

(or perhaps Briggs also fell under her spell). After the interview, he wrote that Mrs. Greene "thinks & acts as she pleases . . . is generally an object of envy and distraction . . . has an infinite fund of vivacity . . . possesses an unbounded benevolence." Briggs also concluded that, contrary to what others said, "I am perfectly convinced that she has a very great share of maternal affection."[71]

Perhaps she did. But what is certain is that whenever Caty Greene received an invitation, or even the smallest hint, that her husband desired her company, she packed herself up and dashed away to the appropriate encampment, often leaving all the little Greenes behind. Even General Greene called his children "almost fatherless and motherless."[72]

CORNELIA LOTT GREENE, 1778–1867

The Greenes' second daughter, Cornelia Lott Greene, was born on September 23, 1778, soon after the Valley Forge encampment. Cornelia, a frail premature baby, had not been expected to live. By her own account, she grew so slowly that her mother feared she would be a dwarf. Her father, too, commented on her short stature. "What makes Cornelia such a short thing?" he wrote in a letter. "I hope she increases in stature as she gets older."[73] By the age of three, however, Cornelia was being described as a charmer and "very well but Very Fat."[74] She grew into a beautiful, intelligent, sought-after young woman.

She also had the gift of storytelling, and, from Cornelia, a sharper picture of Caty Greene emerges. Cornelia told her granddaughter, Martha Littlefield Phillips, a wonderful story about a visit she and Caty made to Mount Vernon. Eight-year-old Cornelia had been thoroughly prepared by the demanding Caty about what was expected from her at the Washingtons' home. Cornelia was to smile, curtsy, modestly answer all questions, but was not to make a show of herself in any way. Caty had drilled her daughter in deportment, for not only was General Washington revered by everyone in the country, but he had also been her husband's good friend and immediate commander. According to Cornelia's later recollections, she, at Mount Vernon, terrified and tongue-tied, was able to give only a stuttering response to Mrs. Washington's kind questions. But when the great man entered the room, Cornelia was so overcome that she fell to the floor before him and burst into tears. Washington used his own handkerchief to wipe her tears, then led her gently away from the outraged Caty. He placed Cornelia beside him at the dinner table, and he, alone, filled her plate with delicious food. After dinner the two walked together in the garden, and as they talked Gen. George Washington gave himself "to the task of making the happiness and charming the confidence of a shy and frightened girl."[75]

Cornelia remembered that Martha Washington "took small note of the children" at that visit. But she did impress the young girl as a handsome woman, with upright posture, who wore a rich silk gown with an embroidered apron and a "dainty kerchief folded about her neck and shoulders."[76]

Several years later President and Mrs. Washington invited Cornelia to live with them for two years in Philadelphia. Cornelia and Mrs. Washington's granddaughter, Nelly, were about six months apart in age, and friends. Cornelia recalled that, at an occasion of unusual importance at the presidential mansion, she wore a gown lavishly adorned with small wreaths that she had fashioned from bright red feathers. Mrs. Washington admired the creation, then gave Cornelia a beautiful piece of Brussels lace to wear with the gown. "With my love," Cornelia remembers Martha Washington whispering as she gave Cornelia a tender kiss and draped the lace around the girl's shoulders. That glorious night at the ball, Cornelia recalled, "in very truth, I was the observed of all observers."[77]

Cornelia also related incidents about her parents. The Greene children, she said, were not in the least awed by General Greene; they laughed and played with him—indeed, he "winked at every atrocity we perpetrated."[78]

But her relationship with Caty was another story. "It was not that I failed in love for my mother," Cornelia shared, "but it was a love mixed with fear." Cornelia remembered Catharine Greene as "undemonstrative" and a mother who "exacted from her children implicit obedience and unfailing deference." Caty expected her daughters to execute a deep curtsy when they came into her presence and demanded that her children ask her permission before they left the room. The Greene girls were assigned the tasks of polishing the silver, arranging flowers in the vases, and dusting the ornaments in the drawing room—all to be done to Caty's exacting standards. Poise and grace of carriage were paramount. Caty placed Cornelia in stocks for an hour a day in an effort to force her feet to turn out properly. Cornelia was also strapped to a backboard until her posture was perfect. And these harsh measures paid off: Cornelia's granddaughter observed that at the age of seventy-five Cornelia still "had the grace and bearing of a queen."[79]

Her mother was, Cornelia remembered, also a strict disciplinarian. When Cornelia was ten, the little girl ran out of her home in an exquisite, fragile party gown, and the dress became torn and dirty during the day. Caty did not appear angry when the disheveled Cornelia returned home. But after examining the ruined gown, Caty looked at her daughter and then calmly said, "Well, my daughter, it must be mended."[80] Cornelia protested that this would be an impossible task, but Caty quietly replied that, with patience and persistence, the task would be accomplished. Ten-year-old Cornelia dutifully took up her needle and worked two hours a day for three weeks to repair the gown to her mother's satisfaction.

On April 22, 1802, Cornelia married Payton Skipwith Jr., a county judge with property and money. The couple (he was twenty-seven, she twenty-four) quickly established a home near St. Marys, on the Georgia mainland. Their first son, George Greene Skipwith, was born nine months after the wedding. Two other sons soon followed. But the prospect of a long, happy marriage was denied the couple. Payton Skipwith died in the autumn of 1808, at thirty-three.

Two years later, in May 1810, Cornelia eloped with Edward Brinley Littlefield, a first cousin. Caty was furious, as she felt Cornelia's new husband to be no more than a "fortunehunter." The marriage ceremony itself infuriated Caty, for Cornelia had thrown decorum and restraint to the wind and had been married in the St. Marys post office by someone Caty referred to as "that cutthroat Ross." The only witness was a man Caty labeled a "Cracker Tavern keeper." The whole business almost drove Caty "to madness," and she vowed never to mention Cornelia's name again.[81] Seven months later, Caty was still distraught. "Cornelia's folly," her friend Eli Whitney wrote, "has broken her mother's heart."[82]

Three years later, in 1813, another incident occurred that made Caty furious with Cornelia once again. Quite by coincidence, she saw Cornelia and Cornelia's six children, followed by a wagonload of servants and slaves, slinking along the back streets of Savannah. Caty quickly realized that while she had been away from the property, her daughter had come to Dungeness and taken some servants and slaves from Caty's estate. Cornelia had wanted them for her own.

Enraged, Caty obtained an order that forbid Cornelia and her entourage from leaving town with Caty's property. The group was arrested and spent several days in jail but was eventually released when they secured bonds that guaranteed Caty cash value for her slaves. All this was again too much for Caty. She took to her bed, then rose up to rewrite her will, granting Cornelia only a token from the estate. She refused to see Cornelia again.

Cornelia Lott Greene Skipwith Littlefield, a child of the Valley Forge encampment, educated in a fine girl's school, who had lived for two years with President and Mrs. George Washington, died at the age of eighty-nine. She is buried at her home in Mississippi.

THE OTHER GREENE CHILDREN

Cornelia had four brothers and sisters who lived beyond infancy.

George Washington Greene (1775–93), who was sometimes referred to as "His Little Excellency," accompanied his mother to several of the army encampments. General Washington wrote this of his namesake when the boy was seven: "He is a fine boy, and I dare say with proper attention, if he lives, will be an ornament to his Country; as his infant genius promises much from mature age."[83] After Nathanael Greene died, when the boy was just eleven, young George was sent to be educated in France with Lafayette's son, also named George Washington. Sadly, George Washington Greene drowned in a swollen river near Mulberry Grove soon after returning home from France. He is buried beside his father.

Martha Washington "Patty" Greene (1777–?) was born with a port wine stain that her father insisted on treating by dabbing it with port; Patty was also encouraged to drink port. Patty married a man of some means in a wedding spectacular in 1795. When he died, she married the brother of Caty's physician, who persuaded her to demand from Caty a large portion of the Greene estate. Caty took offense and, as she had Cornelia, wrote Patty out of her will and her life.[84]

Nathanael Ray Greene (1780–1859) was born at the Morristown encampment. Washington wrote of him, "Nat, I suppose, can handle a musket," when the boy was still in diapers.[85] Caty described her second son as "without exception the most sensible child I ever saw—Even Mrs. Knox says so—but . . . he is much inclined to vixy."[86] Little is known of Nat. An "eccentric good-hearted soul" was how Dr. Daniel Turner, a friend of the family, described him."[87]

Not much is known about Louisa Catharine Greene (1782–1831) either. Caty wrote that Louisa was very shy. When Louisa was with her French tutor, Caty reported (rather unkindly) the girl could only say, "*in English—don't touch me—don't touch me—*[emphasis in original] blushing and trembling lest he should put his hands about her. The other two ladies who took lessons with her laughed ready to die at her fears—and called her a country girl."[88] Louisa had a serious crush on Eli Whitney, but that came to nothing because he admired Caty. Louisa finally married James Shaw at the age of thirty-two. Because Mr. Shaw was a British subject, however, Caty asked that the marriage not be made public. But at the same time Caty thought highly of her daughter's choice. "We all respect, honor, and love him," Caty wrote about James Shaw to Eli Whitney. "He is not only tender and affectionate to her—but *to me* [emphasis in original] the most dutiful son and excellent friend."[89]

MRS. HENRY KNOX: LUCY FLUCKER KNOX, AUGUST 2, 1756–JUNE 20, 1824

At twenty-two, Lucy Flucker Knox was one of the youngest of the officers' wives to come to Valley Forge. Social, audacious, and officious, she was sure of her place and let everyone know it. "I hope you will not consider yourself as commander in chief of your own house," she wrote to her new husband soon after they were married, "but be convinced . . . there is such a thing as equal command."[90] Gen. Henry Knox, who commanded the Continental Army's artillery, adored his big, bossy, brilliant wife.

Lucy Flucker, who came from one of Massachusetts' leading families, grew up surrounded by affluence and high style. Still she set her heart on Henry Knox, a bookseller with no imposing ancestors and no fortune, soon after she saw him in his Boston store. Henry's father had taken off for the West Indies when the boy was nine, leaving young Henry responsible for his mother and little brother William, then three. Henry left school (Boston Public Latin Grammar School) and went to work for a bookbinding company to support his mother and brother. In his spare time he read his employer's books; he found the topic of military artillery particularly fascinating. At twenty-one, the enterprising Henry Knox opened his "New London Book-Store" in Boston. The shop, which offered customers the latest and best in books and magazines, quickly became a magnet for students attending nearby Harvard College. Intelligent and observant, the shop owner began to imitate the manners and behavior of his Harvard customers. Soon Henry Knox, too, appeared the gentlemen.

Always fond of books, Lucy now found herself smitten with the bookseller. When Lucy was around, the charms of this "imperious, spoiled" young woman were such that it was said the besotted and distracted bookseller was unable to give his customers the correct change. But there was a problem. Lucy's parents were Loyalists, and wealthy, prominent ones at that. Her father had served the king as the royal secretary of the Providence of Massachusetts. He and his wife "exploded in wrath" when they realized their pampered and privileged seventeen-year-old daughter was smitten with the twenty-four-year-old shop owner. Not only was the man—oh, the horror of it!—"in trade," but, worse, he actively supported the rebel American colonists.[91]

But Lucy's mind was made up. She wanted her "Harry," as she called him. Eventually Lucy wore her parents down, perhaps because she was "violently emotional and inclined to hysterical scenes."[92] Lucy Flucker and Henry Knox married on June 16, 1774. (To signal their disapproval, Lucy's parents left the city for the day.) The bride was almost eighteen; the groom nearly twenty-five. Lucy had a volatile temper; Henry was "manly and kind, courteous and refined, soldierly and brave."[93] Her parents foresaw only a dire fate for Lucy and Henry, predicting the couple would forever eat "the bread of poverty and dependence."[94]

True, the couple always had financial problems, but Lucy and Henry Knox, because of his involvement in the Revolution and later in Washington's administration, and assisted by her social ambitions and standing, became one of America's most prominent couples. While Lucy thrived on her husband's success, the war tore her from her birth family and its privileges.

The American Revolution has been called the "First Civil War." Families were ripped apart when loyalties split between the British and Americans. Lucy's parents, staunch Tories, sailed to England from Boston early in the war, and she never saw or heard from them again. Lucy was also estranged from her siblings. Thomas, her brother, served as a British Army officer. Hannah, one of her sisters, married a British officer. When she married a Patriot, Lucy was no longer welcome in the family pew of the conservative King's Chapel or invited to fashionable royal soirees. And the loss of her family pained her. "When I seriously reflect that I have lost my father, mother, brother, and sisters, entirely lost them, I am half distracted," Lucy wrote to Henry on August 23, 1777. "True I cheerfully renounced them, for one far dearer to me than all of them—but I am totally deprived of them."[95]

Henry Knox and their children were all the family Lucy Knox had in America. This prompted Lucy, unusual among the wives of the American officers, to habitually follow her husband as he moved up and down the eastern coast during the war. For a woman born of privilege and wealth, living conditions with the Continental Army undoubtedly seemed primitive. Yet Lady Knox remained devoted to the cause and to "her ever dear Harry," her "only friend . . . in the world."[96]

Henry Knox was one of Washington's most trusted and valued generals. In 1776 Knox conceived the ambitious—and successful—scheme to drag artillery pieces captured at Fort Ticonderoga to the needy American troops at Boston. The enterprising and determined Knox organized the soldiers, the forty-two strong sledges, and eighty yoke of oxen to haul the sixty or so cannon and mortars over hundreds of miles of mud, muck, ice, and snow from New York to Massachusetts. This "noble train of artillery," as Knox called it, had a total weight of around 120,000 pounds and traveled over three hundred miles in under two months.[97] Gen. Henry Knox participated in the battles of Brandywine, Germantown, and Monmouth. He championed a training academy, the predecessor to the U.S. Military Academy, at the Middlebrook encampment, and then later commanded West Point itself. Knox directed the artillery for the battle of Yorktown in 1781. He also served as secretary of war under the Confederation and then as Washington's secretary of war until 1794.

These were big tasks, but then both Lucy and Henry were, quite literally, big people. When they were first married, Henry was "tall, built like a heavyweight prize fighter"; Lucy's hefty body was topped by a pretty face.[98] In later years both Knoxes were truly formidable; he weighed in at 290 pounds, she at 250. And people noticed. "She [Lucy] is fatter than ever which is a great mortification to her," Nathanael Greene wrote to his own slim, beguiling wife during the Revolution. But, Greene continued, "The general is equally fat and therefore one cannot laugh at the other."[99] While praising Mrs. Knox's neatness, attentiveness to her family, and fondness for her children, Nabby Adams, daughter of John and Abigail Adams, proclaimed Lucy Knox to be "enormous." "I am frightened when I look at her," Nabby's letter to her mother continued. "I verily believe that her waist is as large as three of yours at least."[100] "Lucy Knox," declared William A. Duer, who knew her well, was "eccentric in character and concentric in figure."[101]

Not only was Lucy's size spectacular, but so was her coiffure. In later years she retained a French hairstylist who charged twenty shillings a month to augment her hair with bows and laces and such. Mrs. Knox's hairdo, wrote a contemporary, "is at least a foot high, much in the form of a churn bottom upward, and topped off with a skeleton in the same form covered with black gauze, which hangs in streamers down her back. Her hair behind is in a large braid, turned up, and confined with a monstrous large crooked cap."[102] The Marquis de Chastellux, in an early, privately printed edition of his memoir, wrote this of Lucy Knox: "Her attire was ridiculous without being neglected; she had made of her black hair a pyramid which rose a foot above her head; this was all decked out with scarves and gauzes in a way that I am unable to describe."[103] (The diplomatic Frenchman omitted this description in his later editions.) Mrs. Knox, wrote another observer, "seems to mimic a military style . . . disgusting in a female."[104] But, as noted before, Catharine Greene received only praise and warm gushes when she appeared in a military jacket and epaulets.

Yet General and Mrs. Knox, Nathanael Greene wrote his own wife, "appear to be extravagantly fond of each other and I think are perfectly happy."[105] During their separations, Henry and Lucy frequently exchanged letters—warm, loving letters. In one, Lucy declares to "her Harry" that she loves him with "the tenderest the purest affection . . . with a love as true as ever entered the human heart."[106] Like the letters of his friend Nathanael Greene to Catharine Greene, Henry Knox's letters to Lucy were sweet and tender. "My dearest and only Love," begins Henry Knox in a letter written from Valley Forge on December 27, 1777. "I am my dear Girl with the utmost purity of affection Your own."[107]

LUCY KNOX AT VALLEY FORGE

Lucy Knox and her two-year-old daughter, also named Lucy, traveled from Boston to the Valley Forge encampment. After twenty-two days on the road, mother and daughter arrived at camp on May 27, 1778, only a few weeks before the army left. "Both Lucys arrived in perfect Health,"

Knox wrote, then proudly trumpeted, they "are situated in my Hut in the centre of the Park and are perhaps better situated than any other Ladies in Camp." Benedict Arnold had met mother and daughter at New Haven and accompanied them to Valley Forge. He had also provided the horses for the trip—"no small service," General Knox acknowledged.[108]

Benedict Arnold and Lucy Knox had had previous dealings. In late 1777 Arnold had sent a gift of a trunk packed with fine clothes to a Miss Betsy DeBlois, who refused the present. Lucy Knox somehow got hold of the trunk, opened it, viewed the finery, and extracted a fine silk scarf for her own use. She wrapped it around her neck and refused to part with it—the fabric was fabulous and impossible to find elsewhere. But Benedict Arnold was unwilling to part with the scarf. "If he intends disposing of it," Arnold's aide wrote diplomatically in his response to Henry Knox's inquiry, "you may be sure that he will give you the preference."[109]

Little is known of Lady Knox's activities once she arrived at Valley Forge. She came to camp after the celebration of both the May 6 French Alliance and the memorable performance of *Cato*, so did not participate in those festivities. Although Catharine Greene had already left for Rhode Island, Martha Washington was still in camp. In spite of the differences in their ages—Martha celebrated her forty-seventh birthday at Valley Forge, Lucy was just twenty-two—the two ladies became friends, and they would have visited back and forth during the few weeks they spent together in Pennsylvania. Like Martha Washington, Lucy Knox had already been inoculated against smallpox before she came to Valley Forge—a necessary prerequisite for camp life.

By late May conditions at camp had improved. "The Army strengthens very fast & both Officers & Men make a much more reputable Appearance than they did formerly," stated a report of June 9, 1778.[110] By mid-June, in anticipation of the start of the summer campaign, all the ladies at camp, except for Lucy Knox, had left Valley Forge. Lucy planned to remain near her husband during the campaign, so the little Knox family traveled together from Valley Forge to Philadelphia where Lucy had decided to stay. The British had just vacated the city, and Washington had placed Benedict Arnold in charge. But when "Lucy and I went in [to Philadelphia]," Knox reported, "it stunk so abominably that it was impossible to stay there, as was her first design."[111] So Lady Knox and her toddler moved on to Morristown, New Jersey, to await the end of the summer campaign.

LADY KNOX AT THE OTHER ENCAMPMENTS

Lucy Knox spent considerably more time at the fourth encampment, at Middlebrook, New Jersey, than she had at Valley Forge.

The Continental Army's 1778–79 winter camp became a far livelier place than Valley Forge had been. Henry and Lucy Knox did their part by staging an extravagant "entertainment" to celebrate the anniversary of the French Alliance—a gala event attended by Mrs. Washington, Mrs. Greene, and a "vast concourse of spectators from every part of the Jersies."[112] Henry Knox proudly wrote his brother that seventy ladies and about four hundred officers and gentlemen attended the festive frisk.

Guests were greeted by a thirteen-cannon salute. Dinner was sumptuous and "would have done honour to the taste and opulence of the most flourishing cities." The magnificent display of fireworks, which was set off by the officers, lasted for over an hour and illuminated the facade of a specially constructed Greek temple. Thirteen paintings, including "Franklin Harnessing Lightning from the Clouds" and "The Battle of Saratoga," could be seen within the thirteen arches of the temple. The fireworks over, the guests proceeded to an elegant ballroom, where Washington led a pregnant Lucy Knox in the first dance. "The power of description," gushed the *New Jersey Journal* on February 23, 1779, of the Knox's extravaganza, "is too languid to do justice to the whole of this grand entertainment."[113]

But all was not fun and frivolity at Middlebrook. Henry and Lucy Knox lost their second child, also a daughter, in early July. They named the infant Julia, "with the addition of Winslow, Waldo, or Campbell," as Henry wrote, "we have not yet determined which."[114] They never did choose the middle name. Julia's tiny grave (with a tombstone engraved, "Julia Knox. Infant Daughter of General Henry Knox and Lucy Knox. Died, July 2, 1779") may be found today at the Middlebrook encampment site. "How our brightest prospects are blasted and our sweetest hopes embittered by disappointment," Nathanael Greene wrote to Caty on July 8, several days after the baby died. "May guardian Angels protect you against such evils."[115] Two weeks later, Greene wrote that Mrs. Knox bore the loss of her daughter "with a degree of fortitude that marks a phylosophick [philosophic] temper."[116]

A few other snippets of information about Lucy Knox during the Revolutionary War survive. We know, for example, that during the

1779–80 Morristown encampment Lucy and Henry Knox and their two children lived on a farm near camp. According to Chastellux, Lucy and the little ones made up a "real family" for General Knox, as she "never leaves her husband."[117] In February 1780 General Washington and Lucy Knox opened the first Morristown Assembly ball. This was to have been another extravaganza, but hostile weather intervened and only sixteen ladies and sixty officers attended. And, as mentioned previously, Chastellux noted seeing General and Mrs. Washington riding out in a carriage to pay a social call on Lucy Knox at the New Windsor encampment.[118]

Martha Washington and Lucy Knox consoled and comforted each other at Mount Vernon during the siege of Yorktown. It is reported that, in later years, Lucy described to her children the suspense, trembling, fear, and hope that gripped the two friends as they waited for the daily express with news of the battle. After the Yorktown victory, a jubilant Henry Knox took the first opportunity to write his wife, "the charmer of my soul." "A glorious moment for America!" Knox exhalted. "This day Lord Cornwallis and his army march out and pile their arms in the face of our victorious army. . . . They [the British] will not be allowed to unfurl their colors or *play Yankee Doodle* [emphasis in original]."[119] General Knox did not mention the slight injury he had received to his ear during the battle.

When the Treaty of Paris was finally signed and the long war over, Congress appointed Henry Knox as the first secretary of war (the title was originally "secretary at war"). The Knox home became a favorite salon for the fashionable, the intellectual, and the cultivated. A contemporary of Lucy Knox described her as a "lively and meddlesome person but an amiable leader of society, without whose cooperation it was believed by many besides herself that nothing could be properly done in the drawing room or ballroom or any place indeed where fashionable men and women sought enjoyment."[120]

AFTER THE WAR

In 1783, after the hostilities ended and the colonies were free, the Knox family returned to Boston where they lived in a house rented from John Singleton Copley, the painter. After Henry Knox became Washington's secretary of war, the family moved to New York; when the capital moved to Philadelphia, so did they. At every location Lucy, always the society belle, placed "herself firmly in the center of all official activity, certain that she was one of the few who knew how to handle it."[121] Meanwhile Henry never stopped worrying about the bills. After Lucy inherited the confiscated Flucker family estate in Maine, Henry Knox left public service to build Lucy's dream house. Montpelier, the first home the couple ever owned, was finally completed in June 1795.

Described as "a combination of a French chateau" and "a fine Virginia mansion," the vast residence with twenty-four fireplaces had been partially prefabricated in Boston.[122] (Montpelier may have been America's first prefabricated building.) The window frames, sashes, shutters, doors, balustrade and cornice, as well as the casings for the doors and windows, had been constructed in Massachusetts and sent by boat to the Thomas Town (now Thomaston) site. But later upkeep became expensive, and in 1837 Nathaniel Hawthorne was already describing Montpelier as but a "large, rusty-looking edifice of wood, with some grandeur in the architecture."[123] The present Montpelier is a reconstruction as the original house was demolished in 1871. The servant's quarters of the Knox estate have been converted into the Thomaston, Maine, railroad station.

The Knoxes entertained lavishly at their new mansion. On July 4, 1795, soon after they moved in, they extended an invitation to the neighbors for a housewarming. Their daughter Lucy, who played the harpsichord for the gala, remembered that crowds of people assembled at dawn to enter Montpelier. Henry Knox, in fact, thought that more than five hundred guests came to the house that day. But the gala brought its problems, as a gold watch and two of Lucy Knox's silver cups disappeared, never to be recovered. And immediately after the event, the Knoxes were forced to order massive amounts of food supplies to refurnish their larder, including a barrel of oatmeal. Henry Knox later invited the Tarrateen Indians of Penobscot County to visit Montpelier, and they remained for weeks in their wigwams on the lawn. Finally Lucy had enough and told Henry to send the Indians home.

Henry Knox was often seen out and about the Thomaston area. He is credited with funding a school, church, and courthouse in the sparsely settled region. The elitist Lucy, however, seemed "unwilling to mix with the country folk" and, it is reported, callously turned her head when her carriage spattered unlucky pedestrians with mud.[124] Nathaniel Hawthorne, who visited Montpelier about fourteen years after Lucy Knox died, wrote in his *American Note-Books* that Lucy Knox at Thomaston, "was a woman of violent passions, and so proud an aristocrat that as long as she lived, she would never enter any house in the town except her own. The General was personally very popular, but his wife ruled him "[125]

Henry Knox had looked beyond Lucy's foibles into her heart. The solid Knox marriage lasted thirty-one years, only to end abruptly and tragically on October 25, 1806. Henry Knox, at the age of fifty-six, succumbed to peritonitis from a chicken bone stuck in his esophagus. (Another account says he died when a chicken bone punctured his intestine.) The Duke of Rochefoucauld recalled Henry Knox as "one of the worthiest men I have ever known; lively, agreeable, valuable equally as an excellent friend and as an engaging companion."[126] "My best of fathers is no more," Knox's son wrote about his death. "Everything that could be was tried, but all in vain. He is gone, I trust, to a happier and better place."[127]

Gen. Henry Knox was buried with military honors at Montpelier. The Knox estate, excluding its extensive properties, was valued at $100,000. The inventory included seven carriages and fifteen horses; one of the horses, obviously a motley one, was valued at a mere fifty cents.

Both the estate and the family spiraled into decline after Henry Knox's death. "The days of show and profusion are all gone and we are a plain, retired country family," wrote daughter Caroline from Montpelier about fifteen years after her father died.[128] Lucy Knox lived for eighteen years after her husband's death—heartbroken, in poor health, with little money, almost a recluse. She died on June 20, 1824, around three o'clock in the morning. "Madame Lucy Knox," the newspaper report stated, "having now outlived her fortune, her pleasures and most of her other friendships, departed this life at the age of 68, after a gradual failure and one month's severe illness."[129] It is said that in her final hours Lucy relived her glory years; she felt herself young and exuberant and fancied herself dancing once again in the arms of her beloved Harry.

THE CHILDREN OF HENRY AND LUCY KNOX

Of the thirteen children born to Lucy and Henry Knox, only three survived to adulthood: their first child, Lucy Flucker, who had come to the Valley Forge encampment at the age of two; Henry Jackson, the cause "of endless heartache" brought on by his "instability"; and their youngest daughter, Caroline Wadsworth.[130]

Lucy Flucker Knox Thatcher, 1776–October 12, 1854

Lucy Flucker Knox, born in Fairfield, Connecticut, in early 1776, was, her mother wrote, "without exception the sweetest child in the world."[131] She was also a well-traveled little girl. As a two year old, Lucy accompanied her mother to the Valley Forge encampment. At four, she traveled to camp at Morristown. At five years old, with the war still on, she was sent for safety to a boarding school near Philadelphia. In January 1804 Lucy married Ebenezer Thatcher, described by a contemporary as an "ornament to any circle, however intellectual, however refined."[132] When this "ornament" died in 1842, however, he left Lucy with an estate valued at only $158.50 and seven adult children. Three of the children were still alive when Lucy Knox Thatcher herself died in 1854.

Her sister Caroline wrote that Lucy, a sweet little child, grew into a woman who was "a singular union of rare intelligence and almost childlike artlessness."[133] As an adult, Lucy Thatcher enjoyed reading, writing letters, and attending religious, musical, and literary gatherings. Serious lectures were of particular interest to her. Lucy was pleased to find a lecture series on the U.S. Constitution a delight—she had thought it would be a "dry subject"—and the speaker, she wrote, recalled "many events in our early history which I knew either personally or from my Parents."[134] After Lucy attended an 1842 lecture by Daniel Webster in Faneuil Hall in Boston, she wrote with admiration of Webster's excellent mind and delivery. At the age of sixty-nine, Lucy still traveled and enjoyed the northeastern states' beauty. She had heard stories about Niagara Falls since childhood; when she finally visited, she found that, although the falls were not as high as she expected, the site nevertheless "far exceeded my anticipations."[135]

Conversely, Lucy Knox Thatcher described the sketch of her mother that Elizabeth Ellet wrote for *The Women of the American Revolution* as both flawed and disappointing. Of Mrs. Ellet, Lucy wrote, she "has said some things which I never thought of saying."[136] (See appendix for more about Lucy Knox Thatcher and Elizabeth Ellet.)

Lucy Flucker Knox Thatcher, who came to Valley Forge as a toddler and lived in a hut near the artillery park, died on October 12, 1854.

Henry Jackson Knox, May 24, 1780–October 9, 1832

Henry Jackson Knox, the only son of Henry Knox to live to adulthood, had a difficult and turbulent life. His schoolmaster reported that Henry, as a youth, beat "a little girl, insulted a man on the street and broke open a closet from which he had stolen some sugar."[137] After a brief time in the navy, he returned home, married, went to debtor's prison, and divorced.

Then Henry Jackson Knox found religion. "You will be much surprised to hear that your Uncle Knox has lately become a pious man," his sister Lucy wrote to her own son in 1828, and "his conversion is one of the most wonderful things I have ever met with."[138] To demonstrate his remorse for causing the family grief, the new convert supported the First Congregational Church of Thomaston, became active in civic affairs, and helped out on the Montpelier estate. Henry Jackson Knox died in 1832. According to local legend, as a sign of penance he had requested to be buried deep in the ground in an unmarked grave at Montpelier, far from his parents' burial site.

CAROLINE WADSWORTH KNOX SWAN HOLMES, JULY, 1791–OCTOBER 17, 1851

Caroline Wadsworth, described to Knox as "the finest and most healthy child of any you have had," was born in Boston in 1791.[139] Her first marriage, to James Swan Jr., a rich but lazy man, ended when Swan died in 1836. Caroline's second marriage, a happy one, was to James Holmes on July 7, 1837. Holmes, a lawyer and a respected public servant who served as a U.S. senator from Maine, died in 1843. Caroline died at Montpelier about eight years later, at the age of sixty of "cancer of the side."[140]

Unlike her mother, Caroline was not flamboyant and boisterous, but gracious and kindly, pleasant and calm. She even dressed serenely; one of her favorite colors was a soft, pretty gray. At the age of forty-six, Caroline described herself as "a quiet unobtrusive sort of woman. . . . My tastes center almost exclusively round home, and the domestic hearth. In my youthful days, I soon became weary of the great world, and the show and parade of life."[141]

It seems that Caroline could not be called handsome or elegant, but she did possess a pleasant, happy, open spirit. Caroline herself wrote that a friend observed that she (Caroline) had the ability to rise above the "troubles of life and pluck such flowers as I might find in my path." She had inherited this trait, Caroline said, from her father, Gen. Henry Knox— or so her mother had told her.[142]

The Other Knox Children

Henry and Lucy Knox had ten other children, but none of them survived to adulthood. Julia, General and Mrs. Knox's second daughter, died in infancy at the Middlebrook encampment. Henry Jackson Knox was born in 1780, and on December 10, 1781, Lucy Knox gave birth to a second son. The proud father wrote his friend Nathanael Greene, "I should name it after you, were it not for the confounded name given you by your Scriptural father. As it is, I shall call him after some fine Roman whose character I think you may like."[143] The chosen name was Marcus Camillus. In spite of this fine name, the baby died nine months later. On July 6, 1783, the Knoxes had another little boy, also called Marcus Camillus. The child lived until September 8, 1791.

The first Caroline Knox, who was born in 1786, died at the age of one of a sickness her father said was "common to children cutting their teeth in summer."[144] Knox wrote to Washington in November 1787 to announce the happy birth of a "fine black-haired, black-eyed boy. . . . As an evidence of our respect and affection for you, which we hope will survive ourselves," the letter continued, "we have done him the honor of giving him your name."[145] But little George Washington Knox lived for only two years.

William Bingham Knox (called Marcus, or Billy) was born in 1785. Lafayette had hoped to take the boy to France with him, but the charming eleven year old died of what was called "putrid sore throat" or "throat distemper" (probably diphtheria) on April 23, 1796, before Lafayette could set sail.

Unbelievably, a Knox daughter, Augusta Henrietta Knox, died the same day—April 23, 1796—from the same disease. In newspaper reports, Augusta was described as having been in "blooming health and beauty personified." The stricken parents laid out both children in the Montpelier "dead room."[146]

Lucy and Henry Knox laid out yet one more son in the dead room in 1796. Another George Washington Knox, born in January 1790, was six years old when he died.

In July 1797, at forty-one years old, Lucy Knox delivered a stillborn child. It was a difficult birth, but Lucy appeared to recover completely. She had no more children.

Lucy did have more sorrow, however. Julia Wadsworth, born in 1784, died on January 21, 1798. What is known of this girl comes from a newspaper obituary: "Julia Wadsworth Knox, fourteen years of age, died in this town of rapid consumption. To support the death of so lovely a child . . . requires the combined efforts of reason, philosophy and religion, for she possessed all the amiable qualities of head and heart to promise the highest satisfaction."[147]

Lucy and Henry Knox had had thirteen children in twenty-one years. Five of the children died within two years of each other. "Our family has suffered great Diminution," Henry Knox wrote in 1798 to Clement Biddle about the loss of his children. "My wife's happiness is impaired while she continues on this globe. . . . But," General Knox continued, ever the optimist, "time works wonders."[148]

5

Rebekah Biddle, Lady Stirling, and Alice Shippen at Valley Forge

"I Should Not Be Sorry to See You Here"

MRS. CLEMENT BIDDLE: REBEKAH CORNELL BIDDLE, 1755–1831

Clement Biddle, the commissary general of forage at Valley Forge, lost his first wife and infant son about 1773. On August 18, 1774, Biddle married Rebekah Cornell, from a prominent Rhode Island family. Rebekah was nineteen years old; the groom thirty-four.

Like Lucy Knox, Rebekah Biddle was a young mother in her twenties when she came to the Valley Forge encampment. Rebekah shared something else with Lucy—both ladies eventually had thirteen children, and both mothers saw only three of their children live to adulthood. One of the Biddle children, Thomas A. Biddle, probably came to Valley Forge with his mother. The Biddles were Philadelphians, and with the enemy occupying the city, Rebekah would have wanted her child with her when she fled from the British Army. Thomas, who was born in 1776, would have been two at the time of the Valley Forge encampment, and so would have been a playmate for two-year-old Lucy Knox. Gen. Nathanael Greene wrote about seeing Mrs. Biddle and her "fine son" at the Middlebrook encampment, so Thomas may have accompanied her there, also.[1]

At Valley Forge, the Biddles may have lived at Moore Hall with Catharine and Nathanael Greene and the Moore family. Certainly Colonel Biddle worked from Moore Hall, as his letters from camp are addressed from "Moorhall."

Colonel and Mrs. Biddle were among the many officers and wives who posed for Charles Willson Peale that spring of 1778. Peale recorded in his diary that their miniatures were ready for delivery on April 26. Later, on May 6, Rebekah Biddle, along with Martha Washington, Caty Greene, and several other ladies, participated in the joyful camp celebration of the French Alliance.

And that, unfortunately, is the extent of what is known about Rebekah Biddle's activities during the Valley Forge winter of 1777–78.

It appears, however, that Elizabeth Ellet, author of *The Women of the American Revolution*, has invented some stories about Lady Biddle at camp. As has already been noted, Ellet wrote that Mrs. Biddle and the Marquis de Lafayette, years after the Valley Forge encampment, reminisced about the flocks of wild pigeons that were seen and killed for food near camp. But no available primary source from the 1777–78 encampment authenticates this event. Only Elizabeth Ellet tells this tale—and she writes about seventy-five years after Valley Forge.

Another Ellet *story* goes that Rebekah Biddle herself cooked for the army near the Brandywine battlefield on September 11, 1777. According to Ellet, Washington ordered the ladies, including Mrs. Biddle, to leave the Brandywine area when British troops were spotted nearby. Instead of obeying orders, Rebekah approached the commander seeking permission to remain behind to prepare food for the exhausted officers when they returned from battle. Permission was granted, but she was ordered to flee should the Americans lose ground. After dispatching a servant to collect all available food in the area, Ellet writes, Lady Rebekah Biddle cooked over the open fires all day and had a hot meal ready for a hundred or so officers when they returned to camp. Ellet states that she got this information from a Biddle family member.[2] But this, too, is oral history, subject to romanticized hindsight and a fallible memory. There is no written reference or record from the period to support Ellet's claim.

Although there is likely no truth to the pigeon and cooking stories, some facts are evident: Clement and Rebekah Biddle paid dearly for supporting the American Revolution. Because Biddle, who had been born into a wealthy Philadelphia Quaker family, supported the Patriot cause—he early raised a company of Philadelphia volunteers, the "Quaker Blues"—he and Rebekah were read out of meeting. Clement Biddle also lost a great deal of money during the war; he declared bankruptcy in 1785, two years after the Revolution ended. Consequently he took on different positions to support his large family. He investigated ships and cargoes that came into the port of Philadelphia, was commissioned a U.S. marshal in 1787, and became a notary public in 1788. Biddle served as justice to the

Pennsylvania Court of Common Pleas and published a street directory of Philadelphia. In 1791 he was appointed quartermaster of the force sent to western Pennsylvania to quell the Whiskey Rebellion. But this job required spending time on a horse, and as Biddle had gout and "another Complaint which has prevented me from riding any distance on horseback," and found "the Expense attending the Execution has been equal to or greater than the Endowments of the office," he asked to be relieved of this position.[3]

Clement Biddle was Washington's factor in Philadelphia during the presidential years. Martha Washington sent to Biddle requesting such items as "knives and forks—and wine, if it is very good" as well as "ginn [sic] and liquors . . . of the best kind" for the New York presidential household. Later she sent for "orrange [sic] flower water" for perfume and cooking, pickled walnuts, Guthries' *Geography* and the *Art of Speaking* (for her grandchildren's lessons) and even "mops and clamps for scouring Brushes."[4] A February 10, 1790, letter signed by Tobias Lear asks Biddle to procure a carpet for the presidential residence in New York City. Lear's request was very specific: the carpet was to be on "Pea Green Ground, with white or light flowers or spots . . . for a Room 32 feet by 22 feet . . . of the best kind."[5] As nothing of quality was available in New York City, Lear asked Biddle to look for the carpet in Philadelphia.

Col. Clement Biddle died July 14, 1814. Rebekah Cornell Biddle died seventeen years later, at the age of seventy-six.

MRS. WILLIAM ALEXANDER, LADY STIRLING:
SARAH LIVINGSTON ALEXANDER, 1722(?)–1791

Rebekah Biddle was one of the youngest ladies at Valley Forge; Mrs. William Alexander, or Lady Stirling, was, at about fifty-six, one of the oldest.

Lady Stirling (Sarah Livingston Alexander) traveled from her beautiful estate in northern New Jersey to share the Valley Forge winter with her husband, Maj. Gen. William Alexander, or Lord Stirling, as even Washington called him. The wealthy Lady Stirling had traveled to Valley Forge with several servants and her daughter, Lady Kitty (Catherine) and Nancy Brown, an orphaned niece. Army camp—with its dashing and eligible young officers—must have been very appealing to the young ladies, as both Lady Kitty and Nancy were in their mid-twenties, and neither was married. At Valley Forge, the lord and his lady and family lived with the Rev. William Currie and his family in a house by the Valley Creek. The residence still stands today.

Lady Stirling's activities at camp, like those of the other officers' wives, are rarely mentioned in the letters, journals, and diaries of the period. Nor is much said about the activities of Lady Kitty or Nancy Brown. Pierre S. DuPonceau did include Lady Kitty and Lady Stirling among the group of ladies who met at each other's homes that Valley Forge winter, and it is known that both ladies also attended the camp production of *Cato*. DuPonceau, years after the encampment, also remembered Nancy Brown as having been a "distinguished belle."[6]

Lady Kitty wrote a bit from Valley Forge about her activities there. A letter written May 3, 1778, records that the family was off attending "divine services," although Lady Kitty doesn't say where. She stayed home, on doctor's orders, although we don't know why. What Lady Kitty does say is how proud and pleased everyone at camp was that day, for France had officially joined in an alliance with the Americans against the British. "From France we have here nothing but rejoicings," she wrote. "Every one looks happy & seems proud of the share he has had in humbling the Pride of Britain & of establishing the name of America as a *Nation* [emphasis in original]."[7] The French Alliance, officially celebrated on May 6 at Valley Forge, was indeed an event of exultation.

More is known of Lord Stirling than his wife. His Lordship was considered by some to be "the most martial in appearance of any general in the army save General Washington."[8] He was also a bit pompous. Born William Alexander, he spent five years in Scotland and England on a quest to reclaim the title "Earl of Stirling" as his own. The gentleman returned to America in 1761 without that prize, but with plenty of baggage: "some fifteen cases of household furniture, much wearing apparel for himself and his ladies, a new coach, a new phaeton, and six cherry trees of a special type he had admired in England."[9]

Soon after he arrived home, the self-proclaimed lord planted his cherry trees and then began construction on an impressive, new manor near Baskingridge (now Basking Ridge), New Jersey. Lord Stirling wanted the estate to appear as a fine countryseat in the European manner. The place was so grand (or perhaps His Lordship's funds were so deficient) that, although construction started in 1761, the mansion was still unfinished in 1775. The residence featured piazzas, painted walls, oak floors, and a library of more than two hundred volumes. The grounds included a deer park, rose garden, Italian vineyard, and an orchard with at least six cherry trees. Lord Stirling had himself a showplace. (The mansion was destroyed by fire in 1920.)

This is not to say the lord was wealthy, or even solvent, although his wife, from the prosperous New York Livingston family, had brought some money to the marriage. Lord Stirling made some income from breeding horses—horses so fine that Washington, who was very particular about his animals, wrote from Mount Vernon to inquire about purchasing a stallion for his mares. But Lord Stirling was also a big spender and slow to pay his debts. In 1772 he tried to raise needed funds by selling off some of his extensive property holdings by lottery, a not uncommon tactic in that time. Washington himself bought thirty lottery tickets. The lottery, however, ended with only one-third of the tickets sold, and Lord Stirling plunged even deeper into debt. These were unsettled times, and there were very few bids when Stirling next attempted to sell the family estate and mansion in New York City. His tangled financial affairs, in fact, almost forced the family into bankruptcy. Through it all, His Lordship's "cheerful readiness . . . courage, faithfulness and unselfishness were unchanging."[10]

And then there was the mother-in-law problem, undoubtedly the cause of more stress and angst between Lord and Lady Stirling. On May 6, 1777, Washington (at headquarters in Morristown, New Jersey) wrote to Lord Stirling (at home in Baskingridge, about ten miles away) that he had received information that His Lordship had behaved in a "degree of roughness & indelicacy" in a "sudden transport of passion" toward Mrs. Livingston. "Mrs. Livingston" was Mrs. Philip Livingston, Lord Stirling's mother-in-law, who lived with Lord and Lady Stirling in New Jersey. Washington had learned that Lord Stirling had attempted to put his wife's mother out of the house. Writing as a friend, Washington begged the lord "to consider your conduct in this affair." Mrs. Livingston's character, connections, sex, and situation all merited Stirling's careful consideration, Washington wrote. Lord Stirling was also to think about how the enemy would take advantage of the situation.[11]

Washington received a response the same day. Lord Stirling was, he wrote, "extremely unhappy to find . . . that my private affairs should have taken up so much of your attention." Then His Lordship shared his side of the story. Because his family had need of more space, the lord had asked his mother-in-law six weeks before to move from his Baskingridge property to one of her own four houses. On May 5 he again asked her "in the most friendly manner" to please vacate his premises as soon as possible. Mrs. Livingston took offense and "behaved very improperly and threatened to move the next morning." Lord Stirling's reply? "I told her she might do as she thought proper."[12]

How this was resolved is uncertain, as there is no more mention of the incident in extant correspondence between the two officers. Nor is there any mention of how Lady Stirling felt about the matter.

William Alexander (who was not yet known as Lord Stirling) had married Sarah Livingston in 1748. The twenty-six-year-old bride was the widow of a prosperous merchant; her new groom was twenty-two. The couple's first daughter, Mary, arrived a year later. Catherine, or Kitty (or Kate, as her mother called her), was born about 1752.

Mary Alexander eventually married Robert Watts, a staunch Loyalist, in a union that brought pain and heartache to her family. The Revolution caused Lord Stirling's family, like the Knox family, to split into Loyalists and Patriots, Tories and Whigs. When Mary dutifully remained with her husband in New York City during the British occupation, Lord Stirling sought and received permission from both the British and Americans for his wife and younger daughter to visit Mary Watts there. They found Mary in "great distress" when they arrived. She had been "brought to bed about ten days before we got there," Lady Stirling wrote to her husband, but had "lost her little boy the funeral just over as we got to the house . . . she longs to see you and wishes to be with you but duty to her husband must keep her where she is."[13] Lord Stirling made no mention of Lady Mary Watts in his will, but by that time her husband had amassed his own fortune. Robert Watts himself died in 1814. Lady Mary Watts died twenty-five years later, in 1839.

The Alexanders' second daughter, Lady Kitty, married William A. Duer, a congressman from New York. (Lafayette thought little of Duer, calling him a "rascal" and "tory." But then Lafayette had also written this about "Miss Ketty" at the time of the Valley Forge encampment: "If she had taken any Notice of what my eyes could have signified, she would have read there the greatest admiration of all her accomplished person.")[14] William Duer was instrumental in thwarting the so-called Conway Cabal, a plot to remove Washington from command of the Continental Army.

Although bedridden with a serious illness, Duer had risen from his sick bed, hired a litter, and was about to travel to Congress to vote against Washington's removal as commander in chief. When the faction opposing Washington heard this, they abandoned their plans—and the Conway Cabal was aborted.

Lady Kitty and Duer wed on July 27, 1779, at the Stirling mansion in a magnificent ceremony attended by George and Martha Washington and a numerous group of "civil and social magnates from New York and New Jersey."[15] The event was all show, as Lord Stirling was virtually bankrupt by this time.

The Duers had several children. Their first, a chubby girl, was described by her proud papa "as fat as a Mole."[16] One of Kitty and William Duer's sons, Robert, rose to become chief justice of the New York Superior Court. William Alexander Duer, another son, was elected president of Columbia University. He also wrote a two-volume biography of Lord Stirling, his grandfather. Duer allotted only a few lines in the biography to his grandmother, Lady Stirling.

Lady Kitty Duer glittered as a hostess in New York City society after the Revolutionary War ended. Although not a beauty, she possessed "the most accomplished manners" and was considered to be "a fine woman"; when presiding over the dinner table, she "performed the honors of the table very gracefully, was constantly attended by two servants in livery, and insisted upon performing the whole herself."[17] Her husband resigned from Congress to make his fortune; by 1783 he was considered "one of the richest men in New York city."[18] Duer was a founder of the Bank of New York and served as assistant secretary of the treasury under Hamilton. But Duer, like his father-in-law, could not hang on to his money. He speculated heavily. On March 29, 1792, it was reported that "Col. Duer they say has failed for three millions of dollars [and] is now in the new jail."[19] And, except for a few months of parole, he remained there until his death in 1799. Lady Kitty, once a belle of the Valley Forge encampment, lived out her last years in a boarding house.

Lady Stirling was a gracious hostess; her manor in New Jersey, both before and during the war, was "the seat of hospitality, refinement and luxury," where "great sociability prevailed."[20] Little is known of her personality, but a fragment from a letter indicates an astute and sensible character. In the letter to her husband, Lady Stirling writes that when she and daughter Kitty visited with Mary in New York City, then behind enemy lines, they were offered "the liberty to take any thing out of town I pleased." Lady Stirling was thankful for the offer but told the British, "I was only come to see my daughter; which I thought most prudent, for I was afraid there would be a handle made of it, if I accepted the offer." The offer was made again by several others, and the last time she was told, "I must take a *box of tea,* but I stuck to my text [emphasis in original]."[21] Lady Stirling, shrewdly, did not want anyone to think that she, an American general's wife, would accept any favors from the British.

Lady Stirling rarely appeared by her husband's side and seemed to fade into the background when he was around. Few contemporaries record anything about her. But she wrote affectionate letters to her "Billie" when they were apart. "My Dear Lord," began one letter from Baskingridge, "I should not be sorry to see you here. How very agreeable a line from you will be to me pray let me have it whenever you have an opportunity for that shall be all my comfort here."[22]

Lord Stirling was a good general and trusted friend to his commander in chief. When Stirling died of gout in 1783, Washington wrote to Lady Stirling that her husband's death had deprived him of "public and professional assistance, as well as the private friendship of an officer of so high Rank with whom I lived in the strictest habits of amity." The entire army regretted Lord Stirling's death, Washington wrote. Further, the commander felt that it would undoubtedly be a "soothing consideration in the poignancy of your grief" for her to know that the general officers were "going into Mourning for My Lord."[23] Lord Stirling was "brave, energetic, intelligent, cautious when caution was required, a good organizer, a fine military engineer."[24] He had, at one time or another, commanded every brigade in the Continental Army but South Carolina and Georgia. When Washington was away for two months during the Middlebrook encampment, Lord Stirling took command of the entire army. But he suffered with physical ailments. "I [am now] laid up," he wrote, "with my old Companion in Winter [gout and rheumatism] and so bad Still in my Right hand that I am now Scarce able to hold my pen."[25]

Lord Stirling was admired by many, but not all. Douglas Southall Freeman, Washington's biographer, writes, "[The soldiers] did not consider him incompetent; they liked him and enjoyed his company and admired his social qualities; at the same time they did not expect of him the strategical sense with which they credited Nathanael Greene. . . . The category of Stirling was one of the largest in an army—the comprehensive class of those a Commander-in-Chief never would think of demoting—or of advancing."[26] Lafayette called him "braver than wise." Dr. Benjamin Rush, however, found him "a proud, vain, lazy ignorant drunkard."[27] There is, too, evidence of an elicit tryst in the 1760s. A brother-in-law wrote His Lordship that someone he described as the hairdresser planned to visit Lord Stirling's New Jersey home to present him with an "account of things furnished Miss Stephenson by your order, wh. [which] remained unpaid." As the brother-in-law realized that the hairdresser's visit would be both "expensive" and "troublesome to you," and that there would "be an impropriety in his visit," he delivered the account to Stirling himself.[28] There is no record of Lady Stirling's reaction to all of this.

Lord Stirling, once the master of one of the finest manor estates in the land, left essentially nothing for his family when he died. Lady Stirling died, destitute, in 1791.

MRS. WILLIAM SHIPPEN: ALICE LEE SHIPPEN, 1735–1817

Two prominent Virginia ladies—Martha Dandridge Custis Washington and Alice Lee Shippen—both traveled to the 1777–78 Valley Forge encampment. Lady Shippen's husband, Dr. William Shippen, was chief physician and director of the Continental Army hospitals.

Alice Lee was one of eleven children, and the youngest daughter, of the illustrious Thomas Lee family of Stratford Hall, Virginia. Two of her brothers, Richard Henry Lee and Francis Lightfoot Lee, signed the Declaration of Independence. Henry "Light Horse Harry" Lee, the father of Robert E. Lee of Civil War fame, was Alice's nephew. Light Horse Harry, like Alice, came to Valley Forge.

Although she had a distinguished family background, Alice Lee did not have a pampered and privileged childhood. After her mother died in 1749, and her father passed away in 1750, the teenager found no joy at the plantation. At the age of twenty-four, Alice Lee, still unmarried, had had enough of Stratford Hall and its quiet, rural setting. She renounced any claim to her father's estate, collected forty pounds sterling, gathered up some of her belongings, and set sail for England. There she met and, two years later, married Dr. William Shippen Jr. The elder Dr. William Shippen was a founder of both the University of Pennsylvania and Princeton University.

Alice's new husband had been sent to England by his father "to be perfected in the medical art"; he rose to become one of the foremost physicians and medical innovators of the time.[29] Dr. Shippen Jr. presented the first medical lectures by an American doctor, in Philadelphia. (Ten students signed on.) Later he wrote and put into practice a highly regarded plan to reorganize the army's medical service. Like his wife, Dr. Shippen came from a renowned colonial family: his great-grandfather was the first mayor of Philadelphia. But, as in many families, loyalties split the Shippen family. Dr. Shippen was related to Peggy Shippen, the wife of the turncoat Benedict Arnold. He was also related to Elizabeth Powel, another Philadelphian and close friend to both George and Martha Washington.

After returning to America from England, William and Alice Shippen moved into a substantial Philadelphia home—Shippen House—that eventually became the northern headquarters of Virginia Patriots. The couple had eight children, but only two lived beyond infancy: Anne Home "Nancy" Shippen, born on February 24, 1764, and Thomas Lee Shippen, born two years later. The two children became the "objects of almost idolatrous devotion and the center around which the world of Shippen House revolved."[30] Nancy and Tommy were away at their respective schools—Nancy in New Jersey, Tommy in Maryland—when the British marched into Philadelphia on September 26, 1777. Although General Howe had sent word that the good citizens of Philadelphia would be safe and should remain in their homes during the occupancy, Alice Shippen closed up her home and left. Once-elegant Philadelphia had already been struck by smallpox and yellow fever, and the war brought the sick and wounded soldiers of the Patriot army to the city. It was common to see the "shocking sight of a cart with five or six coffins in it. . . . The poor creatures die without number . . . and forty or fifty coffins are put in the same hole."[31]

Alice Shippen retreated to her childhood home in Virginia when she left Philadelphia, then ventured out to travel with her husband to army camps. She wrote a letter to her sister from Manheim, Pennsylvania, in May 1777 and sent letters from Reading, Pennsylvania, in September and November 1777. Alice Shippen came to the Valley Forge encampment, and a June 7, 1778, letter written by Dr. Shippen from camp informs fourteen-year-old Nancy that as soon as the enemy left Philadelphia—and this was expected soon—her parents would visit her at school in Trenton, New Jersey. Shippen added that your Mamma "longs to see you much" and that "Your Mamma has bought you many clever things for ye summer."[32] What Shippen does not say in that letter to his daughter is that Alice was pregnant, for three months later, he wrote to his brother that Alice "was confined to her room and I am afraid will lose another patriot for me."[33] In April 1779 Nathanael Greene recorded seeing Alice and Nancy at the Middlebrook encampment.[34]

In 1774 John Adams described Alice Shippen as "sensible," a "deep thinker," and a "religious and reasoning lady" who believed the people of Boston would not have been able to bear their trials "if they had not been influenced by a superior power."[35] She was also a woman much taken with her daughter's deportment and needlework skills, no matter what was happening in the country or with the army. Alice Shippen's letters to her daughter at school are full of phrases such as "do remember my dear how much of the beauty & usefulness of life depends on a proper conduct" and "Needle work is a most important branch of a female education." Lady Alice of the Lees of Virginia also implored her daughter to "tell me how you have improved in holding your head & shoulders, in making a curtsy, in going out or coming into a room, in giving & receiving, holding your knife & fork, walking & sitting. These things contribute so much to a good appearance that they are of great consequence."[36] From Valley Forge, Nancy's father wrote, "Your Mamma desires you will never wear a ribbon on your Shoulder because it is apt to make the person crooked."[37] At all times, her daughter's deportment and carriage were *very* important to Alice Lee Shippen.

Nancy learned to carry herself beautifully, converse easily, sing and play several instruments, speak some French, recite English poems and essays, and, if needed, pickle and preserve. She was also admonished to improve in humility, patience, and love. And why was all this so important? Because, as her mother said, "These are absolutely necessary to make you shine."[38] Because, as her father wrote, your mother "loves you & wishes to make you one of the finest women in Philadelphia."[39]

At the age of fifteen, in 1778, Nancy Shippen was "finished." And Nancy did shine, attracting many beaus. At eighteen she married Col.

Henry Beekman Livingston, the son of Robert R. Livingston of the wealthy, illustrious New York House of Livingston. (Sarah Livingston Alexander, Lady Stirling, was the bridegroom's aunt.) The colonel had served in the ill-fated expedition to Quebec—where he "has by no means given any offense, though some uneasiness, by some little imprudence."[40] (One wonders what that was about.) Later Livingston served as a colonel in the Fourth New York Regiment at Valley Forge—where to "all those under his Command," a soldier wrote, he exhibited "unbounded Pride and thirst." "I find myself treated like a slave," the soldier continued, "& cant bear it no longer."[41] As an officer, Livingston was a disaster—he was rich, yes, but annoyingly prone to fits of outlandish expressions of rage. He was also selfish and licentious and produced several children by several alliances. Not surprisingly, his marriage to Nancy was also disastrous, forcing her to flee New York for Philadelphia and her parents. Nancy and Henry Livingston's only child, Margaret "Peggy" Beekman Livingston, was born December 26, 1781, at Shippen House in Philadelphia.

But in spite of the chaotic, choleric atmosphere in New York, both Nancy and Peggy shuttled back and forth between the Shippens in Philadelphia and the Livingstons in New York. Mother and daughter also occasionally visited with Lady Kitty Duer or General Knox's family while in New York City. As Nancy wrote in her journal, they traveled to New York only because her father, Dr. Shippen, had determined that "he could not be answerable for the Childs [Peggy] losing her fortune . . . if I kept her from her Grandmother."[42] The Livingstons were very wealthy, and Dr. Shippen wanted to be sure his granddaughter would receive her inheritance from the Livingston family.

The behavior of Nancy's husband, Henry, however, became ever more bizarre and terrifying. He launched an ugly smear campaign against Nancy and several times attempted to snatch up his daughter Peggy from her. Nancy finally sued for divorce. (Did the words her father wrote to her in 1781—"Never forget that it should be your first care to please & make your husband happy"[43]—ring in her ears as she did so?) But when Nancy refused to give up custody of their daughter, Livingston refused to consider the divorce. Finally Peggy herself, yet a teenager, took control of the situation. In the spring of 1797, at the age of sixteen, she renounced her expected Livingston fortune, turned her back on the luxuries of living with that family in New York, bid farewell to her adoring Livingston grandmother, aunts, and cousins, and set out for Philadelphia. But life did not become easy for the girl. Nor did it go well for her mother, Nancy, or grandmother, Alice Shippen.

Dr. William Shippen Jr. and Alice had left their Philadelphia mansion around the turn of the nineteenth century to move into a smaller house in Germantown. Their son Tommy married in 1791; in 1792 Mrs. Washington came to call on Tommy's new baby boy. (President Washington visited soon afterward.) But Tommy—so much had been expected of him!—died in 1798, as did one of their grandsons. Long before Tommy's death, Alice Shippen had begun to exhibit signs of debilitating physical and mental illness. Nancy wrote that her mother's spirits were "extremely low, her mind is much affected" in February 1784, just after the Revolution ended.[44] In 1787 Alice Shippen began "to think it is too great an indulgence for her to live with us [the family] any longer," as her husband put it, and she moved to the country to be alone.[45]

Toward the end of her life, Alice, by now overcome with religious fervor, moved from one relative's house to another, carting her furniture with her. She died on March 25, 1817, a troubled, sightless woman. Her tombstone reads, "Endowed with great talents, she was also a liberal friend of the poor, a Sincere Christian. Hark, the trumpet sounds and the tombs burst. Awake, arise, the Savior of the world calls."[46] Dr. William Shippen Jr., who had been so helpful to the medical department during the Revolution, had passed away several years earlier, on July 11, 1808.

By this time Nancy Shippen Livingston had long slipped into the same state of religious melancholia that had tormented her mother. Nancy was struck another blow when her dear friend, the French diplomat Louis Otto—who had waited eight years for Nancy to divorce—decided he could wait no longer and remarried.

And so Nancy Shippen Livingston, a cherished daughter who had once shared breakfast with Martha Washington and tea with General Washington, a girl who had been trained to be "one of the finest women in Philadelphia," spiraled into a decline. As a girl, Nancy had been asked by her father to "work a pair of ruffles for General Washington if you can get the proper muslin."[47] Dr. Shippen had also praised her for behaving "like a Virginian like her mother."[48] As a woman, Nancy shared her mother's manners as well as her hopeless melancholy. In her later years she took to putting the first five books of the Bible into verse, composing hymns, and collecting cash to evangelize slaves.[49] Nancy Shippen Livingston died on August 23, 1841, at the age of seventy-eight.

Peggy Livingston, whose grandmother and grandfather had come to the Valley Forge encampment, shared her mother and grandmother's mental illness. There were some funds, as Grandmother Livingston displayed a magnanimous frame of mind and left her favorite grandchild a part of the Livingston fortune that Peggy had renounced years ago. But the Livingston monies dwindled after swindlers, posing as clergy, appropriated the funds. Peggy lived for twenty-three years after her mother passed away—secluded, despairing, mentally ill. She died in 1864, at the age of eighty-two.

Nancy and Peggy, nearly inseparable in life, lie buried together on the grounds of a Philadelphia estate.

6

The Women with Washington's "Family"

Slaves, Servants, and Spies

General Washington traveled with his military family throughout the Revolution. The members of this select group—gentlemen all—were handpicked, intelligent, and hardworking, fiercely devoted to Washington and the cause. At Valley Forge, family members included military secretaries, aides-de-camp, and two members of Washington's guard, Capt. Caleb Gibbs and Lt. George Lewis, the general's nephew. The commander in chief, an exceedingly busy man, found the assistance of his family members indispensable.

The duties of these gentlemen were many and varied. They attended to the voluminous army correspondence, wrote up the general orders, and kept up the expense reports. They also participated in court-martial proceedings and examinations of American camp deserters and prisoners. The aides met with the visitors who came to talk with the commander. Sometimes Washington sent an aide or two off to hand-deliver a message. Sometimes he gave the men special assignments. He sent Col. Richard Kidder Meade, for example, to meet Martha Washington's carriage on the road and escort it to the Valley Forge encampment. At camp, Col. Alexander Hamilton and Col. John Laurens, aides who were both fluent in French, translated Steuben's new military training manual from French to English.[1]

A few women of the "common sort"—an eighteenth-century term for those regarded as lower class—also traveled with the general throughout the Revolution. Although only gentlemen belonged to Washington's military family, he did consider the women he traveled with, as he once wrote, "of his family."[2] Cooking, sewing, washing, and supervising the commander's households were some of the tasks performed by these female servants and slaves.

Because Washington's entourage numbered twenty-five or so people, conditions were crowded at headquarters. The stone Isaac Potts House, headquarters during the Valley Forge encampment, was constructed with five small rooms plus an attic, basement, and separate kitchen—tight quarters indeed for the twenty-five or so of Washington's family who worked and lived there during the six-month encampment. Col. Timothy Pickering, in fact, wrote from camp that Washington's family was "exceedingly pinched for room" at the Potts House.[3] Lieutenant Colonel Laurens said he worked in a "small, noisy, crowded room."[4] Martha Washington, too, wrote from Valley Forge, "The Generals appartment [sic] is very small."[5] Because headquarters was crowded, some of the commander's military family probably slept in nearby farmhouses, in the dining hut Washington had built near headquarters, or in the nearby guard huts. Additional huts for sleeping may have also been built near Washington's headquarters. The slaves and servants with Washington's family would have slept in the halls, attic, basement, or kitchen of the Potts House.

As in every family group, not everyone with Washington's military family got along. Although the general declared himself "entirely destitute" when one woman left his employment,[6] he wrote of another that he "never wished to see her more."[7] And "Negro Hannah," as she was called in Washington's expense books, so provoked the general that, she said, he pronounced her a "fool."[8]

WASHINGTON'S HOUSEHOLD HELP

Fifty-six-year-old Negro Hannah worked with her husband Isaac as a cook at Valley Forge headquarters. Occasionally she also purchased items for headquarters' kitchen—evidence that she was a trusted, responsible servant. (In the eighteenth century, "servants" was a general term referring to free servants, indentured servants, and slaves.)

Hannah was permitted to keep forty shillings a month from her wages for clothing and necessaries. The remainder of her salary went directly to her master, Rev. John Mason of New York; he allowed that, after he had been paid fifty-three pounds, Hannah would be set free. She earned her freedom sometime between December 1778 and June 1780, as on December 19, 1778, Rev. Mason received thirty-two pounds New York currency in "full for my servant Hannah's wages who was in the service of His Excellency General Washington."[9] Indeed, a June 23, 1780, receipt for eighty-six dollars for Hannah's service "in full for two months' wages at His Excellency General Washington's family" does not mention Mason.[10] And this 1780 receipt is signed, not by Hannah Mason as the other had been, but by Hannah Till. (Her actual signature was a big, proud X.) Hannah used her master's surname while a slave. Once free, she proudly signed as "Hannah Till."

In March 1824 John Watson interviewed Hannah for his *Annals of Philadelphia.* Although Hannah was 102 years old at the time, Watson found that she spoke "in a good strong voice all the things she saw in her long life, with better recollection and readier utterance than any other narrator with whom I have had the occasion so to converse." During the interview, Hannah related that she had been sold at the age of fifteen and brought to Pennsylvania from Delaware. At twenty-five, she was purchased by a Rev. Henderson. At thirty-five, she was purchased by Rev. Mason, a Presbyterian minister in New York, who lent her out to Washington. Hannah worked as a cook for seven years during the American Revolution, serving both Washington and Lafayette. After the war ended, Isaac and Hannah Till lived in Philadelphia, at 182 South Fourth Street, a little south of Pine Street. Washington's former cook died in 1825 at the age of 104.

Hannah's recollections give a unique perspective on General Washington, for she is speaking as one of his slaves. Hannah recalled that General Washington required compliance to his orders, "but was a moderate and indulgent master." He would occasionally give a "moderate laugh" and was also "moderate" in his eating and drinking habits. Hannah said Washington "always had his lady with him in winter." She had never seen the general at prayer but "expected he did" pray. In times of "high excitement," Hannah remembered, Washington did not "strictly guard" against swearing. He, in fact, had once called her "a c—d [colored] fool." Hannah, however, does not say what provoked Washington to do so.

For six months during the war, Washington loaned Hannah out to General Lafayette, whom she seems to have greatly admired. Hannah remembered Lafayette as being "very handsome, tall, slender and genteel, having a fair white and red face, with reddish hair." His English was "plain enough," and she thought him to be "always kind." All in all, Hannah believed Lafayette to be "Truly a gentleman to meet & to follow."[11] Years later, so Watson says, this kindly French gentleman paid off the mortgage on Hannah's house in Philadelphia.

As mentioned, Hannah's husband, Isaac, who had been loaned to Washington from Capt. John Johnson, also worked as one of Washington's cooks at Valley Forge. Isaac apparently joined Washington's family in July 1776 and remained with him at least through June 1780. At Valley Forge, Isaac also occasionally received money from Captain Gibbs to purchase cooking supplies and food for headquarters. Isaac's salary was seven pounds a month. Of this amount, Isaac kept forty shillings a month in New York currency for his clothing and expenses; the remainder of the salary was forwarded to his owner, Captain Johnson. Isaac eventually also paid off his master and, like Hannah, earned his freedom.

Another woman with Washington's family at Valley Forge was Margaret Thomas, a washerwoman and a free black woman. Margaret was attached, or perhaps married, to William Lee, Washington's faithful body servant. It was unusual for a male slave to be attached to a free black woman, but William Lee himself was unusual. Like his master, William was an expert horseman and, to keep up with the general on the field, would have had a fine horse. Israel Trask, who at ten years old volunteered for army service as a cook and messenger, recalled seeing General Washington and his "colored servant" decisively diffuse a confrontation between the Marblehead regiment and riflemen recruited from Virginia. Trask remembered that what had begun as a small skirmish over military uniforms early in the war quickly deteriorated into a fierce struggle and snowball fight with, Trask recalled, "more than a thousand combatants." When William and Washington came upon the fracas, Washington allegedly leapt off his horse, threw the reins to his slave, rushed into the center of the melee, and seized "two tall, brawny, athletic, savage-looking riflemen by the throat." The other combatants abruptly fled when they recognized the commander in chief in their midst. Satisfied, Washington and William jumped on their horses and galloped away.[12] (This wonderful vignette of Washington and William in action must be considered oral history, however, as it was recounted by Trask almost seventy years after it occurred.)

At Valley Forge, Margaret Thomas washed and mended the bed and table linen. With William Lee, she cared for General Washington's clothing. She also looked after the clothes of Mrs. Washington and members of the military family. Margaret Thomas was paid for sewing for the commander in February 1776. A receipt from Valley Forge dated February 1778, also indicates she was paid for "'washington' [an amusing slip of a quill pen] done for His Excellency General Washington from the 20th Day of Oct. 1776 to the 20th day of Feb. 1778."[13]

In 1784, after the war ended, Washington wrote to Clement Biddle in Philadelphia for assistance in reuniting William Lee (then with Washington at Mount Vernon) and Margaret Thomas (then living in Philadelphia with Isaac and Hannah Till). Washington had not initiated this reunion. He did not even like Margaret Thomas—he wrote Biddle that he "never wished to see her more"—but William had asked she be allowed to join him at Mount Vernon. Margaret had been "in an infirm state of health" for some time and had also been, Washington allowed, "of my family." Because William Lee had "lived with me so long and followed my fortunes through the War with fidelity," Washington felt he could not refuse his servant's request if it could be reasonably accomplished. Biddle was asked to arrange transportation for Margaret Thomas from Philadelphia to Mount Vernon, whether by sea or stage, "as you think cheapest and best."[14] It is not clear if Margaret Thomas actually came to Mount Vernon.

In addition to cooks, a seamstress, and a laundress, Washington also employed a housekeeper at the Valley Forge encampment. Mrs. Mary Smith had been employed as Washington's housekeeper from April 12 to June 26, 1776. But after an anonymous letter was received suggesting that Mrs. Smith was part of a Loyalist plot to capture New York City, she was abruptly dismissed. It is said that, after her dismissal, Mrs. Smith promptly sailed off to England, where she received a pension for services rendered during the Revolution.

After Mrs. Smith's discharge Washington had no housekeeper, and the commander in chief found himself to be "entirely destitute, & put to much inconvenience." When Mrs. Elizabeth Thompson was recommended to him as a "fit person," he sent for her to be interviewed for the position.[15] On July 4, 1776, Washington received word from New York that Mrs. Thompson had been found and was "very willing" to work for him. Washington was to "Expect her the first Opportunity."[16]

Mrs. Thompson began to "keep house" for General Washington on July 9, 1776, when she was seventy-two years old. Then, just nine months after she was hired, the housekeeper was let go. Mrs. Thompson must have made an excellent impression on Mrs. Washington during this time, however, for the general soon wrote around inquiring about Mrs. Thompson's whereabouts. "Mrs. Washington," the commander's inquiry letter to Captain Gibbs reads in part, "wishes I had mention'd my intentions of parting with the old Woman, before her, as she is much in want of a Housekeeper."[17] (This is a rare glimpse into the famous couple's relationship. One can almost picture the six-foot-two-inch General Washington gazing down at his five-foot wife as she gently chastised him for making a household decision without first consulting her.) Captain Gibbs found Mrs. Thompson, and the housekeeper soon returned to work—but again for General Washington, not for Mrs. Washington.

The housekeeper was referred to as "Mrs. Thompson" in the military account books. At Valley Forge, Mrs. Thompson, now seventy-four, was very busy supervising Isaac and Hannah; she also made sure that dinner was served promptly at three each afternoon, just as the commander in chief wanted it. She took charge of the laundresses and other household servants. Mrs. Thompson wanted the housework done to her satisfaction, inspected the linens and the cutlery, and ordered the food. She arranged the settings of each room so each guest had a comfortable place to stay and had the beds made up just right.[18] As part of her responsibilities, Mrs. Thompson supervised the packing and unpacking of the household each time General Washington shifted locations—and about ninety different buildings served as headquarters during the war. She also purchased small items for General and Mrs. Washington, the household, and members of Washington's military family. When Martha Washington came to headquarters, Mrs. Thompson took orders from her.

Like many of the soldiers and officers, Mrs. Thompson did not stay for the entire six months at Valley Forge. On March 10, 1778, a wagon and driver were sent out from camp to "fetch" her from Newtown, Pennsylvania, where she seems to have been visiting relatives.[19]

In December 1781, at age seventy-seven, Mrs. Thompson reluctantly retired. "Age made it necessary" for her to do so. She had served in General Washington's family for five years.[20]

Washington did not forget her, nor did she forget him. In September 1783, two years after her retirement, Washington found himself wanting a "*good* Cook, German I should prefer." Mrs. Thompson, he wrote to Daniel Parker in New York City, "probably can assist in the enquiries and

Martha Washington traveled to all eight of the Revolutionary War winter encampments. Portrait by Charles Willson Peale, 1795. *Courtesy of Independence National Historical Park*

Gen. George Washington— beloved commander in chief of the Continental Army. Portrait by Rembrandt Peale, 1848. *Courtesy of Independence National Historical Park*

An unfinished portrait of Catharine Greene, Gen. Nathanael Greene's wife. Attributed to James Frothingham, 1807. *Courtesy of Telfair Museum of Art, Savannah, Georgia*

Gen. Nathanael Greene revolutionized the quartermaster's department at Valley Forge. Portrait by Charles Willson Peale, 1783. *Courtesy of Independence National Historical Park*

The only known silhouette
of Lucy Knox, the wife
of Gen. Henry Knox.
No formal portrait of
Lucy exists. *Courtesy of
the Massachusetts
Historical Society*

Gen. Henry Knox, a
former bookseller, took
command of the artillery
for the Continental Army.
Portrait by Charles Willson
Peale, 1784. *Courtesy of
Independence National
Historical Park*

Elizabeth Ellet, author of the groundbreaking *The Women of the American Revolution.*
Courtesy of Wikipedia Commons

Benson J. Lossing, a prolific, though unreliable, nineteenth-century author. Drawing ca. 1865.
Courtesy of Vassar College

BENSON JOHN LOSSING.

The Isaac Potts House, where Gen. and Mrs. Washington stayed during the encampment. *Courtesy of Valley Forge National Historical Park*

Gen. and Mrs. Nathanael Greene lived in Moore Hall during the Valley Forge winter. *Printed by permission of French and Pickering Creeks Conservation Trust, Inc.*

The stone farmhouse of Elizabeth and David Stephens.
Courtesy of Valley Forge National Historical Park

Lord and Lady Stirling stayed in the Rev. William Currie house.
(Photograph taken ca. 1900.) *Courtesy of C. Herbert Fry*

The soldiers and women with the army lived in huts
during the Valley Forge winter. (Huts pictured are reconstructions.)
Courtesy of Valley Forge National Historical Park

"We are better hutted than any army in the world."
Courtesy of Valley Forge National Historical Park

At least four hundred women came to camp with the army on December 19, 1777.
Courtesy of Laura Kostyk

examination" of candidates. Incidentally, Washington's specifications for a cook required a "Person that has understanding in the business, who can order, as well as get a dinner; who can make dishes, and proportion them *properly* [emphasis in original], to any Company which shall be named to him to the amount of 30."[21] Isaac and Hannah would have been very busy at Valley Forge.

On October 10, 1783, a letter was written to General Washington on Mrs. Thompson's behalf. From the communication, it is evident that this "very worthy Irish woman" had a cordial relationship with Washington. The letter also gives up some hints as to why Mrs. Thompson was so well considered. She was an enthusiastic and devoted worker, as she had come to work for the general, so the 1783 letter says, "with a zealous Heart to do the best in my Power." She was a modest woman, as she writes that her service, "was never equal to what your Benevolence has thus rated them." She had a good relationship with General Washington, as she wrote with confidence, "should I ever want, which I hope will not be the Case, I will look up to Your Excellency for Assistance, where I am sure I will not be disappointed." And she must have had a sense of fun about her, as she signed herself, "Your Excellency's Old Devoted Servant, Elizabeth Thompson."[22] Two months later Mrs. Thompson received $240.00 "in full of Account for Services" with General Washington's family. [23]

Another letter with her signature was sent to Congress on February 17, 1785, asking for a small sum for the former housekeeper, now eighty-one, to enable her to "close her eyes in peace." The next day Congress, displaying an uncharacteristic burst of speed, awarded Elizabeth Thompson an annual pension of $100.00 for life. Washington had invited his former housekeeper to live out her days at Mount Vernon, but Mrs. Thompson declined. She was living in New York at the time and wrote, "With a heap of infirmities upon me, such a journey appears impossible."[24] It is unknown when or where Washington's faithful housekeeper died.

THE WOMEN WITH WASHINGTON'S GUARD

Because they traveled with Washington and his military family, Mrs. Elizabeth Thompson, Hannah Till, and Margaret Thomas, women of the common sort, were all afforded some status in camp. A few other women of the common sort also received a modicum of respect at Valley Forge. These were the women with Washington's personal guard.

In the eighteenth century, it was common for senior officers to surround themselves with both a military family and a cadre of guards. (In Washington's words, "In the Course of the Campaign, my Baggage, Papers, and other Matters of great public Import, may be committed to the Sole Care of these Men.")[25] A woman or two was attached to the guard to do the laundry and some cooking.

Major General Lord Stirling's guard at Valley Forge, for example, had Peggy Brindley, who did the men's washing and cooking. "A List of Shoes Delivered to the Men Belonging to Major General Lord Stirling's Guard" identifies twenty-one men who received shoes on February 4, 1778, at the Valley Forge encampment. At the bottom of the list is the name of one more person who received shoes: "Peggy Brindley."[26]

A woman also served Washington's guard. An order dated August 16, 1777, before the Valley Forge encampment reads, "Let the Bearer have 1 Day's provision for 48 men & 1 Woman of His Excellency's Guard."[27] A second order, dated August 26, 1777, calls for provisions for "43 men & 1 wash woman" for "His Excellency General Washington's Guard."[28] As one woman was with the commander's guard the summer before Valley Forge, undoubtedly there was at least one woman who washed the linen and helped cook for Washington's guard during the Valley Forge encampment.

But—like so many of the women, and ladies, who came to the Valley Forge encampment—her name has been forgotten.

7

Camp Women at Valley Forge

"A Caravan of Wild Beasts"

"One Accident happened this Day a wagon overset and killed one woman," Col. Israel Angell wrote in his diary on December 19, 1777. The day the Continental Army marched into Valley Forge had dawned clear, cold, and very windy. It was a Friday, and the army had marched eight miles from Gulph Mills, from dawn to darkness, to reach their 1777–78 encampment site. The troops were hungry—no rations had been issued for the march—and some of the ravenous soldiers and camp women devoured "Suppers of raw Corn" snatched from fields along the way. As for the army horses, there was no fodder to be found.

The fourteen thousand or so soldiers and officers and their "very poor and weak horses" moved slowly along the treacherous, rutted roads that led to winter camp.[1] Soldiers and officers took the lead; the common soldiers on foot, the officers on horseback. Then came the slow, creaky baggage wagons. About four hundred camp women and their numberless children trudged along behind, bent over against the wind.[2] Little has been recorded about this journey of Washington's army. Nothing more has been recorded about the woman crushed by the wagon on the march. She may have been riding on the wagon, although orders forbade this. Perhaps she was expecting a child, or had small children with her on the wagon. She may have been married to one of the soldiers. Col. Israel Angell supplied no details; nor did he name her.

It is surprising that Colonel Angell commented on the woman's death at all. She was, after all, only a camp woman, one of the four hundred or so bedraggled beings who tramped into Valley Forge with the baggage on that winter day. This entire collection of hundreds of hungry, destitute camp women clung to the very fringes of respectability and followed the

113

troops because the army afforded them, and the children with them, their best chance for survival. The camp women reflected the army, for there were both black and white camp followers at Valley Forge.

The months, even years, of camping out during the long war took a toll on every woman with the army. Pvt. Joseph Plumb Martin, a Revolutionary War soldier whose autobiography first appeared in 1830, compared the women at Valley Forge and the other encampments to wild beasts, with a "bodily appearance" that was "odd and disgusting." Martin wrote that some had "two eyes, some one, and some, I believe with none at all. . . . The furies who inhabit the infernal Regions [could] never be painted half so hideous as these women." Martin remembered the camp women speaking many dialects: Irish brogue and Scottish burr, murdered English, and "flat insipid Dutch and some lingoes which would puzzle a philosopher to tell whether they belonged to this world or some 'undiscovered country.'"[3] But Private Martin's scorn for the army's women did not prevent him from employing them to wash his shirt or mend a tattered pair of stockings. Some of these "hideous" camp women nursed the soldiers when they were wounded in battle or stricken with disease. And many of these women were married to men in Martin's own regiment.

Private Martin was not the only one to write disparagingly of the army's women. On August 23, 1777, Washington issued detailed orders about the Continental Army's upcoming march through Philadelphia. The soldiers were to be adorned with sprigs of greenery on their hats—the only uniformly "uniform" part of their attire. He prescribed how the men would parade (in one column), the order of march, and the distance between divisions. The drums and fifes were ordered to play, but not too quickly, as the commander did not want the soldiers "dancing along, or totally disregarding the music, as has been too often the case." The baggage, wagons, and extra horses were forbidden to be on view during the march. And orders for the army's women were clear: "Not a woman belonging to the army is to be seen with the troops on their march thro' the city."[4] But the women despised being siphoned off to the little streets and dirty alleys. Barely had the troops passed through the main thoroughfares, when, it was later said, "these camp followers poured after their soldiers again, their hair flying, their brows beady with the heat, their belongings slung over one shoulder, chattering and yelling in sluttish shrills as they went, and spitting in the gutters."[5]

The women who traveled with the British Army were no more appealing. "I never had the least Idea that the Creation produced such a sordid set of creatures in human Figure," Hannah Winthrop wrote in a letter to Mercy Otis Warren on seeing the British Army prisoners from the battle of Saratoga. "Poor, dirty, emaciated men, great numbers of women, who seemed to be the beasts of burden, having a bushel basket on their back, by which they were bent double, the contents seems to be Pots and Kettles, various sorts of Furniture, children peeping thro' gridirons and other utensils, some very young infants who were born on the road, the women bare feet, cloathed in dirty rags, such effluvia filled the air while they were passing, had they not been smoking at the time, I should have been apprehensive of being contaminated by them."[6]

The most familiar today of all camp women of the Revolution, Molly Pitcher, was probably one of the women who struggled into Valley Forge on December 19. During the war, however, "Molly Pitcher" was a general term for women who carried water to the soldiers during battle. Molly Pitchers were everywhere on the field and went everywhere with the troops. There were many Molly Pitchers with the Continental Army.

Usually today, however, Molly Pitcher is used only to refer to Mary Hays. Sgt. John Casper Hays, Mary's husband, enlisted before the Valley Forge encampment, came to winter camp, and then took up his famed artillery piece at the battle of Monmouth, the first major engagement following the 1777–78 encampment. It is likely, then, that Sergeant and Mrs. Hays wintered at Valley Forge.

There is no record of Mary Hays's activities at camp that Valley Forge winter, but Pvt. Joseph Plumb Martin may have been describing Mary and John Hays when he wrote about a husband-and-wife team working the artillery during the battle of Monmouth. Martin remembered that a cannonball passed directly between the woman's legs, fortunately "without doing any other damage than carrying away all the lower part of her petticoat." Martin wrote that the woman looked down at her petticoat, shrugged, and then observed in a cheeky way that "it was lucky it did not pass a little higher, for in that case it might have carried away something else." Like other camp women, Mary Hays had no education, smoked continuously, and, it is said, "swore like a trooper."[7] At Valley Forge she was cold, dirty, and hungry, and clung to the very edge of survival, as did every other woman who traveled with the army. The private soldiers, along with some of the lower ranking officers, did the same.

Mary Hays is a distant figure, but some idea of her contribution to the American Revolution is known. We also know her name. Most of the hundreds of women with the Valley Forge encampment, however, remain only as shadowy, anonymous figures of a bygone war. We will never know their names. We will never know their stories, or how they individually contributed to America's freedom. Accounts of the women's activities are rare, for at the Valley Forge encampment—indeed, during the entire Revolutionary War—camp women were of little consequence to most soldiers and officers. Unless, of course, the soldier was married to one of the women. Or if he needed his laundry done.

CAMP WASHERWOMEN

Because Washington ordered the men under his command to display a "soldierly" appearance, many of the hundreds of women who came to Valley Forge worked for the army as laundresses. The commander wanted every military uniform, no matter how ragged, to be kept clean. Both the officers and common soldiers were also expected to be clean-shaven. This was actually a practical consideration, as facial hair could blaze up if a musket sparked when fired.

But Washington's soldiers did not always look sharp. In May 1775 one observer (admittedly a British surgeon) described the rebels, as he called them, as nothing more than a "drunken, canting, lying, praying, hypocritical rabble, without order, subjection, discipline, or cleanliness."[8] In November 1775 another observer looked at the passing parade of Continental soldiers and pronounced them "as dirty a set of mortals as ever disgraced the name of a soldier." The army, he wrote, "have no women in the camp to do washing for the men, and they [the soldiers] in general not being used to doing things of this sort, and thinking it rather a disparagement to them, choose rather to let their linen, etc. rot upon their backs rather than be at the trouble of cleaning 'em themselves." In this observer's opinion, more camp women were needed to keep the men from becoming even more "nasty."[9]

The camp women who worked as washerwomen would also have had a difficult time looking fresh and neat. The Continental Army, although it attempted to supply the soldiers with uniforms, provided almost no clothing to the women who marched and camped with the men. During the six-month Valley Forge encampment, for example, records show that only four items—three petticoats and one pair of shoes—came into camp for the women. The lack of clothing forced the women to wear an eclectic mishmash of shirts and shifts and petticoats, often scrounged and snatched from the soldiers, battlefields, camps, huts, or neighborhood homes. Samuel Hay observed in November 1777, soon before marching into camp at Valley Forge, that a "great many" of the soldiers "have lost their clothes by whores & rogues that went with the baggage."[10]

Although many women worked as laundresses at Valley Forge, only a few of their names are known. Mrs. Mary Geyer worked for the army as a washerwoman; she, with her family, marched from Gulph Mills to winter camp on December 19. Mrs. Geyer was forty-two years old when she, along with her husband and eleven-year-old son, came to camp. Both Mary's husband, Peter, and her son, John, had enlisted in the army for twenty-one months in the spring of 1776. All three members of the little family traveled and served in the army: Peter as a rifleman, John as a drummer, and Mary as a washerwoman for the Thirteenth Pennsylvania Regiment. Peter Geyer was wounded in the groin by a bayonet and took a ball to his leg at Germantown, the battle before Valley Forge. John, who drew pay and rations even as a boy, was wounded in a heel during the hotly contested confrontation. Father and son served out their enlistments at Valley Forge, and both were discharged on January 1, 1778, about two weeks after the army marched to Valley Forge. Mary and John, however, remained at Valley Forge, where she continued to work as a washerwoman.[11] The family needed the income.

Mrs. Milliner was another laundress at camp. She apparently came to Valley Forge with her son, Alexander, who may have been a drummer with Washington's Guards. Nothing is known of her activities at camp, but it is said that she followed Alexander in the army "for the sake of being near her boy."[12] (More information about Alexander Milliner is in the appendix.)

Mrs. Maria Cronkite also worked as a washerwoman at Valley Forge. Her husband, Patrick, a private soldier in the First New York Regiment, enlisted in the Continental Army in early 1777, and she joined him. Private Cronkite fought in the battles of Brandywine, Monmouth, and Yorktown, and was with the regiment in Valley Forge. According to Maria's pension deposition, throughout the Revolution she served "in the capacity of washerwoman for the officers until the close of the war when her husband was duly discharged." Her deposition introduces another reality for the women with the army, for "she had while in said service several children."[13]

Not all washerwomen at Valley Forge were women. Lt. Joseph Hodgkins had his servant Thomas, who was "good for all most Everything," with him during the early part of the Valley Forge encampment. Thomas served not only as a "washwoman," but also as a nurse and a cook for Hodgkins. Soon after arriving at Valley Forge, however, Thomas asked to leave camp—we can only guess why—and Hodgkins reluctantly agreed to let him go. I am "dull" for "losing Thomas," Hodgkins wrote his wife on January 11, 1778, "but he is Going home & I wish him well with all my hart [sic]."[14]

Not every washerwoman was as diligent as Thomas, as examples from other camps attest. Two years after Valley Forge, a group of women received a reprimand when they set up their wash tubs directly in front of the tents and then proceeded to throw the dirty water, soapsuds, and other kinds of "filth" on the Regimental Parade grounds.[15] In October 1778 the Second Pennsylvania Regiment, realizing that the laundry was not getting done, did not allow its camp women to "draw rations from the continent in this regiment unless they make use of their endeavors to keep the men clean."[16] In 1783 the commanding officer at New Windsor reprimanded the Second Massachusetts Regiment because its soldiers were "so very dirty." Orders were given that unless the women who drew rations for washing attended to their jobs, "their rations would be discontinued."[17] If you did no work for the army, you did not receive rations from the army.

At Valley Forge, an officer, or several officers, could group together and hire a washerwoman to wash exclusively for them. This is what Col. Ebenezer Huntington did at a later encampment. Huntington's dilemma was this: Should he pay someone to wash for him piecemeal, or should he try to hire a woman to live in camp and wash exclusively for some of his officers and himself? Huntington believed that it would be less expensive to hire a woman to stay at camp but was well "aware that many Persons will tell the Story to my disadvantage." Nevertheless, to save money—and he wrote his "washing bill is beyond the limits of my wages"—Huntington planned to employ a woman to stay at camp "if I can hire one on better terms than hiring my Washing."[18]

Officers and soldiers alike paid for laundry services from their own pockets. But because the men were neither well paid, nor regularly paid, they had little available cash to pay the washerwomen. The troops gave off a pungent odor, and the Valley Forge camp itself reeked as the months wore on and milder weather moved into southeastern Pennsylvania. To relieve the stench and let in fresh air, Washington ordered at least two windows to be cut in each hut in May. On June 9 he ordered the army to abandon the huts and move into what was described as a "new Camp," possibly on the north side of the Schuylkill River. (The army had been camped during the winter on the south side of the Schuylkill River.) In May the soldiers were excused from exercise on Friday afternoons to wash their linens and to bathe in the Schuylkill River. The men, however, were admonished to soak for no more than ten minutes; such an indulgence was thought to be "unhealthy."[19]

CAMP NURSES, MEDICINE, AND HOSPITALS

Between fifteen hundred and three thousand men died at Valley Forge and in the nearby army hospitals during the encampment of 1777–78, far more than at any other of the seven encampments.

"Hospitals are the sinks of human life in the army. They robbed the United States of more citizens than the sword,"[20] wrote Dr. Benjamin Rush, a surgeon general of the Middle Department during the Valley Forge period. The killers at the 1777–78 winter encampment were not battle wounds. Instead, the soldiers were defeated by dysentery (an infectious disease marked by ulceration and inflammation of the lower bowel); typhus (an acute, infectious disease, transmitted by lice and fleas, causing severe nervous symptoms and an eruption of reddish spots over the body); and typhoid (an infectious disease marked by intestinal inflammation and ulceration, caused by the typhoid bacillus). "Camp fever" (any epidemic that spread throughout the camp) and venereal diseases were also rampant. Poor sanitation, lack of cleanliness, crowded conditions, deficiency of clothing and blankets, and poor nutrition all contributed to the death rate. Because Washington ordered his army to be inoculated against smallpox, that dreaded disease never spread through the camps. But every one of the three thousand or so soldiers who took the smallpox inoculation at Valley Forge was "unfit for duty," as the expression went, for at least a month after being inoculated.

The smallpox inoculation program is a little-known success story at Valley Forge. Smallpox, a highly contagious viral disease, ran rampant in the eighteenth century. Washington, who had the disease as a young man, bore facial scars from smallpox for life, and so it is not surprising that he advocated inoculation. To allow the troops to recover, they underwent inoculation during an encampment period when the army was not on the move. The winter of Valley Forge was an ideal time for smallpox inoculation.

At Valley Forge, guards were posted around the camp perimeter to keep out both enemy soldiers and those carrying smallpox. Inoculation began in late January, as General Huntington wrote on January 16, "The Troops who have not had the Small Pox are to receive the Infection [inoculation] in Camp in a few days."[21] But the efforts were in vain, for Gen. Enoch Poor wrote in March that the dreaded disease "so got into our Camp," that at least five hundred men from New Hampshire were under inoculation. (And, Poor continued, "not more than One half of them [under inoculation] have a blanket or any kind of covering except Straw, how they will live through this cold season God only knows.")[22] Gen. Elias Boudinot wrote later that month from Valley Forge that three thousand soldiers had taken the smallpox inoculation with, he trumpeted, "not one lost by Inoculation."[23] Although there is no record of either women or children undergoing inoculation at Valley Forge, both camp women and children were inoculated against smallpox in April 1781 at West Point.[24]

These sick, dying, and inoculated soldiers, patients in both the camp hospitals and those established in the surrounding communities, required nurses to care for them. But few women felt called to the task. Nursing was hard work. It paid very little. The danger of catching an infectious disease was high. The demand for nurses far outstripped the supply at Valley Forge; this was also true throughout the war. In August 1778 Washington wrote that any women who wanted to work in the Albany area could "come and attend as Nurses to the Hospitals," where "they would find immediate employ."[25] Few responded.

With female nurses in short supply, soldiers were sometimes pressed into nursing duty. The commander, however, ever mindful of the number of men required on the field, objected to his enlisted men serving as nurses. Soldiers would be "entirely lost in the proper line of their duty" if they took up nursing, Washington wrote, "with but little benefit rendered to the sick."[26]

Nursing in the eighteenth century was not the respected profession of today. Then hospital nurses provided only custodial care. Duties included bathing the newly admitted patients with warm water, washing hands and faces, and combing the patients' hair. Nurses emptied chamber pots, swept out the wards, and sprinkled hospital floors with vinegar several times a day. When the surgeon ordered them to do so, nurses changed the bed linen. Some nurses cooked for their patients. Nurses were also required to keep themselves clean and sober, and they could not be absent without leave. Stealing clothes from a patient was forbidden. But stealing must have occurred, for Washington wrote to Congress from Valley Forge saying that hospital patients had recovered, but could not return to duty because they had no clothing. Orders also forbid stealing from a corpse. This, too, would have been tempting, as another task of the nurse was to collect the effects of the dead for the ward master.[27]

Military nurses worked hard, but, for all their efforts, at the start of the Revolution army hospital nurses received only two dollars a month. (In contrast, enlisted soldiers received six and two-thirds dollars a month; one hospital chief physician was paid four dollars a day.) By September 1776, with nurses in short supply, Washington recommended to Congress that they be paid a dollar a week. In 1777 nurses' salaries were set at eight dollars a month.

But Alice Redman still received only two dollars a month in 1780. Her petition for higher pay presents a rare, firsthand account of the duties of a Revolutionary War military nurse. Nurse Redman worked in an Annapolis, Maryland, military hospital that had once functioned as the city poorhouse. In the petition, she described herself as a "diligent and careful" nurse with "sixteen men for to cook and take care of." The work hours were long, and Alice was "obliged to be up day and night with some of the patients." In spite of her diligence, however, Alice never had "been allowed so much as a little tea or coffee." Supplies were so short that Alice was "obliged to buy brooms and the soap we wash with" from her own scant salary.[28] It is not known whether Alice Redman received her requested raise.

The army employed some Valley Forge camp women to serve as nurses in the brigade hospitals, also called "flying hospitals." These structures—fifteen feet wide, twenty-five feet long, and nine feet high—

were considerably larger than the soldiers' huts. A fireplace was placed at one end, the entrance at the other. To "catch the air," windows were located on each side of the building. Each brigade was to have two hospitals, ideally located, if the "ground permits," at the center of the brigade encampment.[29]

These camp hospitals were used for emergency care and housed soldiers not seriously ill. At Valley Forge, Gen. Johann de Kalb ordered hospitals—or "barracks," as he called them—to be built for those in his regiments who suffered from "the itch," a distressing disorder that covered the men "over and over with scab."[30] Seriously ill soldiers, however, were transported to temporary hospitals located in neighboring communities, often miles away from camp. These outlying hospitals had not been built as hospitals but were, instead, available public buildings and homes that had been taken over for army patients. During the Valley Forge period they were located in Pennsylvania towns, including Reading, Easton, Lititz, Ephrata, Bethlehem, North Wales, Skippack, Allentown, Manheim, Rheimstown, Warrick, and Schaeferstown.

In Reading, Pennsylvania, the Trinity Lutheran Church, the First Reformed Church, the Friend's Meeting House, the Reading Court House, "the Brick House," and "the Potters Shop" were all confiscated for army hospitals. The Reading facilities, like other hospital facilities during the war, were packed: over nine hundred soldiers were cared for in buildings that would have been comfortable for five hundred.

There is some information about some of the nurses who served in the temporary hospitals in Reading. Mary Reed worked as a nurse during the Valley Forge period. An army document dated November 17, 1777, about a month before the Valley Forge encampment, lists Margaret Senix, Hannah Crooks, Sarah Burk, Ann Chamberlain, Martha Mitchel, Catherine West, Ann Doyle, and Elizabeth Southerland as hospital nurses at the Reading court house, brick house, and potter's shop.[31] What is intriguing here is that the last name of every one of these nurses matches the last name of a hospital patient. Which makes one wonder: Did the women leave their homes to travel to the hospital to care for their loved ones? Had the women been traveling with the army and moved to the hospital when their husbands became ill? Or had some of the women been working as hospital nurses, only to see their husbands come in as patients? It is also interesting that the "List of the Sick in the Potters Shop at Reading" includes several husband and wife pairs: Thomas Finetree and wife, William Pinkfield and wife, David Kelly and wife. Had both husband and wife been with the army when they became sick? Had, perhaps, the wives who served as nurses become infected and afflicted their husbands? Unfortunately, these questions will never be answered.

Not unexpectedly, the army's sick were not always welcome in the little Pennsylvania towns. "A few days ago," the January 8, 1778, minutes of the Uwchlan Monthly Meeting read, "the key of the Meeting House was demanded by some of the physicians of the Continental Army in order to convert the same into an hospital for their sick soldiers. The Friend who had care of the house refusing to deliver it, forcible entry was made into the house and stable."[32] Quakers, or Friends, remained neutral during the conflict—thus their reluctance to surrender the meeting house key.

A chilling petition reveals the misery suffered by Ephrata, Pennsylvania, when the town was forced to care for sick soldiers. Soon after the Continental Army arrived at Valley Forge, open wagons bound for Ephrata lumbered away from the encampment. The carts were stacked with sick soldiers, "almost naked; many of them without shoes, stockings, or blankets to cover them." According to the 1780 deposition, "many died from the effects of the journey." The "waggoners," who were "without orders what to do with them," deposited the human cargo in the center of Ephrata, then returned to their empty wagons and drove away. The drivers had been paid to deliver the soldiers to Ephrata, and they had done so. No nurses or other attendants accompanied the men. As the night was cold, "the sick crept into . . . homes in a piteous condition, affecting to humanity, and entreated to be saved from perishing."[33]

Something had to be done. Washington was losing his army to disease and illness. Patients were receiving inadequate care, and there were too few places to care for the many sick soldiers. The Pennsylvania communities did not want the sick, infectious soldiers in their homes. So, in January 1778 construction was begun on the first permanent military hospital in the United States. It was located in Yellow Springs, about ten miles from Valley Forge, and, when completed, hosted thirteen hundred patients.

To reach Yellow Springs, as well as the other outlying hospitals, the suffering soldiers of the Valley Forge encampment bobbed along, sometimes for hours, over rutted, icy roads in uncomfortable wagons that were sprinkled with meager cushions of straw. Few blankets were available for the ride. Once the patients arrived at their destinations (and many died on the way), they found the hospitals already crowded with the sick and dying.

Yet the hospital chaplain of the army's Middle Department, which included hospitals in the Valley Forge area, gave a high rating to the Yellow Springs hospital. He described it in April 1778, as "very neat, and the sick comfortably provided for."[34] On April 27, 1778, Dr. Samuel Kennedy, the hospital director, wrote that the Yellow Springs hospital was "neatly arranged, clean, and healthy." Dr. Kennedy, however, also wrote that the hospital desperately needed supplies. Wine was necessary—lots of wine—as well as sheets, shirts, iron spoons, candles, soap, writing paper, wrapping paper, pots, and every kind of medical supply. It would have been difficult for Abigail Hartman Rice and Christina Hench, two of the local women who worked as nurses, to adequately care for the hospital patients with the meager supplies they had on hand. Dr. Kennedy noted, too, that money to purchase food for the patients was in short supply.[35]

Sadly, Dr. Samuel Kennedy, like so many of his patients, succumbed to typhus. He died on June 17, 1778, two days before the army marched from Valley Forge.

By late May preparations were well under way at Valley Forge for the Continental Army to leave camp. By this time it was obvious that the British Army was preparing to vacate Philadelphia, and the spring campaign would begin soon. General Washington ordered a report of the number of sick in camp so that "proper nurses may be provided as soon as possible."[36] On May 31, after looking over the numbers, Washington ordered each brigade to leave two officers and a surgeon behind at camp to care for its sick. Every twenty sick men required an orderly, who was pulled from among the soldiers who "for want of clothing, from lameness and the like, are least fit to march with the Army, but at the same time, capable of this duty." Nurses, drawn from the "women of the Army as can be prevailed on to serve as Nurses," were to remain at Valley Forge. For their duties, they would be paid the "usual Price."[37] John Laurens, one of Washington's aides, wrote that some military nurses had come from the encampment's collection of "camp whores"—a group, Laurens observed dryly, that had become "more numerous" as the encampment wore on.[38]

On June 19, 1778, the Continental Army marched about twenty thousand strong from Valley Forge to begin the new campaign. Close to three thousand sick soldiers remained behind at camp under the care of the officers, surgeons, orderlies, and nurses. All the "Bad cases" had already been removed to the hospitals in the surrounding areas.

OTHER WOMEN AT VALLEY FORGE

Not all the camp women at Valley Forge legitimately worked for the army as nurses, washerwomen, seamstresses, or cooks. Some of the camp women did no legitimate work at all. One Valley Forge officer even penned a poem about them:

> What! though there are, in rags, in crepe,
> Some beings here in female shape
> In whom may still be found some traces
> Of former beauty in their faces.
> Yet now so far from being nice
> They boast of every barefaced vice.
> Shame to their sex!
> Tis not in these one e'er beholds
> These charms that please.[39]

The verse does not describe hardworking army women diligently washing or nursing to make money for themselves or their families, but rather the camp prostitutes. In spite of Washington's orders to keep them away, the number of camp whores, as previously noted, had become "more numerous" by the spring of 1778. Gen. Charles Lee may even have smuggled a strumpet into the commander in chief's headquarters—an audacious move, indeed.

According to Gen. Elias Boudinot, an American general who was in charge of British prisoners, General Lee brought a "miserable dirty hussy with him" into Washington's headquarters at Valley Forge. General Lee, who was not related to Civil War Gen. Robert E. Lee, was an interesting man. Born in England, Lee had a great deal of military experience, and Washington initially respected him. "He is the first Officer in Military knowledge and experience we have in the whole Army," Washington wrote enthusiastically of Lee on March 31, 1776. "He is zealously attach'd to the Cause, honest and well-meaning, but rather fickle and violent I fear in his temper. However . . . he possesses an uncommon share of good Sense and Spirit."[40]

Washington vigorously negotiated for Lee's release after he was captured by the British on December 13, 1776. When Lee finally arrived at Valley Forge in late April 1778, Washington greeted him like a brother. At the encampment Lee, after the appropriate approbations, was escorted to headquarters. There the newly released prisoner was entertained with "an elegant Dinner" and selected musical renderings by the army's fife and drum corps. Lee, an eccentric man who traveled with an entourage of dogs, was assigned a little room at headquarters "back of Mrs. Washington's sitting room." Lee "lay very late" the next morning, General Boudinot reported, "and Breakfast was detained for him. When he came out, he looked as dirty as if he had been in the Street all night. Soon after I discovered that he had brought a miserable dirty hussy with him from Philadelphia (a British Sergeant's wife) and had actually taken her into his Room by a Back Door and she had slept with him that night."[41]

She was not the only loose woman at camp. On May 15, according to court-martial records, Col. George Nagle of the Tenth Pennsylvania Regiment was seen "drinking either Tea or Coffee in Sergeant Howcroft's Tent with his Whore, her Mother, the said Howcroft and his Family." Not surprisingly, this combination was felt to be "to the prejudice of good Order and Military discipline."[42]

Sarah Van Kirk was another woman at Valley Forge with a questionable reputation. Col. Israel Angell wrote on December 23, 1777, that a woman was drummed out of camp (that is, dismissed in disgrace to the beat of a drum) for stealing. John Smith wrote the same day that a "whore" was drummed out of camp. Sarah Van Kirk was sentenced to be drummed out of camp on December 23, and the sentence was approved. From the records it is hard to know whether Sarah Van Kirk was a thief, whore, or both, or whether different women are being described in each account. What is certain is that, by Christmas, Sarah Van Kirk was gone from Valley Forge.[43]

Gen. George Weedon's orderly book of January 29, 1778, records that Mary Johnson was "Charged with laying a plot to Desert to the Enemy." The court found her guilty, and she was sentenced to receive "100 Lashes and to be drum'd out of the Army by all the Drums & Fifes in the Division." The punishment was to take place at 4 o'clock that afternoon; as was the usual practice, the entire division would be "paraded for that purpose."[44]

Ann McIntosh came with her husband to the winter encampment. Both Mrs. McIntosh and her husband, William, a member of the Second Virginia Regiment, were imprisoned for "mutiny and desertion" at Valley Forge. But at their January 29, 1778, trial, both were "acquitted by the Court of the Charge exhibited against them." Washington approved the acquittal and ordered them released from their confinement.[45]

Mrs. Lendell came to camp—and was left there by her husband. After Corporal Lendell of the guards disappeared from his post in late January, a group of officers went to his tent to inquire after him. His wife reported that Lendell had left camp, taking his clothes with him, and that he had threatened to kill her if she "told of him."[46] Whether or not Mrs. Lendell also left Valley Forge herself is not known.

Sarah, also known as Rachael, and described as a "lusty wench" and a mulatto woman "big with child," likely came to camp. Sarah, who had been stolen (or had run away) from her slave master and had taken up with a soldier from the First Maryland Regiment, presented herself as a free married woman. She traveled with her son, Bob, who was six, a boy with a "remarkable fair complexion" and "flaxen hair." Sarah remained with the army for more than two years. The October 1778 *Pennsylvania Packet* carried two advertisements offering rewards for her return. Her master first offered thirty dollars for her return on October 15, 1778. Less than ten days later, on October 24, 1778, he raised the ante to fifty dollars.[47] It is not known if Sarah ever returned to her master.

Pvt. Joseph Plumb Martin wrote of not having "a morsel of anything to eat" for the first two nights and one day after arriving at Valley Forge "save half of a small pumpkin, which I cooked by placing it upon a rock, the skin side upper-most, and making a fire upon it."[48] The women coming into camp on December 19, 1777, would also have had only scraps of food, and they shared the same harsh camp conditions with the soldiers. Many, if not most, of these destitute women worked for the army as cooks, nurses, seamstresses, and washerwomen. And hundreds of them traveled with the army because it offered them and their children their best chance for survival.

And the reward?

The order of march from Valley Forge issued on June 1, 1778, makes no mention of the army's women. But the women knew their place. They would leave the third winter encampment as they entered it—at the end of the line, with the baggage.

Pvt. Joseph Plumb Martin compared the women with the army to a "caravan of wild beasts." [49] But to many soldiers, they were wives.

8

Camp Women with

the Continental Army

Cannonballs and Cooking Kettles

Gen. George Washington danced for three hours with Lady Catharine Greene at the Middlebrook encampment. He paid a social call on Lady Lucy Knox at Newburgh. "General Washington," wrote Lady Martha Bland on May 12, 1777, from a Morristown encampment, "commands both sexes; one by His Excellent Skill in Military Matters, the other by his ability, politeness and attention."[1]

The commander was also comfortable with at least one woman with his military family. He so appreciated elderly Mrs. Elizabeth Thompson, his housekeeper during most of the Revolution, that she received an invitation to spend her final days at Mount Vernon.

But Washington's relationship with the army's hundreds of women of the common sort was not as easy. Throughout the long Revolutionary War, neither Washington nor Congress formulated clear policies about the women who traveled with the Continental Army. No woman who worked as an army cook, laundress, seamstress, or nurse signed a contract. No camp women swore an oath of allegiance to the United States of America. Army women were often regarded as a nuisance, and, worse, the commander feared that they brought disease and debauchery to the troops, encouraged the men to desert, and spied on the entire operation. When the army was on the move, its women were directed to remain with (but not on) the wagons at the rear of the march. When the troops paraded through town, the women were told to stay away. The war went on for years before Washington acknowledged that any woman with the army—even if she washed or cooked or mended or nursed for the troops, or carried water to the soldiers during battle—should be counted in the official reports.

SARAH OSBORN BENJAMIN

Yet the assistance of the army's camp women to the war effort should not be dismissed. Washington may even have spoken directly with Sarah Osborn Benjamin, a camp woman, during the October 1781 siege of Yorktown. Sarah recalled, about fifty years after Yorktown, that she had met up with General Washington as she slowly trudged to the entrenchments with food for the soldiers. The commander saw her and asked if she feared cannonballs. "No," she reported she replied, "the bullets would not cheat the gallows." Then she added that she was taking food to the soldiers because "it would not do for the men to fight and starve, too."[2]

Sarah Osborn Benjamin was eighty-one years old when she related her account of this long-ago encounter, and it may be suspect. Nevertheless, her November 12, 1837, pension deposition for service in the Revolutionary War remains a remarkable and invaluable autobiographical account of a hard-scrabble camp woman who spent more than three years in army trenches, tents, and huts. Because two of Sarah's husbands served with the Continental Army, she eventually received twice the usual army pension. Sarah, however, received no compensation for her own efforts as a camp woman.

Sarah had not expected to be part of any army; her husband, Aaron Osborn, signed up for the service without her knowledge. When Aaron, in 1780, "desired deponent [Sarah] to go with him" to war, Sarah, then twenty-four, agreed—but only after she was told that she could travel by wagon or horseback when the army was on the move. Her husband's position with the commissary guard of the Third New York Regiment gave her this privilege; most camp women trudged along with the wagons.

Sarah remembered three other women with the company, including Letta, a black woman. In her deposition, Sarah recalled that when her husband's company camped near Philadelphia, several Quaker women came out from the city and urged her to stay with them. Sarah's husband, however, would not permit this, so she dutifully remained at camp to help bake bread for the troops. When the army left camp, Sarah did, too.

Sarah related that she, like other camp women, washed, mended, and cooked for the men during the October 1781 siege of Yorktown. As the soldiers were throwing up entrenchments, she cooked and then carried the beef, bread, and coffee ("in a gallon pot") to the soldiers. Although retold more than fifty years after the event, Sarah's account of Cornwallis's surrender of the British Army on October 19 is stunning in its details. That day the enemy drums "beat excessively" until, suddenly, the American "officers hurrahed and swung their hats" around in the air when the British capitulated. (She again dutifully carried the provisions she had prepared "to the entrenchments that morning, and four of the soldiers whom she was in the habit of cooking for ate their breakfasts.") Sarah recalled the British drums covered by black handkerchiefs, the fifes tied with black ribbon, the tears running down the cheeks of a "large, portly" British general. This was not General Cornwallis, who she saw later and described as "being a man of diminutive appearance and having crossed eyes." Sarah also related that, near the time of the battle of Yorktown, the governor of Virginia gave her a "pewter cover to a hot basin that had a handle on it," the last in a set of twelve. It was useless to him, but treasured by Sarah, who, nevertheless, later sold it. She regretted doing this, she later lamented, "a hundred times" over.

After Yorktown, Sarah and her husband Aaron, now a corporal, traveled with the main army to Pompton Plains, New Jersey, where Sarah busied herself "cooking and sewing as usual." The Osborns first "lived in a tent made of logs but covered with cloth," and later in a private home. When the spring campaign began, the soldier and his wife went on to West Point. Aaron Osborn was finally discharged at New Windsor, New York. After discharge, the Osborns remained in one of the army's log huts and took in soldiers as boarders. Aaron Osborn worked for the farmers in the area, as did some of the soldiers who boarded with them.

Two children, a girl (Phebe) and a boy (Aaron Jr.), were born to the Osborns at New Windsor. Then, although Sarah had faithfully followed him around for years, Aaron left Sarah several months after their son's birth. Sarah and Aaron never divorced, but both eventually remarried. Aaron's second wife, Polly, "died dead drunk, the liquor running out of her mouth after she was dead," according to Sarah's deposition. After Polly's death, Aaron Osborn married once again. Sarah herself later married John Benjamin, who had also served in the Continental Army. Sarah and John Benjamin eventually moved to Pleasant Mount, Pennsylvania; he died at least ten years before she did.

NUMBERS OF CAMP WOMEN WITH THE ARMY

Through her pension deposition, Sarah Osborn Benjamin, an eighteenth-century woman of the common sort, has permitted us a rare glimpse into the life of a Revolutionary War camp woman. Most women with the Continental Army, however, remain but anonymous shadows to us today.

Notable exceptions are the washerwomen who remained behind at Fort Sullivan, Pennsylvania, in 1779 when General Sullivan and General Clinton's troops marched west to fight the Indians. We know who these camp women were, for they are actually named in a "Return of the Women & Children Left in Charge of Baggage Necessary to Wash for Genl Clintons Brigade."[3] This return (that is, a record or accounting) shows that eight single women, five married women, and three children stayed behind to launder for General Clinton's troops. Not only does this unusual return list the names of the jettisoned washerwomen, but, surprisingly, it also dignifies each with the title of Mrs. or Miss. Furthermore, the surname of all but one of the camp women matches that of a soldier in Clinton's brigade. There is, for example, the laundress Mrs. Lambertson and a Sgt. Simon Lambertson in the Second New York; the washerwoman Mrs. Canby and child and a Pvt. James Cambee in the Fourth New York; a Miss Sherlock and a Pvt. John Sherlock in the Third New York. Here is compelling evidence that camp women traveling with the army (at least in Clinton's brigade) were the soldiers' wives, mothers, and sisters.

Most accounts of the women with the army were not as specific as the Fort Sullivan return. On August 11, 1778, for example, about two months after the Continental Army left Valley Forge, British Intelligence reported on Washington's forces at White Plains. The spy reported that the Continental soldiers numbered "14000 that is the outside of them" and that "Women and Wagoneers make up near the half of their Army."[4] How many of these thousands of "Women and Wagoneers" were female followers? How many were male wagon drivers? Today only a guess can be made because, to that long-ago British agent, it apparently made little difference.

As for the number of camp women with the army, no Revolutionary War return available today shows that women comprised anywhere "near the half" of Washington's forces. The commander, in fact, did not want women with the troops; he sanctioned only those who were "necessary" and "useful." In early August 1777, for example, Washington ordered the officers to "get rid" of all camp women who were, as he put it, "not absolutely necessary," especially those "who shall, or may have come to the army since its arrival in Pennsylvania."[5] In late August 1777 the officers were directed to forbid women who were not "absolutely necessary, and such as are actually useful, to follow the army."[6] If the woman did not wash, cook, sew, or nurse for Washington's army—if she did not contribute to the welfare of the troops—she could not be allowed to share in the army's meager rations and resources. (But this is not to say that women who were not "absolutely necessary" did not follow the army. As already mentioned, the prostitutes at the Valley Forge encampment became "more numerous" as the encampment went on.)

It is obvious from the few Revolutionary War returns that include women that hundreds of women and an untold number of children traveled with the Continental Army. The previously mentioned "Account of Rations Drawn by the Infantry of Ye Standing Army per Day," for example, lists 400 women with about 14,000 soldiers fit for duty. The June 1781 "Return of Women That Draw Provisions in Several Brigades and Corps of the Army, New Windsor" states troop strength at 4,410 with 137 women.[7] Another record, the January 24, 1783, "Return of the Number of Women and Children in the Several Regiments and Corps Stationed at, and in the Vicinity of West Point and New Windsor," has troop strength at 10,443 with 405 women and 302 children.

As the long war continued, it seems that more and more women sought refuge in, and so traveled with, the Continental Army. Some companies reported no camp women when the American Revolution began. There was perhaps one woman for every forty-four enlisted men at Valley Forge the winter of 1777–78.[8] In January 1783, near the war's end, the proportion of women to men in the Continental Army rose to one in twenty-six. Throughout the war, on the average, it has been estimated that there was one camp woman for every thirty-three soldiers in the Continental Army. If, say, 120,000 Continental soldiers fought in the war, approximately 3,500 to 4,500 camp women followed the army.[9]

Fewer women traveled with the Continental Army than with either the British Army or the Hessians, the German troops who fought for the British. Early in the war the British carried about one woman for every eight soldiers; in 1781 the New York troops reported one woman to every four or five British soldiers. The Hessians initially reported one woman for every thirty men. Later the ratio at New York was about one woman for every fifteen soldiers. And, like the troops, the women who came to America with the British and Hessian armies had spent arduous weeks in wind-tossed ships while crossing the Atlantic Ocean to reach America's shores.

ORDERS ABOUT WOMEN

Only a small percentage of the thousands of orders issued during the Revolution directly concerned the army's women. Although many related to food and shelter for the camp followers, most orders about women related to the army on the move. Some orders, as might be expected, also focused on venereal disease. At Valley Forge, for example, both officers and private soldiers were fined if found to be infected with gonorrhea or syphilis. Earlier, on July 1, 1777, all women with Capt. Robert Kirkwood's Delaware company were paraded and ordered to undergo an examination for venereal disease by the company surgeon "except those who are married, & the husbands of those to undergo said examination in their Stead." Any one who did not comply was to be immediately drummed out of the regiment. Later that month, Capt. Kirkwood's company ducked (that is, punished by plunging the head under water) and drummed a women from the encampment "for giving the men the Venereal Disorder."[10]

But usually the directives about camp women concerned the camp women's behavior when the army was in motion. The commander, for example, did not permit camp women to ride in the wagons. On July 4, 1777, General Orders from Morristown stated that "no woman shall be permitted to ride in any wagon" unless she had permission from her brigade commander.[11] On August 27, 1777, the women were again ordered to keep off the wagons.[12] The next year, as the army prepared to leave Valley Forge, Washington admonished the officers to "pay the strictest attention" and not permit any woman to climb into the wagons on "any Pretence" whatsoever.[13] But camp women obviously ignored these directives, for on June 19, 1778, the day the army left Valley Forge, it was noted that the "indulgence of suffering Women to ride in wagons had degenerated into a great abuse." Now women would be allowed in the wagons only if they could prove an "inability to march." Furthermore, Washington asserted, violations would not "pass unnoticed."[14] A year later, in June 1779, "the pernicious practice of suffering the women to encumber the wagons still continues notwithstanding every former prohibition."[15] But nothing changed. On September 19, 1780, the army women were once again ordered to keep out of the wagons unless "their peculiar circumstances require it."[16]

Not only did Washington struggle with keeping camp women off the wagons, but he also had difficulty in keeping them with the wagons. The army women were not interested in trudging along at the end of the line with the cumbersome wagons loaded with baggage. They wanted to talk with, and walk with, the soldiers—many of whom were their husbands, brothers, or sons. Nevertheless, on July 10, 1777, the commander ordered the women to stay with the baggage wagons when the army was on the move.[17] On July 23, 1777, the wagons and the women were assigned their place in the march; both were directed to "follow on after the army."[18] Orders issued September 13, 1777, after the battle of Brandywine, directed the army women to follow the baggage.[19] But later the presence of hundreds of women with the baggage presented new problems, for in 1779 orders declared that "the General was sorry to see . . . a much greater proportion of men with the baggage than could possibly be necessary."[20]

Other orders confirm that the women were left behind with the baggage when the troops went off on campaign. On June 18, 1777, the women, baggage, and guards left on the "other Side of Corrells ferry" were ordered to be "brought forwards immediately" to Flemington, New Jersey.[21] In late September 1777, in preparation for the Philadelphia campaign, the army parked nine hundred army wagons behind a Bethlehem, Pennsylvania, inn. The army women—an unsavory group described as a "crowd of low women and thieves" that necessitated "a watch at the Tavern"—accompanied the wagons.[22] On November 29, 1777, the "crowd of camp-followers who have been here [near Nazareth, Pennsylvania] so long" were ordered forward to camp.[23] In August 1781, soon before the army left for Yorktown, Washington ordered his officers to leave "such of their Women as are not able to undergo the fatigue of frequent marches" at West Point. The baggage, all that the army could "dispense with," was also to be kept back with the women.[24]

Sometimes feisty camp women, however, refused to be left behind and made their own way—walking hundreds of miles—to join the men. In February 1781 Lafayette, realizing that his detachment would be in Virginia for several months, sent for the baggage that had been left behind in New York and New Jersey. Some wives seized that chance to travel south with the baggage. Other women traveled with General Wayne to meet up with Lafayette in Virginia, but the journey was not without incident. "The artillery passed over [the Potomac River] first," an officer recorded about the effort to join Lafayette. "The second flat-boat had left the shore about forty yards, when the whole sank. Several women were on board; but as hundreds of men were on the bank, relief soon reached them; none was lost—got all over." It is perhaps not surprising that, although this mishap was recorded in five separate journals, only one reporter noted that women were on the boat that sank.[25] The other soldiers wrote only about what was important to them—the boat's cargo.

Food was important for survival, and orders were eventually issued about rations for the army's women. There is no evidence that women "on the strength" routinely received a half ration.[26] (Because women who worked as cooks, laundresses, seamstresses, or nurses were issued rations and pay, they were considered "on the strength" of the army.) Instead, the food allotment for American camp women fluctuated between a whole ration and none at all, depending on location, circumstances, tasks performed, and the time period. Consider, for example, the "Returns of the Daily Issues of Provisions to the Troops at the Post of Wyoming, from May 9th to the [27th], 1779," which records that every camp woman received a full ration.[27] In 1780 an Albany hospital matron was allotted one ration for herself and one for her son, while nurses in the hospital, several of whom had children, received one or two rations each. The sick in the hospital were less well fed, for nineteen patients—nine women and ten children—shared a total of twelve rations.[28] The 1781 return of Vose's Light Battalion allowed two rations per officer and one for every soldier and woman. Each of the 405 camp women at New Windsor received a full ration, and every child received a half ration. A 1783 return issued under the "Late regulations" on rations also permitted women a full ration and each child a half ration.

Not that a full ration was a lot of food. In April 1778, two months before the army left the Valley Forge encampment, the daily ration was established as "a pound and a half of flour or bread, one pound of beef or fish or three quarters of a pound of Pork & 1 Gill whiskey or Spirits; or a pound and a half of flour or bread, half a pound of pork or bacon, half a pint of Peas or Beans one Gill of whiskey or Spirits."[29] (A gill is a quarter of a pint.) Even this standard, however, was not often attainable; it was especially difficult to find vegetables and meat for the army. Locating and transporting spirits, too, was at times, impossible.

Indeed, years after the Valley Forge encampment, Pvt. Joseph Plumb Martin recalled that his usual daily fare at camp was nothing more than a pound of fresh beef—by his account, reduced to three-quarters of a pound after cooking—and a pound of bread or flour, plus sometimes whiskey or spirits.[30] Surgeon Albigence Waldo also reported a hungry winter of 1777–78, punctuated with the cry of "No Meat! No Meat!" from more than one Valley Forge hut. At times Waldo himself had nothing but a diet of "Fire cake & Water" for breakfast, dinner, and supper.[31] On Christmas Day 1777, Gen. Johann de Kalb wrote, "The soldiers have had for four days neither flour nor meat."[32] (The British Army fared no better in Philadelphia that winter, and deserters reported that the troops in the city "had been placed on an allowance and were in extreme want of provisions.")[33] With food so scarce for the soldiers training to fight the battles, sustenance for the army's women and children became almost an afterthought. Although camp markets were eventually established at Valley Forge to sell fruit and vegetables to the army, the Continental soldiers, who received but a pittance in pay, and that irregularly, had little money to purchase food for themselves and for the families who traveled with them.

It was not until December 1782, near the end of the war, that an attempt was made to standardize the amount of food the army's women received. "For every fifteen men actually in a regiment or corps," General Orders stated, "there shall be allowed a draught for sixteen rations, so as to supply the women of the regiment or corps."[34] This meant that one additional ration would be allotted for every fifteen men. But women were not spread uniformly throughout the army. Sometimes two or three women, plus several children, traveled with fifteen men. Were they to share that one ration?

In January 1783, just one month later, Washington publicly admitted this plan of allowing one extra ration for fifteen men was ill-conceived and unworkable. Sometimes fifteen soldiers carried more women—Washington referred to them as "the extra Women"—and could not survive on one puny additional serving of food. Washington wrote that the soldiers remarked, with "too much justice. . . . If pay is withheld from us, and Provisions from our Wives and Children, we must all starve together or commit acts which may involve us in ruin." Washington's soldiers complained further that their wives could earn their rations, but the "Soldier, nay the Officer, for whom they [the laundresses] Wash has naught to pay them." Indeed, the commander feared himself about to "loose by Desertion, perhaps to the Enemy, some of the oldest and best Soldiers in the Service" because the families traveling with them were hungry. And so, after listening to "the Cries of these women," witnessing the "sufferings of their Children" and being subjected to "the complaints of the Husbands," Washington found himself with "no alternative" but to order up more rations for the army's women and children.[35] This he did.

Finally, although there is no record of hut accommodations for the women at the 1777–78 Valley Forge encampment, there are a few hints about possible sleeping arrangements that winter. On May 24, 1777, about six months before the Valley Forge encampment, Capt. Robert Kirkwood's Delaware regiment ordered six men per sleeping tent, or one tent for every five men and one woman. Three months later, Kirkwood allocated one tent "to 6 Privates including corporals, as Well as Wagoners women &c."[36] Later, in September 1777, as supplies became fewer, Kirkwood allotted one tent to each field officer, while all others slept eight to a tent.

Private soldiers slept twelve to a hut at Valley Forge. Based on conditions in Kirkland's regiment, attached women probably slept together with their mates in a hut, along with other soldiers. Unmarried women slept in separate huts. Available orders do not mention sleeping arrangements for children traveling with the army.

CONTEMPORARY ACCOUNTS OF WOMEN WITH THE CONTINENTAL ARMY

There are only a few eighteenth-century descriptions of any of the hundreds of camp women with the Continental Army. Most officers did not consider these women of the common sort worth their precious ink and paper. Many of the private soldiers were married to women who traveled with the army, but only a few of the private soldiers could write or read.[37] Jacob Nagle wrote about one soldier's wife at the battle of Brandywine stirring porridge in "the camp kettle on a small fire about 100 yards in the rear of the Grand Artillery." Suddenly, to Nagle's surprise and distress, a British cannonball ripped through camp and smashed the kettle, scattering the contents everywhere.[38] Nagle went hungry that morning, for his breakfast had been simmering in that pot.

There are vivid, revealing descriptions from both American and British soldiers of the army women's actions during the 1777 battles at Saratoga, New York. After the British loss at Saratoga, Ens. Thomas Anburey, a British officer, wrote that he "met with several dead bodies belonging to the enemy, and amongst them were laying close to each other, two men and a woman, the latter of whom had her arms extended, and her hands grasping cartridges."[39] (Anburey's description affirms that the "Molly Pitchers" of the army carried more than water on the battlefield.) Years after Saratoga, a member of the Connecticut militia recalled watching camp women, "doubtless the basest of their sex," desperately attempting to strip the dead while the battle still raged. One woman did not complete her task, for she was "struck by a cannon ball and literally dashed to pieces." Another soldier wrote he witnessed "women attempting to strip a wounded Hessian officer. One woman was attempting to get his watch. He was able to speak and although they could not understand what he said he made so much resistance that they left him."[40] It is also said that forty dead British soldiers at Saratoga were thrown into a common pit after unceremoniously "being stripped of their clothing by the women of the American camp."[41]

Also from Ensign Anburey, the British officer, comes a description of a British soldier's wife giving birth on a march—another reality for women of both the British and American armies. "We were two days in crossing the Green Mountains," Anburey wrote as the British marched to Cambridge after surrendering at Saratoga, "the roads . . . were almost impassable, and to add to the difficulty when we got half over, there came a heavy fall of snow. . . . In the midst of the heavy snow-storm, upon a baggage cart, and nothing to shelter her from the inclemency of weather but a bit of an old oil-cloth, a soldier's wife was delivered of a child, she and the infant are both well. . . . It may be said, that the women who follow a camp are of such a masculine nature, they are able to bear all hardships; this woman was quite the reverse, being small, and of a very delicate constitution."[42]

The camp women described by Nagle and Anburey remain anonymous —as most camp women of the Revolution are today. Something is known of Sarah Osborn Benjamin's life as an army woman only because she applied for a government pension. It is also through pension applications and government records that we know the names of several other women who followed the army. Margaret Corbin, for example, was awarded a pension even before the American Revolution ended.

Margaret Corbin (also known as "Captain Molly") was another Molly Pitcher who carried more than water to the men on the field. Like the more famous Mary Hays who wintered at Valley Forge, this Molly Pitcher also took up her husband's artillery position when he went down. When

John Corbin enlisted at the beginning of the war in the First Company of Pennsylvania Artillery, Margaret, who was childless, accompanied him to the field. After a cannonball struck and killed John at Fort Washington on November 16, 1776, Margaret took over his artillery piece. She was seriously wounded for her efforts (an arm was almost torn off and a breast mangled), awarded full rations by the army, and later assigned to the Invalid Corps. On June 29, 1779, the Supreme Executive Council, recognizing that Margaret had been "wounded and utterly disabled" while assisting the artillery and had "not been provided for as her helpless situation really required," granted her $30.00. On July 6, 1779, Congress voted that since she "heroically filled the post of her husband, who was killed by her side, serving a piece of artillery" she was entitled to receive half-pay for life, or until she no longer was disabled. She would also receive a one-time gift of a "complete suit of clothes" or the equivalent value in currency. In late July 1780 Congress, learning that Margaret continued in a "deplorable situation in consequence of her wound," voted to continue awarding her a set of clothes, or its cash value, annually.[43]

Margaret settled in Westchester County, New York, drank heavily, then died at the age of forty-eight. In 1926 her body was moved from an obscure gravesite to a place of honor at the U.S. Military Academy at West Point, and a statue of "Captain Molly" can still be seen there today. Margaret Corbin received an army pension in 1779, years before the American Revolution ended. She was the first camp woman with the Continental Army to be acknowledged by a pension.

The application of Deborah Sampson, who also traveled with the army, was denied when she applied for a pension about fifteen years after the Revolutionary War ended. And Deborah Sampson had fought in the war as a *soldier*. Deborah was born December 17, 1760, the fifth of seven children. Her father deserted the family when she was a small child, and her mother, unable to care for the children, sent Deborah to live with a distant relative. When the relative died, a pastor's elderly widow cared for her. After the widow died, Deborah, as was common in the eighteenth century, was bound out as a servant. At the age of eighteen, Deborah, now free from bondage, worked as a spinner and weaver. She also worked for a time as a teacher, for, surprisingly, she could both read and write. Then, wearing borrowed clothes, the five-foot-seven Sampson enlisted in the army as Timothy Thayer, probably in April 1782. The would-be soldier, however, was quickly discovered to be female, booted out of the service, and threatened with legal action.

Deborah's behavior so incensed the Third Baptist Church of Middleborough, Massachusetts, that the congregation removed her from the rolls. On September 3, 1782, the church "considered the case of Deborah Sampson, a member of this church, who last spring was accused of dressing in men's clothes, and enlisting as a Soldier in the Army." Because Deborah had acted in a "very loose and unchristian like" manner, the Third Baptist Church concluded it was its "duty to withdraw fellowship until she returns and makes Christian satisfaction."[44] There is no record of Deborah ever returning to the fold.

Deborah was more successful in staying in the army the second time around. Now masquerading as Robert Shurtlieff (a common New England name, also seen as Shurtleff, Shirtliff, Shurtliff), twenty-two-year-old Deborah reenlisted in the Continental Army on May 20, 1782, and promptly received a bounty of sixty pounds. (There is some uncertainty about the enlistment date. Deborah herself, under oath, swore that she enlisted in May 1782. Years later, Deborah, again under oath, stated that she had fought at Yorktown and had enlisted in April 1781.)[45] While serving the Continental Army in the light infantry, she received several wounds—and insisted on treating them privately. But Deborah could not take care of everything herself. When she was treated for—as a newspaper reported— a "violent illness," her true identity was discovered.[46] Gen. Henry Knox granted her an honorable discharge at West Point on October 23, 1783.

Deborah Sampson married Benjamin Gannett Jr., a farmer, on April 7, 1785. Their son, Earl Bradford Gannett, was born seven months later. The couple eventually had three children, then adopted one more. The Gannett family, so noted Paul Revere, possessed only "a few acres of poor land, which they cultivate, but they are really poor," so Deborah sought financial compensation for her Revolutionary War service.[47] In 1792 Massachusetts finally awarded Deborah back pay plus interest for serving in the Revolution. In September 1797 she gained celebrity status with the publication of a memoir. On November 28, 1797, Deborah's petition as a soldier "while in the actual service of the United States" for "pay and emoluments granted to other wounded and disabled soldiers" was brought before Congress; it was considered and denied.[48] In June 1802 the enterprising former soldier took to the lecture circuit—and it is said she was the first American woman to do so. This did not go well, however, for she was sick and destitute less than a year later. In 1805 Congress finally awarded Deborah a monthly pension of $4.00, which gradually increased to $6.40 a month. But this amount was not enough to sustain the family, and the impoverished woman had to borrow money several times. Finally in 1821, after attesting that her only property was wearing apparel valued at $20.00, Deborah was awarded a general service pension. She died about six years later, on April 29, 1827. On July 7, 1838, Congress approved a bill issuing the surviving heirs of this "soldier of the Revolution" (as Congress phrased it) benefits of $466.66.[49] But Congress had moved too slowly for her husband to benefit; by that date Benjamin Gannett was dead.

Deborah Sampson Gannett, a rare woman of the common sort who could both read and write, exhibited "female heroism, fidelity and courage" during the American Revolution.[50] Acknowledged as a soldier, she survived a battle wound that bothered her for life, married, raised children, and then lectured about her experiences. "This extraordinary woman," the *Dedham Register* stated about eighteen years before she died, "is now in the sixty-second year of her age; she possesses a clear understanding and a general knowledge of passing events; is fluent in speech, and delivers her sentiments in correct language, with deliberate and measured accent; is easy in her deportment, affable in her manners, robust and masculine in her appearance."[51] After seeing her stage performance, a man identified as Gill Blass praised her as a woman of "charms," not at all what he had expected. Instead, Deborah was, Blass gushed, "beautiful in an eminent degree," with easy manners, a fair complexion, and a modest blush. "And when she smiles," Blass continued, Mrs. Gannett displays "a beautiful row of Chinese [porcelain] teeth."[52] But the soldier's fame dimmed, and when she died she received only scant mention in a country paper.

Deborah Sampson Gannett fought as a soldier longer than any other woman during the Revolutionary War. She enlisted in the army to serve as a warrior, not in the traditional woman's role of washerwoman, nurse, cook, or seamstress. And she was not alone; several other women also wore the uniform of the Revolutionary soldier.

After Anna Maria Lane's husband enlisted in 1776, at the age of forty, she traveled with him to the battles of White Plains, Trenton, Princeton,

Germantown, and Savannah. Sometimes Mrs. Lane dressed as a common camp woman; at other times she dressed as a soldier. Anna Maria Lane fought alongside her husband at the battle of Germantown and was rewarded with a serious leg wound that bothered her for years. In 1808 the Virginia General Assembly awarded John Lane an annual, lifetime pension of $40.00. That same year, the assembly awarded Anna Maria a pension of $100.00 annually for life because she, "in the revolutionary war, in the garb, and with the courage of a soldier, performed extraordinary military services, and received a severe wound at the battle of Germantown."[53] There is, unfortunately, no record of what "extraordinary military services" she performed to merit this unusually large government pension.

Anna Maria Lane signed her May 20, 1808, pension receipt with an "X." She signed the next receipt the same way. But soon John Lane (who also signed with an "X") came to Richmond to collect the funds alone, as his wife was too ill to travel. Anna Maria Lane, an acknowledged soldier of the American Revolution, died on June 13, 1810. John Lane died at the age of eighty-seven, on July 14, 1823, in the Richmond city poorhouse.

Both Deborah Sampson and Anna Maria Lane are well documented as fighting as Revolutionary War soldiers, in army uniforms. Both received government pensions for their efforts. A woman who presented herself as "Samuel Gay" also served several months as a soldier, but when she was discovered, she was fined and sent to jail for three months. Anna Smith's efforts to appear as Samuel Smith were futile; she, too, spent time in jail. Other women who attempted to present themselves as soldiers could not even get to the field. When discovered, the would-be patriots in their makeshift soldier's uniforms were thrown out of town, accompanied only by the sounds of a woeful whores' march.

But most women who traveled with the Continental Army were like the four hundred or so women of the common sort who straggled into the Valley Forge encampment on December 19, 1777. They struggled merely to stay alive and dressed as best they could in tattered petticoats and shifts, not army uniforms. They lived in huts or tents during an encampment and sometimes slept on the ground. Their months with the army were spent bent to the arduous tasks of washing, cooking, mending, and nursing. The women worked for rations or scrounged food from the soldiers or farmer's fields. They received pay for their labors—when the soldiers and officers had the funds to give them. But for all their efforts, the army's hundreds of women were always considered to be *with* the army, never *of* the army.

These camp women also followed the beat of the army drum and served to help keep Gen. George Washington's army fed, clothed, healthy, and clean—and on the field.

9

The General Returns to Valley Forge

A Distinguished Officer's Musings

On June 20, 1778, Elizabeth Stephens's family, like the other families that lived on Mount Joy and Mount Misery, heaved a collective sigh of relief. The Continental Army had marched away from the Valley Forge area the day before. Gone were the thousands of soldiers who had practiced their maneuvers and tramped over the farmers' fields. Gone were the shouts of the officers, the sounds of the men, the calls of the women, the wails of the babies. No more would the screech of fife or the rattle of drums or the rumble of the wagons split the air. The muskets' retort and smoke were no more, and the hundreds of campfire lights had been extinguished. What was left was the devastated land, about two thousand log huts, and an unmistakable stench. But the Continental Army had marched out at last, and the farmers were finally alone with their wasted fields and what animals they had been able to keep from the army.

As quiet descended on gentle, rolling hills of the area surrounding the destroyed forge in the valley, the Stephens family, like the other farm families, busied themselves with preparing the fields for planting. Army huts were torn down for fencing. Trenches were filled in. The land was plowed and readied to receive the seed. Two years later, farm output was about what it had been before the army assaulted the ground.

The story is told that, in the last summer months of 1796, eighteen years after the Valley Forge encampment, an elderly figure of dignified appearance, on a fine horse, rode up the rutted road through the former encampment area. One black servant, also on horseback, accompanied the gentleman. As he rode along, the observer eagerly looked to the right and left, and noted the conditions of his surroundings in a little black book he carried with him.

Spotting someone in a field, the gentleman dismounted, threw his reins to his servant, and inquired of the farmer about the region's agriculture practices. The gentleman was curious about such things as what crops were grown, when the fields were planted, farming methods, and crop output. The stranger also inquired about the area's inhabitants. He listened to the answers attentively and wrote them in the little book.

The farmer apologized for not being able to give as informed answers to the questions as he would have liked, for he had not grown up in the area. He allowed that he had first come to Valley Forge during the winter of 1777–78, when he had been a soldier with the army. The distinguished gentleman nodded attentively, said that he was in Philadelphia on business, and shared that he had come to the encampment area to see how the farms and people were faring. This would be his last visit, he said. He added that he had also been in the army. He gave his name as George Washington.

The farmer expressed his surprise, as he had not recognized his former commander and the country's first president. Washington replied that he was particularly pleased to see a former comrade in arms. It gave him great satisfaction to see that the land was again productive and to hear that the people were happy. He had pressing business, he said, otherwise he would have liked to visit others in the area. After a cordial handshake, Washington and his servant left Valley Forge forever.[1]

As he rode away, Washington surely reflected on that Valley Forge encampment of 1777–78. About fourteen thousand soldiers had trudged into camp on December 19. In spite of all efforts, the army wore ragged clothing, ate meager rations, and received only sporadic pay for much of their time at camp. And, he remembered regretfully, some soldiers had no shoes; their movements in camp could be traced from the blood from their feet.[2] Conditions were so difficult at Valley Forge that hundreds of officers resigned their commissions, and many of the soldiers deserted. Yet, somehow, the army had held together. Washington recalled ruefully that soon after coming into camp he himself had predicted, "Unless some great and capital change suddenly takes place . . . this Army must inevitably be reduced to one or other of these three things: Starve, dissolve, or disperse."[3] The fierce loyalty of his officers and soldiers had kept the Continental Army intact.

Yes, the general recalled, the camp had some successes. Because of new recruits and reenlistments, about twenty thousand soldiers left Valley

Forge on June 19, 1778. At Valley Forge, the inspired and tireless General von Steuben taught the soldiers to fight together—and the men proved themselves at Monmouth just a few days after leaving camp. Gen. Nathanael Greene, who had reluctantly accepted the quartermaster general position, rejuvenated that office and ensured that troops were better supplied. *Cato* had been performed at camp, some portraits had been painted, and Washington could not have helped but smile when he remembered the exuberant May 6 celebration of the French Alliance. And Mrs. Washington had again come to him.

Sadly, Gen. Nathanael Greene, one of Washington's most trusted friends and officers, had passed away in 1786, soon after the Revolution ended. Lord Stirling died during the war. Gen. Charles Lee was gone; so was General de Kalb. Col. John Laurens, an aide to Washington, was killed in one of the war's last battles.

The former commander gave the reins of his horse an inadvertent shake. The long Revolutionary War had brought so much death and destruction, but—oh, the glorious outcome! The colonies had united to become free and independent states, carrying the proud name of the United States of America. Now life, liberty, and the pursuit of happiness were the right of all.

Unlike her husband, Martha Washington never returned to the site of the third winter encampment. Her granddaughter later wrote that Martha Washington did not speak of her experiences during the American Revolution. She preferred to forget those times, to focus instead on the present and her family.

"The difficulties, and distresses to which we have been exposed during the war must now be forgotten," Martha Washington wrote soon after the Revolution ended and she had returned to Mount Vernon. "We must endeavor to let our ways be the way of pleasantness and all our paths Peace."[4]

Appendix

Making the Myth of Martha Washington

Nineteenth-Century Fantasy vs. Eighteenth-Century Reality

From eighteenth-century journals, letters, diaries, and records we know that Martha Washington directed the household, acted as hostess, socialized with the camp ladies and officers, and participated in official military functions while at the 1777–78 Valley Forge encampment.

By mid-nineteenth century, however, the Martha Washington of Valley Forge is portrayed very differently. Nineteenth-century writings do not mention that Lady Washington attended the camp theater, accepted portraits of her husband, or hosted elegant dinners while at camp. Nor is it noted that she raised her voice in song over a saucer of tea or coffee with the elite ladies and officers. Instead, according to nineteenth-century writers, Lady Washington filled her days bringing solace to the soldiers in their huts. These writers would have us believe that the purpose and duty of this Virginia lady, on the highest rung of society in the class-conscious eighteenth century, was to enter the Valley Forge army huts to cheer and comfort the Continental Army soldiery.

Did she? Or are Martha Washington's visits with the private soldiers at the Valley Forge encampment nineteenth-century fantasy, not eighteenth-century reality?

Mercy Otis Warren, who corresponded and visited with Lady Washington during the American Revolution, had firsthand knowledge of Martha's activities at camp. Warren's three-volume *History of the Rise, Progress, and Termination of the American Revolution* was published in 1805, twenty-seven years after Valley Forge. Mrs. Warren writes, "The commander in chief, and several of the principal officers of the American army, in defiance of danger, either to themselves or to such tender connections, sent for their ladies from the different states to which they belonged, to pass

149

the remainder of the winter, and by their presence to enliven the gloomy appearance of a hutted village in the woods, inhabited only by an hungry and half-naked soldiery." To this Warren adds a note: "Nothing but the inexperience of the American ladies, and their confidence in the judgment of their husbands, could justify this hazard to their persons, and to their feelings of delicacy."[1] Eighteenth-century ladies, Warren writes, would find the private soldiers a "hazard to their persons" and a threat to their "feelings of delicacy." Did any eighteenth-century lady venture out among this "hungry and half-naked soldiery"? Warren does not indicate that she knows any lady—including Lady Washington—who did so.

Martha Washington is also mentioned later in Warren's *History*. After a brief look at the "magnanimous and disinterested" Washington resigning his commission in 1783 as commander of the Continental Army, Warren writes that his return to Mount Vernon was "hailed by the joyous acclamation" of everyone, especially the "crown of his domestic felicity," Martha Washington. "Mrs. Washington had long sighed for the return of her hero, whom she adored as the saviour of her country, and loved as the husband of her fond affection," Warren writes. "In this lady's character was blended that sweetness of manners, that at once engaged the partiality of the stranger, soothed the sorrows of the afflicted, and relieved the anguish of poverty, even in the manner of extending her charity to the sufferer."[2] Mercy Otis Warren is extolling Martha Washington's general goodness, kindness, and charity. Her words, and the context, offer no hint or suggestion that she is describing Lady Washington soothing the afflicted and poor of the Continental Army.

Col. David Humphreys, an aide-de-camp at Valley Forge, describes Martha Washington as a young widow as being "handsome & amiable . . . possessed of an ample jointure." He says nothing of her being out among the Valley Forge camp soldiers.[3] Capt. John Marshall, later chief justice of the U.S. Supreme Court, wintered at Valley Forge, too. Marshall's *The Life of George Washington* includes a few words about Martha but also makes no mention of her with the private soldiers.[4] Pierre DuPonceau, also at Valley Forge with Martha Washington, writes about her at the head of the dining table, where she appeared to him as a "Roman matron." He does not write of her in the soldiers' huts.[5] Martha Washington never writes that she visited the soldiers in their huts or even knitted for the men, and neither does George Washington. Nor does any account from either a soldier or officer at any army camp.

Others, including Mrs. Theodorick Bland, wrote about Martha Washington's activities at other encampments. Mrs. Bland rode with her friend, Mrs. Washington, in a carriage from Mount Vernon to Philadelphia. She also went out on riding parties with General and Mrs. Washington at the Morristown encampment. Mrs. Bland, however, says nothing about Mrs. Washington out among the army.[6] Capt. John Steele, one of Mrs. Washington's guards at Morristown, does not mention Mrs. Washington visiting the soldiers.[7] Elizabeth Schuyler (soon to be Mrs. Alexander Hamilton) met Martha Washington at Morristown; the two ladies later exchanged gifts. Miss Schuyler, however, does not write of Mrs. Washington spending time at Morristown in the military huts.[8] Neither does the Marquis de Chastellux, who visited with General and Mrs. Washington at several encampments,[9] nor Julian Niemcewicz, who visited with the Washingtons at Mount Vernon.[10]

There is no mention of Lady Washington out among the soldiers in other early nineteenth-century writings. Mason L. Weems's *The Life of Washington* (1800) found Mrs. Washington to be "the nearest heaven of all on earth I knew; And all but adoration was her due," but never in the soldiers' huts.[11] Jared Sparks's *The Life of George Washington* (1839) depicted Mrs. Washington as "affable and courteous, exemplary in her deportment, remarkable for her deeds of charity and piety, unostentatious and without vanity."[12] Sparks, however, does not write that Lady Washington practiced her "deeds of charity and piety" on the private soldiers.

But George Washington Parke Custis changed everything. Fifty-six years after the Valley Forge encampment, Custis wrote the descriptive text to accompany his grandmother's portrait for *The National Portrait Gallery of Distinguished Americans* (1834). In the memoir, Custis wrote that Martha Washington's arrival at camp was "deemed an epoch in the army" and "served to diffuse a cheering influence amid the gloom which hung over our destinies at Valley Forge, Morristown, and West Point."[13] (It is noteworthy that this statement has factual errors, for Martha Washington never traveled to West Point.)

On February 22, 1847, the *Daily National Intelligencer* printed Custis's "The Birth Date of Washington." For this annual piece on Washington,

Custis recalled that Martha Washington was "Greatly . . . beloved in the army. Her many intercessions with the chief for the pardon of offenders; her kindness to the sick and wounded; all of which caused her annual arrival in camp to be hailed as an event that would serve to dissipate the gloom of the winter quarters."[14] In 1834 Custis had written that his grandmother's arrival broke the gloom of camp. In 1847, thirteen years later, Custis was more expansive. Now he wrote that she also interceded for prisoners at camp and showed "kindness to the sick and wounded." But did she?

George Washington Parke Custis, who might be granted some credibility as Martha Washington's grandson, was only a toddler—not yet three—when the Revolutionary War ended. He had not been born at the time of the Valley Forge encampment. Growing up, he was thought to be charming, though lazy. When Custis was sixteen, his step-grandfather, General Washington, wrote to the president of Princeton, "From his [young Custis's] infancy I have discovered an almost unconquerable disposition to indolence in everything that did not tend to his amusement."[15] There was nothing really wrong with the boy, Washington continued later, except for Custis's "aversion to study . . . mere indolence, & a dereliction to exercise the powers of his mind."[16] Custis had some problems with judgment as an adult, also. When correspondents begged him to supply them with "any thing that bears the impress of his [George Washington's] venerated hand," he obliged by "cutting up fragments" of Washington's writings "from old letters & accounts," some from as early as 1760.[17]

One twenty-first-century historian calls Custis a "mythologist," second only to Mason Weems.[18] (Weems dreamed up the story that Washington chopped down the cherry tree.) Another author states that "many of Custis' statements had to be taken with various grains of salt."[19] It has also been said that Custis spent considerable time painting "huge canvases depicting historic scenes" and writing epic poems, for which he did not "display talent."[20] Marcus Cunliffe, in Weems's *The Life of Washington*, notes that Custis "wrote historical plays as a pastime . . . and does not carry conviction as a historian."[21] In short, Custis, justifiably recognized as an orator, collector of all things Washington, and genial host at his home in Arlington, Virginia, is not a credible historian. Nevertheless, as we shall see, others who write about Martha Washington take Custis's comments about his grandmother as truth. Then they expand and embellish them.

ELIZABETH ELLET, MARGARET C. CONKLING, AND NATHANIEL HERVEY

Elizabeth Ellet used and expanded Custis's memoir in her popular and influential *The Women of the American Revolution*. The first two volumes of the set were published in 1848; the third was added in 1850.

In her ground-breaking work, Ellet sketched the life stories of about 150 women of the Revolutionary period. She promised her readers that "the deficiency of material has in no case been supplied by fanciful embellishment. These memoirs are simple and homely narratives of real occurrences. . . . No labor of research, no pains in investigation—and none but those who have been similarly engaged can estimate the labor—have been spared in establishing the truth of the statements."[22]

Ellet, however, had an agenda. She wrote to spotlight both the domesticity and patriotism of the women of the Revolutionary period for her romantic mid-nineteenth-century female audience. She wrote to portray women during the Revolution as demonstrating "decency, and their respect for ceremony and propriety in the midst of horror."[23] She also wrote to encourage the women of her time to look to the past—specifically, to look to the women of the American Revolution—as the guide and inspiration for their present, and their future. [24] Ellen Moore, a young woman who read *The Women of the American Revolution* during the Civil War period, found the stories inspirational, just as Ellet had hoped. Mrs. Ellet's book, Miss Moore enthused, "quite nerves me up to undergo anything."[25]

In spite of Ellet's vow to spare no effort in establishing the truth, *The Women of the American Revolution* is the source of several questionable tales. The account of Mary Hooks Slocumb going to the field for her injured husband, for example, is in doubt.[26] The tradition of courier Emily Geiger, who tore up and then ate a message rather than allowing it to fall into enemy hands, has little substance.[27] As noted before, Ellet extolled the virtues of Mrs. Clement Biddle cooking for the soldiers near the battle of Brandywine. She also writes of General Lafayette and Rebekah Biddle catching pigeons for consumption at Valley Forge. But no primary sources authenticate these events, and Ellet is writing about seventy-five years after Brandywine and Valley Forge.

Elizabeth Ellet also shares some whimsy about General Knox's wife in her book. Mrs. Henry Knox and her daughter Lucy (later Lucy Knox Thatcher) traveled together to the Valley Forge encampment. When Lucy

Knox Thatcher later found Ellet's first account of her mother in *The Women of the American Revolution* "brief—& in some respects very inaccurate," she sent along family recollections and correspondence, which Ellet "kindly expressed herself well satisfied with." But Ellet's revision did not satisfy Mrs. Thatcher. "Mrs E has given the substance of what I wrote in many instances in her own language," Lucy Thatcher wrote after reading the next edition of *The Women of the American Revolution*, "and has said some things which I never thought of saying—such as the influence my Mother possessed over the minds of General & Mrs. Washington which I certainly never asserted—As she [her mother, Lucy Knox] was a woman of powerful mind—it might have been so—but I knew it not—and should be sorry to have it supposed to come from me."[28]

All this indicates that Elizabeth Ellet was a storyteller, not a historian. During "that dreadful winter of 1777-8," Mrs. Ellet writes, Mrs. Washington's "presence and submission to privation was strengthening the fortitude of those who might have complained, and giving hope and confidence to the desponding. She soothed the distresses of many sufferers, seeking out the poor and afflicted with benevolent kindness, extending relief wherever it was in her power, and with graceful deportment presiding in the Chief's humble dwelling."[29] George Washington Parke Custis, in 1847, had Martha Washington showing "kindness to the sick and wounded." Elizabeth Ellet, in 1848, had Martha Washington *"seeking out"* (author's emphasis) the soldiers *at the Valley Forge winter encampment.* It is noteworthy that this portrayal does not appear in print until seventy years after Valley Forge. It is based on no primary documentation whatsoever.

Elizabeth Ellet readily acknowledges her reliance on Custis's description of Martha Washington in *The National Portrait Gallery of Distinguished Americans,* and her vocabulary echoes Custis's. Custis wrote that his grandmother had thought it "her fortune to hear the first cannon at the opening, and the last at the closing, of all the campaigns of the revolutionary war."[30] Ellet wrote that, after the war, Martha Washington was accustomed to saying "that it had been her fortune to hear the first cannon at the opening, and the last at the closing, of all the campaigns of the Revolutionary war."[31] Ellet's word choice also echoes that found in Mercy Otis Warren's history of the American Revolution. Mrs. Warren wrote that Mrs. Washington "soothed the sorrows of the afflicted, and relieved the anguish of poverty, even in the manner of extending her charity to the sufferer."[32] Elizabeth Ellet wrote that Mrs. Washington "soothed the distresses of many sufferers, seeking out the afflicted with benevolent kindness" —*at the Valley Forge encampment.*[33] Ellet stretches the truth, then makes Warren's generalization specific as to time, place, and manner.

Mrs. Ellet also writes that in addition to Custis she cites "Thacher's Journal and other authorities" as her source of information.[34] But no known diary or journal from the Valley Forge period suggests that Martha Washington sought out the private soldiers. Nor do the editions of Thacher's journal available to Ellet at the time.

James Thacher served as a surgeon's mate and regimental surgeon during the war. His *Military Journal of the American Revolution*, first published in 1823, about fifty years after the Valley Forge encampment, underwent several revisions. In the *Military Journal*, Thacher relates that the Virginia officers told him, "Mrs. Washington has ever been honored as a lady of distinguished goodness . . . full of benignity, benevolence and charity, seeking for objects of affliction and poverty, that she may extend to the sufferers the hand of kindness and relief."[35] (Note the similarity to Mercy Otis Warren's words.) Thacher does not suggest that Lady Washington is seeking out "objects of affliction and poverty" in the army. He does not even mention the word "army." Instead Thacher, like Mercy Otis Warren, writes about Mrs. Washington being generally helpful to others.

An 1862 edition of Thacher's *Military Journal* does contain one line about Mrs. Washington assisting the private soldiers. (As Ellet published her work in 1848 and 1850, however, this edition was not available to her.) "Mrs. Washington still remained in camp," reads the 1862 "Life of Washington" appendage to Thacher's work, "doing numberless kind offices for the soldiers, preparing them clothing which they very much needed, and rendering aid whenever possible."[36] This seems straightforward enough. The reader would think that Thacher had seen, or heard, that Lady Washington personally aided the troops. However, this information about Lady Washington remaining in camp and rendering aid to the men does not appear in the 1861 edition of the book. Nor does it appear in any of the earlier editions. As Thacher died in 1844, it is obvious that he did not write about Lady Washington performing kind offices for the soldiers, preparing clothing for them, or rendering aid for them. An eager, enthusiastic editor wrote these words—and these words were added almost one hundred years after the Revolutionary War, during the Civil War period.

Throughout her lifetime Mrs. Washington clearly demonstrated largesse, as did General Washington. In 1775, for instance, she wrote to a Mr. Devenport telling him to allow "Mrs. Bayly," whose husband was ill, a barrel of corn and half a barrel of wheat and to "give her a fat hog."[37] During the presidential years, she received a note from an anonymous writer that began, "I am induced from your well known generosity of heart, and charitable disposition," and then went on to ask Mrs. Washington for thirty dollars for a young man in difficult circumstances.[38] Sister St. Mary wrote to Martha Washington in 1796 asking her to become a "Patron" of an elephant that the sister was exhibiting in Philadelphia to raise funds for victims of a Savannah fire. The good sister was confident of a warm response—she had even included a few tickets for the event—because, as she wrote, Martha Washington was known "every where by those qualities of humanity which makes the only difference amongst Mankind." Besides, the sister continued with assurance, "Those who make 'their fortune by the Public' are obliged to contribute to public charity."[39]

There is, however, a wide gap between the impersonal act of giving money to a religious sister and the very personal act of donning a cape and going into soldiers' huts. Mrs. Washington was an eighteenth-century Virginia lady; she followed a prescribed class role. The concept of the benevolent lady out among the poor and suffering soldiers belongs in the romantic nineteenth century, not the tradition-bound eighteenth century. It belongs to the Civil War, not the Revolutionary War. It is what Mary Ann Custis Lee, Robert E. Lee's wife and Martha Washington's great-granddaughter, could have done, if she had been so inclined.[40] It is not what Martha Washington would have done. Or what she did.

Margaret C. Conkling's *Memoirs of the Mother and Wife of Washington* was published in 1850. Conkling readily acknowledges Elizabeth Ellet's "elegant and highly entertaining volumes" as a source for some anecdotes and details in her own work.[41] Conkling, writing in the florid, romantic style of the mid-nineteenth century, embroiders and embellishes Ellet's vision of Martha Washington and the soldiers. Now "Lady Washington's time and attention during much of the many seasons of her residence with the army . . . were chiefly devoted to the humane purposes of benefiting and relieving the suffering soldiers. She visited the sick, ministered to their wants, and poured that sympathy which is the 'oil of joy' into their desponding hearts." Further, Conkling continues, Martha Washington at the camps "is described by those who witnessed and partook her efforts as having been unwavering in her zeal and earnestness in this, her noble and womanly purpose. No danger delayed, no difficulty or hardship prevented the fulfillment of these benevolent duties."[42]

Mrs. Conkling reports of witnesses to Martha's ministration. It is no surprise that Conkling has been described and criticized as yet another in the parade of nineteenth-century writers who wrote "worshipful" biographies, "embellished with doubtful anecdotes."[43]

But Nathaniel Hervey, also a mid-nineteenth-century writer, pronounces Conkling's *Memoirs* "excellent" and acknowledges his reliance on her text for anecdotes and incidents about Martha Washington. Hervey's *The Memory of Washington: With Biographical Sketches of His Mother and Wife* was published in 1852. Hervey depicts Martha Washington in the winter camps shining "with the luster of the true woman. She gave hope and confidence to the desponding, sought out the afflicted, honored and dignified every station she occupied."[44]

Influenced by these nineteenth-century writings, the myth of Martha Washington visiting among the soldiers in the army encampments became part of American lore.

BENSON JOHN LOSSING

Benson John Lossing (1813–91) propelled the myth to new heights. Lossing was a multitalented self-promoter who began as a wood engraver, morphed into a popular writer, and marketed himself as a historian. During his career Lossing published more than fifty-four articles in *Scribner's Monthly* and *Harper's New Monthly Magazine*, among others. Lossing wrote or edited at least six books related to Washington, including *Recollections and Private Memoirs of Washington, by His Adopted Son, George Washington Parke Custis* (1860), *The Home of Washington or Mount Vernon and Its Associations* (1870), and *Mary and Martha: The Mother and the Wife of George Washington* (1886). One of the last products of his lengthy career was *The Marriage of Pocahontas* (1890). The man published, and did so prodigiously, during a writing career that lasted almost half a century.

Lossing is known for his many popular publications, not for his solid research and stellar scholarship. He has been cited for his "frequent untrustworthiness."[45] His books are "frequently embellished with doubtful anecdotes."[46] Lossing himself wrote that some of his stories about Martha

Washington are based on traditions, not on factual research. "Many are the traditions concerning her beauty, gentleness, simplicity, and industry," Lossing wrote, "which yet linger around the winter-quarters of the venerated commander-in-chief of the armies of the Revolution"[47]

Lossing edited George Washington Parke Custis's *Recollections and Private Memoirs of Washington* (1860); the work notes that Martha Washington was much loved in the army, interceded for prisoners, and showed kindness to the sick and wounded. Her arrival at camp was an event destined to "dissipate the gloom" of the winter encampments.[48] In the late 1860s Lossing, in a memoir that accompanied a steel engraving of Martha Washington for the J. C. Buttre Company of New York, writes that Mrs. Washington was an "honored guest" each winter at army headquarters; that "Lady Washington, God bless her!" was the toast of every "convivial assemblage" of the army; and that "she was ever the delight of the camp and of the neighborhood, wherever the flag of the Great Leader was unfurled."[49] Lossing's declarations, however, are based solely on George Washington Parke Custis's musings and are supported by no primary documentation whatsoever.

But it is in *Mary and Martha: The Mother and Wife of George Washington* (1886) that Lossing's imagination really soars. For this book, he allegedly interviewed a "Mrs. Westlake," who, he wrote, had accompanied Lady Washington into the soldiers' huts at Valley Forge. Lossing writes that he interviewed Mrs. Westlake sometime before 1856. Here is Mrs. Westlake's account of Martha Washington at Valley Forge, according to Lossing:

> I never in my life knew a woman so busy from early morning until late at night as was Lady Washington, providing comforts for the sick soldiers. Every day, excepting Sundays, the wives of officers in camp, and sometimes other women, were invited to Mr. Potts's to assist her [Mrs. Washington] in knitting socks, patching garments, and making shirts for the poor soldiers when materials could be procured. Every fair day she might be seen, with basket in hand, and with a single attendant, going among the huts seeking the keenest and most needy sufferers, and giving all the comfort to them in her power. I sometimes went with her, for I was a stout girl, sixteen years old.
>
> On one occasion she went to the hut of a dying sergeant, whose young wife was with him. His case seemed to particularly touch the

heart of the good lady, and after she had given him some wholesome food she had prepared with her own hands, she knelt down by his straw pallet and prayed earnestly for him and his wife with her sweet and solemn voice. I shall never forget the scene."[50]

There are problems with this recollection. If there was a Mrs. Westlake, she was an elderly woman—ninety-four years old—when she spoke about the Valley Forge encampment to Benson Lossing. She is recalling events that had occurred seventy-eight years prior. As stated previously, no one else at Valley Forge, or at any of the other seven winter encampments, reported that Lady Washington visited the soldiers, prayed with the dying, or patched, knitted, and sewed. Could Westlake's memory have deceived her? Could it be that these scenes never occurred, but were the figment of an old woman's wishful imagination? Or, could this "interview" have been a figment of Lossing's imagination?

Certainly Lossing's books, sprinkled as they are with half-truths and stories, must be evaluated carefully. *Mary and Martha*, the same book in which the Westlake story is found, is full of several downright lies, some of which are contained in letters allegedly written by Martha Washington herself during the Revolution. These "Lady Washington" letters contain interesting anecdotes, but the sprightly style is different from Mrs. Washington's usual formal diction. The spelling is better. Also, as will be shown, an examination of the letters reveals errors that Martha Washington would never make. Not surprisingly, the original copies of the letters in question have never been found. I would suggest that many of the popular images of Martha Washington—of the lady visiting among the soldiers, praying for them, knitting for them—come from the pen of Benson John Lossing, who embellished or even made up stories to tell a good tale—and sell his books. Lossing was a storyteller, not a historian.

In *Mary and Martha*, for example, Lossing quotes two letters he attributes to Martha Washington that were written, he states, during, or near, the time of the 1777–78 Valley Forge winter encampment. The first was supposedly written sometime after December 7, 1777. In this letter, Mrs. Washington, allegedly in camp at Whitemarsh, Pennsylvania, writes that, because of the deep winter snows, she was forced to leave her "chariot" and hire a sleigh to get to camp at Whitemarsh. In spite of her difficulties, however, she found "nothing but kindness everywhere on my journey." Once at the

Whitemarsh camp, she reported finding the General "well, but much worn with fatigue and anxiety." The letter expresses Martha's distress for the "poor soldiers . . . without sufficient clothing and food, and many of them barefooted. Oh, how my heart pains for them!"[51]

The details make this appear to be an authentic letter from the general's wife. Washington's army camped at Whitemarsh before going into winter quarters at Valley Forge. The army had insufficient supplies, clothing, food, and shoes. It is reasonable to think of the commander as worn and anxious. We would like to believe that people were kind to Lady Washington on her travels and that her heart pained for the soldiers. Lossing writes that his authorities for Mrs. Washington being at Whitemarsh were verbal communications from the aforementioned Mrs. Westlake, George Washington Parke Custis, and an unknown, Dr. Auneas Munson of New Haven.[52]

There is, however, no evidence that Martha Washington traveled to the Whitemarsh encampment. In the late fall and early winter of 1777, Martha Washington was sitting by her own hearth, at her own Mount Vernon home. Letters written by Martha Washington from Mount Vernon — authentic ones — are dated late November and late December 1777. Washington himself writes that his wife left Virginia for Valley Forge on January 26 and came directly to the 1777–78 winter encampment. It is perhaps not surprising that, in the 1886 edition of *Mary and Martha*, Lossing also included a full-page drawing of Martha clinging to her husband as they gallop along on a faithful steed between Whitemarsh and Valley Forge. The text about the illustration reads, "On that cold, wintry journey of a few miles Mrs. Washington rode behind her husband on a pillion."[53]

Can we not consider that this "Martha Washington" letter depicting Mrs. Washington at Whitemarsh was written, not by the lady herself, but by Benson Lossing?

Mary and Martha also contains a letter that is allegedly written by the general's wife from the Valley Forge encampment. In this letter, addressed to Mrs. Lund Washington at Mount Vernon in March, "Martha" comments that headquarters was "made more tolerable by the addition of a log-cabin to the house, built to dine in." She notes the size of the "the apartment for business" (sixteen feet square) and says it has a large fireplace. The general, she writes, could look over the encampment from the east window, below which, "he had a box made, which appears as a part of the casement, with a blind trap door at top, in which he keeps his valuable papers."[54] All this is accurate. (Benson Lossing had visited and sketched the house in 1848, seventy years after the encampment.)

But there is, however, little chance that Martha penned this letter. Lossing declares that Mrs. Washington wrote this letter in March to Mrs. Lund Washington at Mount Vernon. However, Lund Washington, Washington's manager, was unmarried at this time: there was no Mrs. Lund Washington in March 1778—something Martha Washington certainly would have known. (Elizabeth Foote and Lund Washington married in 1782.)[55]

Lossing's accounts of Martha Washington at the other encampments reveal more errors. Of the Morristown encampment (1776–77), Lossing states, "The accommodations were so limited, and the movements of his [Washington's] troops were so uncertain, that he did not think it prudent for Mrs. Washington to come to the camp." Instead, "She remained quietly at Mount Vernon," Lossing writes, "until he [Washington] thought he was well provided with good winter quarters in a spacious house at Whitemarsh," and then Washington sent for her to come there.[56] Martha Washington never traveled to the Whitemarsh encampment, but she did travel to both Morristown encampments during the American Revolution.

Lossing also attributes a letter from the Middlebrook encampment to Martha Washington. In it, Lossing has Lady Washington describing the visiting Indians at camp as terrifying "mounted savages" and "like cutthroats all."[57] This "Martha Washington" letter is suspiciously similar to a legitimate one penned by Dr. James Thacher, also from Middlebrook, and is referred to in an earlier chapter of this book.

Another dubious Martha Washington letter, also mentioned previously, comes from the Newburgh encampment. It contains the information that, on February 7, 1783, Martha wrote to her sister, Anna Maria Bassett, describing a group of newly pardoned army prisoners who had knocked on the door of headquarters. Martha greeted the men with tears in her eyes, then handed the leader of the group a small amount of money. "God bless Lady Washington!" cried the grateful man, his own eyes teary.[58] But all this is nonsense, as Anna Maria Bassett, the supposed recipient of this letter, had died in 1777, soon before Martha left for the Valley Forge encampment. I would suggest that this is yet another example of a fanciful letter penned by Benson J. Lossing. It depicts an incident in Martha Washington's life—and an image of Martha Washington interacting with the common soldiers—that never occurred.

In summary, I would argue that Martha Washington's visits among the soldiers at camp is nineteenth-century fantasy, not eighteenth-century reality. In 1834, we read, for the first time, that Mrs. Washington's visit diffuses a "cheering influence" at army camp. This, however, is written fifty years after the war ended by the unreliable George Washington Parke Custis and cannot be substantiated. In 1847 Custis goes a step further— now his grandmother is showing "kindness to the sick and wounded" in winter camp. In 1848, about seventy years after the 1777–78 winter encampment, Elizabeth Ellet writes that Mrs. Washington is "seeking out the afflicted with benevolent kindness" at Valley Forge—marking the first time that Lady Washington is portrayed as being out among the camp soldiers at the Valley Forge encampment. In 1850 Margaret C. Conkling writes, "Lady Washington's time and attention during much of the many seasons of her residence with the army . . . were devoted to benefiting and relieving the suffering soldiers." Now Martha Washington is assisting the soldiers at many encampments. And why is it necessary for her to do this? As Nathaniel Hervey writes in 1852, Martha Washington, as she spreads her cheer throughout the army camps, is "shining with the luster of the true woman"—an important romantic mid-nineteenth-century ideal.

In *Mary and Martha* (1886), Benson J. Lossing published an "interview" with a Mrs. Westlake, who, Lossing writes, visited with Lady Washington among the soldiers' huts at Valley Forge. Mrs. Westlake also recalls Martha knitting, patching, and sewing for the soldiers. She is cooking for them, too. But, as has been argued, Benson Lossing is not a credible historian, and his books contain many fabrications.

Some would say there is another side of the story, and it is only fair to consider this. Some would cite Lady Washington herself as writing that she visited among the soldiers. In a March 7, 1778, letter to Mercy Otis Warren from Valley Forge, Martha Washington does write that the "men are cheifly [sic] in Hutts [sic], which they say is tolarable [sic] comfortable."[59] Could the "they say" suggest that she personally asked the soldiers about their living conditions? I would argue instead that the general's wife is sharing information about hut conditions she learned from the general's officers, the aides in his military family, or from the commander himself—perhaps in discussion around Washington's dining table. Certainly other letters of Mrs. Washington's demonstrate that she knows something of military affairs.[60]

Fifty years after the Valley Forge encampment, Colonel DuPonceau, who camped at Valley Forge—and dined at headquarters—talked about conditions at the encampment. He also wrote a bit of Martha Washington, of her "mild but dignified countenance," of her "grave, yet cheerful" manner. DuPonceau writes, too, "Her presence inspired fortitude, and those who came to her with almost desponding hearts, retired full of hope and confidence in the wisdom of their rulers, in the talents of their chief; and in the high destines of their country."[61] Would Colonel DuPonceau be describing the private soldiers, men of "the common sort," approaching an eighteenth-century Virginia lady for comfort and courage? Lossing and other nineteenth-century writers would like us to believe this would occur. In the class-conscious eighteenth century, however, it seems extremely unlikely.

Finally, there are the recollections of Alexander Milliner, who was interviewed in 1864 at the age of 104. Milliner remembers serving in Washington's Life Guard as a drummer for four years. Milliner also enlisted for two years as a private soldier.

In the mid-nineteenth-century interview, conducted about eighty years after the Revolution ended, Milliner recalled that he was a "great favorite" with the commander in chief, so much so that Washington would "come along and pat him on the head, and call him his boy." One bitter day, Milliner recalled, the commander even "gave him a drink out of his flask." Another time Washington gave him three dollars for entertaining with his drum. Milliner also recalled some things about Mrs. Washington. She was, he remembered, "a short, thick woman, very pleasant and kind. She used to visit the hospitals, was kind-hearted, and had a motherly care." About Valley Forge, Milliner said, "Lady Washington visited the army. She used thorns instead of pins on her clothes. The poor soldiers had bloody feet."

Milliner also related a story about General and Mrs. Washington for the interview. "One day the General had been out some time," Milliner said. "When he [Washington] came in, his wife asked him where he had been. He answered, laughing. 'To look at my boys.' 'Well,' said she, 'I will go and see *my* children [emphasis in original].'" When she returned she told the general "that there are a good many" of them.[62]

All this is interesting, but Milliner's statements must be carefully considered. First, Milliner says he was "young" when he enlisted as a drummer. If his stated birth date (1760) is correct, he was eighteen years old when he came to Valley Forge. This is not a young soldier, and it seems unlikely that General Washington would "pat" an eighteen-year-old "on the head and call him his boy." And would the commander actually give a drummer a drink from his own flask?

Second, Milliner, at the age of 104, is recollecting events at Valley Forge that had occurred more than eighty years before. At best, this falls into the category of oral history. As one reviewer notes, *The Last Men of the Revolution* "has interest for those who are curious to know how little a man can remember in 75 years."[63] Is Milliner reciting fact? Or mid-nineteenth-century fiction?

Can we not consider that the portrayal of Martha Washington visiting among the soldiers at Valley Forge is but a myth? I would argue that the story belongs to the nineteenth century, not the eighteenth century. There is no credible evidence to support the tradition. Visiting among the private soldiers is not what Martha Washington, an eighteenth-century lady, would have done. Or, I would argue, what she *did* during the extraordinary winter of the 1777–78 Valley Forge encampment.

Notes

CHAPTER 1: SETTING THE STAGE

1. Paul K. Walker, *Engineers of Independence: A Documentary History of the Army Engineers in the American Revolution, 1775–1783* (Washington, DC: Historical Division, Office of the Chief of Engineers, 1981), 177.

2. When Benjamin Franklin, then in Paris, learned that Gen. William Howe and the British Army had entered and taken Philadelphia, Franklin allegedly quipped, "Say, rather, that Philadelphia has taken General Howe." Jared Sparks, *The Life of George Washington* (New York: Perkins Book Company, 1902), 255.

3. Ebenezer Crosby to Norton Quincey, April 14, 1778, in Joseph Lee Boyle, *Writings from the Valley Forge Encampment of the Continental Army, December 19, 1777–June 19, 1778* (Bowie, MD: Heritage Books, 2000), 1:105.

4. Hugh F. Rankin, ed., *Narratives of the American Revolution as Told by a Young Sailor, a Home-Sick Surgeon, a French Volunteer, and a German General's Wife* (Chicago: Lakeside Press, 1976), 204.

5. Tench Tilghman to John Cadwalader, January 18, 1778, in *Pennsylvania Magazine of History and Biography* 32:2 (1908): 168. Lt. August Wilhelm Du Roi the Elder, an adjutant with the Prussians who fought at Saratoga and then came through Valley Forge in late 1778 as a prisoner with the Convention Army, did not share Tilghman's high opinion of the Valley Forge huts. "These huts, about 3000 . . . are built in lines, and are made of beams covered with glue. . . . These huts had been built in three weeks and the camp looks like a badly built town. It is remarkable that the [American] army should stand these quarters for a whole winter without many of the necessities of life, as shoes and stockings, etc." John F. Reed, "The British at Valley Forge and Norriton," *The Bulletin of the Historical Society of Montgomery County* 22:1 (Fall 1979): 82–83.

6. "Account of Rations Drawn by the Infantry of the Standing Army," no date, Item 192, Roll 199, Publication M247, Papers of the Continental Congress, National Archives and Records Administration (hereafter NARA), Washington, DC, http://www.footnote.com/documents.php.

7. General Orders, Roxboro, PA, August 4, 1777, in *Writings of George Washington from the Original Manuscript Sources*, ed. John C. Fitzpatrick, *George Washington Papers at the Library of Congress, 1741–1799*, Manuscript Division, Library of

Congress (hereafter LOC), Washington, DC, http://memory.loc.gov/cgi-bin/query/r?ammem/mgw:@field(DOCID+@lit(gw090027)).

8. George Washington to Col. James Clinton, June 28, 1776, in *The Papers of George Washington, Revolutionary War Series*, ed. Philander D. Chase (Charlottesville: University Press of Virginia, 1993), 5:132.

9. George Washington to Continental Congress, December 23, 1777, *Writings of George Washington, Washington Papers*, LOC, http://memory.loc.gov/cgi-bin/query/r?ammem/mgw:@field(DOCID+@lit(gw100200)).

10. Friedrich Kapp, *The Life of John Kalb: Major-General in the Revolutionary Army* (New York: H. Holt and Co., 1884), 139.

11. Alexander Scammell to Timothy Pickering, February 6, 1778, in Boyle, *Writings from the Valley Forge Encampment*, 3:61.

12. Joseph Plumb Martin, *Private Yankee Doodle: Being a Narrative of Some Adventures, Dangers and Sufferings of a Revolutionary Soldier*, ed. George E. Scheer (Fort Washington, PA: Eastern National, 1998), 111.

13. Ibid., 112. But General Washington may not have felt as kindly toward the people of Pennsylvania. Soon before the army left camp, an officer wrote that Washington was "unwilling (to use Washington's own words) to leave any thing of his in this d—n'd State." Samuel Shaw to William Knox, June 3, 1778, in Boyle, *Writings from the Valley Forge Encampment*, 4:165.

14. Lt. Thomas Anburey, a British prisoner from the battle of Saratoga who traveled though the area to Charlottesville, Virginia, in late 1778, found the Valley Forge encampment fortifications to be "exceedingly weak, and this is the only instance I ever saw of the Americans having such slight works." Anburey thought the fortifications to have been "by no means difficult of access." However, Lieutenant Du Roi the Elder had a different opinion: "The place is fortified with lines and batteries," he wrote, "making this camp insuperable." Although the British came out from Philadelphia to forage and engaged Lafayette at Barren Hill, about thirteen miles from Valley Forge, they never attacked the Continental Army at Valley Forge. Reed, "British at Valley Forge and Norriton," 81–83.

15. John P. Brucksch, *Historic Furnishings Report: Varnum's Quarters, Valley Forge National Historical Park* (Harpers Ferry, WV: Division of Historic Furnishings, Harpers Ferry National Park, 1993), 12.

16. Brig. Gen. James Mitchell Varnum to Maj. Gen. Nathanael Greene, February 12, 1778, in notes, George Washington to George Clinton, February 16, 1778, *Writings of George Washington, Washington Papers*, LOC, http://memory.loc.gov/cgi-bin/query/r?ammem/mgw:@field(DOCID+@lit(gw100435)).

17. Brucksch, *Historic Furnishings Report: Varnum's Quarters*, 6.

18. Ibid., 7.

19. Israel Shreve to Mary Shreve, January 15, 1778, in Boyle, *Writings from the Valley Forge Encampment*, 6:29.

20. John Joseph Stoudt, *Ordeal at Valley Forge: A Day-by-Day Chronicle from December 17, 1777, to June 18, 1778* (Philadelphia: University of Pennsylvania Press, 1963), 259.

21. Anne Jones to Whom It May Concern, March 3, 1779, in Boyle, *Writings from the Valley Forge Encampment*, 1:11–12.

22. W. R. T. Saffell, *Records of the Revolutionary War: Containing the Military and Financial Correspondence of Distinguished Officers*, 3rd ed. (Bowie, MD: Heritage Books, 1999), 359–60.

23. Sarah Moore, "Deposition Claim against British and American Armies," December 21, 1786, Cadwalader Papers, Historical Society of Pennsylvania, Philadelphia.

24. Rowland Evans to Edmund Physick, March 2, 1778, in Boyle, *Writings from the Valley Forge Encampment*, 6:80.

25. Ebenezer David, "Another Viewpoint," in *An American Revolutionary War Reader*, ed. Donald J. Sobol (New York: F. Watts, 1964), 95–96.

26. Jedediah Huntington to his father, January 7, 1778, in Wayne K. Bodle and Jacqueline Thibaut, *Valley Forge Historical Research Report* (Valley Forge, PA: Valley Forge National Historical Park, 1980), 1:156.

27. George Weedon, *Valley Forge Orderly Book of General George Weedon of the Continental Army under Command of General George Washington, in the Campaign of 1777–8* (New York: Dodd, Mead, 1902), 183.

28. William Currie, "An Account of Damages Sustained by Ye Subscriber from Ye British Army September 19, 1777," November 15, 1782, Chester County Historical Society, West Chester, PA.

29. Mary Howel, "An Estimate of Damages Sustained by the British Army under the Command of General Howe and His Army on Their March through the Great Valley Tredyffrin Township, Chester County, on the 17th of September 1777 by Me, Mary Howel," November 17, 1782, Chester County Historical Society, West Chester, PA.

30. John Havard, "An Inventory of Ye Goods & Chattels Taken from Ye Subscriber . . . by Ye Hessians & Others of Ye British Army during Their Encampment Here upon the Eighteenth, Nineteenth and Twentieth Days of September AD 1777 upon Command of General Howe," November 18, 1782, Chester County Historical Society, West Chester, PA.

31. During the Valley Forge period, patriotic city women in Philadelphia assisted the American prisoners in the filthy city jails. According to a Philadelphia newspaper of the time, a poor free black woman, who worked herself as a laundress, spent two dollars to purchase ingredients for soup for American prisoners. She had no money to purchase bread for the prisoners, so persuaded a local baker to give her six loaves on credit for the men. Elizabeth Evans, *Weathering the Storm: Women of the American Revolution* (New York: Scribner, 1975), 14.

   In February, the officers of the Virginia line who were stationed at Valley Forge took up a collection to assist two Philadelphians, Mrs. Hay and her daughter, who had shown great tenderness to brother officers confined in the city jails. John Marshall, *The Papers of John Marshall*, ed. Herbert A. Johnson (Chapel Hill: University of North Carolina Press, 1974), 1:13–14.

CHAPTER 2: MARTHA WASHINGTON AT VALLEY FORGE

1. Martha Washington to Burwell Bassett, December 22, 1777, in *Worthy Partner: The Papers of Martha Washington*, comp. Joseph E. Fields (Westport, CT: Greenwood Press, 1994), 176.

2. Martha Washington to Anna Maria Dandridge Bassett, November 18, 1777, in *Worthy Partner*, 174.
3. Walter Blumenthal, *Women Camp Followers of the American Revolution* (Philadelphia: G. S. MacManus Company, 1952), 86.
4. Martha Washington to Mercy Otis Warren, March 7, 1778, in *Worthy Partner*, 177.
5. Nathanael Greene to Gen. Alexander McDougall, February 5, 1778, in *The Papers of General Nathanael Greene*, ed. Richard K. Showman (Chapel Hill: University of North Carolina Press, 1980), 2:276.
6. James Mitchell Varnum to Alexander McDougall, February 7, 1778, in Boyle, *Writings from the Valley Forge Encampment*, 1:46.
7. Washington to Warren, March 7, 1778, 177.
8. Martha Washington's first camp visit was to Cambridge, Massachusetts, in 1775. The following year she traveled to Morristown, New Jersey. The third winter of the Revolution found Martha Washington at Valley Forge, Pennsylvania. She next journeyed to Middlebrook, New Jersey, then again to Morristown. Martha Washington made her sixth trip north to New Windsor, New York. Her final two visits were to Newburgh, New York. From John C. Fitzpatrick, "When Mrs. Washington Went to Camp," *Daughters of the American Revolution Magazine* 59:3 (March 1925): 135–47.
9. George Washington Parke Custis, *Recollections and Private Memoirs of Washington* (Bridgewater, VA: American Foundation Publications, 1999), 504.
10. Washington to Bassett, December 22, 1777, 175.
11. Fitzpatrick, "When Mrs. Washington Went to Camp," 144.
12. George Washington to John Parke Custis, February 1, 1778, in *Writings of George Washington from the Original Manuscript Sources, 1745–1799*, ed. John C. Fitzpatrick (Washington, DC: Government Printing Office, 1933), 10:414.
13. Washington to Warren, March 7, 1778, 178.
14. Martha Custis to John Hanbury & Company, August 20, 1757, in ibid., 6.
15. Martha Custis to Robert Cary & Company, 1758, in ibid., 25–28.
16. Martha Custis to John Hanbury & Company, August 20, 1757, in ibid., 6.
17. Martha Custis to John Hanbury & Company, December 20, 1757, in ibid., 21.
18. Martha Custis to John Hanbury & Company, June 1, 1758, in ibid., 44.
19. Unsigned letter, probably John Chaloner to Robert Dodd, undated, but appears between two letters dated March 3, 1778, Mss. 17137, Series 8D, #12, container 6, Ephraim Blaine Letterbook, Roll 75, Frame 1217, Peter Force Collection, LOC, Washington, DC.
20. Peter S. DuPonceau, "Autobiographical Letters of Peter S. DuPonceau," *The Pennsylvania Magazine of History and Biography* 40 (1916): 181. Music could also be heard on the Valley Forge campgrounds. On December 23, 1777, just days after the army marched into Valley Forge, Albigence Waldo, an army surgeon, wrote that an "excellent Player on the Violin" was playing soft music in the tent next to his, airs "finely adapted to stir up the tender Passions." Much as Waldo wanted to have the music stop, he also "dreaded its ceasing." Rankin, *Narratives of the American Revolution*, 189.

Tea was enjoyed throughout the Revolutionary period. As DuPonceau writes in the letter cited above, tea was even served at Washington's Valley

Forge headquarters. Col. John Mitchell also made a special effort to get tea for Martha Washington's use in Philadelphia during the fall of 1779.

21. Washington to Warren, March 7, 1778, 178.

22. Richard Fish, "Master Report of Washington's Headquarters," (unpublished manuscript, Horace Willcox Memorial Library, Valley Forge National Historical Park, PA, February 9, 1976), 6.

23. Elias Boudinot, *Journal or Historical Recollections of American Events during the Revolutionary War* (Philadelphia: F. Bourquin, 1894), 78. Just what was elegant about the meal? The food? The table appointments? The service? James Thacher, a regimental surgeon, recalled sharing an "elegantly" dressed dinner table with General and Mrs. Washington at the Middlebrook encampment, the year after Valley Forge. "The table was elegantly furnished, and the provisions ample, but not abounding in superfluities . . . the general and lady being seated at the side of the table." James Thacher, *Military Journal of the American Revolution, 1775–1783* (Gansevoort, NY: Corner House Historical Publications, 1998), 160.

24. DuPonceau, "Autobiographical Letters of Peter S. DuPonceau," 179.

25. Pierre DuPonceau, "Harvest Home Oration," *Republican Star and General Advertiser*, August 19, 1828, 2.

26. Elizabeth Sandwith Drinker, *The Diary of Elizabeth Drinker*, ed. Elaine Forman Crane (Boston: Northeastern University Press, 1991), 1:297. "She appeared to be an agreeable fine woman," Drinker wrote in her diary when she learned of Martha Washington's death. We "dined with her at the Valley Forge when G. Washington's Camp was there, the General and 22 officers also dined there—we were on our way to Lancaster, when our husbands were in Banishment at Winchester." Drinker, *Diary of Elizabeth Drinker*, 2:1519.

27. Ibid., 1:271.

28. Ray Raphael, *A People's History of the American Revolution: How Common People Shaped the Fight for Independence* (New York: Perennial, 2002), 171.

29. DuPonceau, "Harvest Home Oration," 2.

30. John B. B. Trussell Jr., *Birthplace of an Army: A Study of the Valley Forge Encampment* (Harrisburg: Pennsylvania Historical and Museum Commission, 1998), 21.

31. Caleb Gibbs and Mary Smith, "Revolutionary War Household Expenses, 1776–80," Image 72, Series 5: Financial Papers, *Washington Papers*, LOC, http://memory.loc.gov/cgi-bin/ampage?collId=mgw5&fileName=gwpage028.db&recNum=71.

32. "The Commander in Chief's Guard," *The Pennsylvania Magazine of History and Biography* 38 (1914): 85–86, 87.

33. Charles Willson Peale, *The Selected Papers of Charles Willson Peale and His Family*, ed. Lillian B. Miller (New Haven, CT: Yale University Press, 1983), 1:266.

34. John Laurens to Henry Laurens, March 9, 1778, in *The Army Correspondence of Colonel John Laurens in the Years 1777–8* (New York: New York Times, 1969), 139. John Laurens was fiercely devoted to Washington and to the cause of freedom. "You ask me, my dear father," Laurens wrote from Valley Forge to his father, the president of Congress, "what bounds I have set to my desire of serving my country in the military line? I answer glorious death, or the triumph of a cause in which we are engaged" (Ibid., 110–111). Laurens was killed in one of the last skirmishes of the war.

35. *Peale Papers*, 1:271.
36. William Bradford Jr. to Rachel Bradford Boudinot, May 14, 1778, in Boyle, *Writings from Valley Forge*, 2:125.
37. Journals of the Continental Congress, vol. 12, *A Century of Lawmaking for a New Nation: U.S. Congressional Documents and Debates, 1774–1875*, LOC, Washington, DC, http://memory.loc.gov/cgi-bin/ampage?collId=lljc&fileName=012/lljc012.db&recNum=161.
38. George Washington, General Orders, May 5, 1778, *Writings of George Washington, Washington Papers*, LOC, http://memory.loc.gov/cgi-bin/query/r?ammem/mgw:@field(DOCID+@lit(gw110349)).
39. Joseph Bloomfield, *Citizen Soldier: The Revolutionary War Journal of Joseph Bloomfield*, ed. Mark E. Lender and James Kirby Martin (Newark: New Jersey Historical Society, 1982), 134.
40. Paul Brigham, "A Revolutionary Diary of Captain Paul Brigham, November 19, 1777–September 4, 1778," ed. Edward A. Holt, *Vermont History* 34:1 (January 1966): 22.
41. Bloomfield, *Citizen Soldier*, 134.
42. John F. Reed, *Valley Forge: Crucible of Victory* (Monmouth Beach, NJ: Philip Freneau Press, 1969), 56.
43. James Abeel to Jacob Weiss, June 3, 1778, MSS 17.402, Manuscript Division, LOC, Washington, DC.
44. George Washington to William Gordon, February 15, 1778, *Writings of George Washington, Washington Papers*, LOC, http://memory.loc.gov/cgi-bin/query/r?ammem/mgw:@field(DOCID+@lit(gw100428))
45. Lafayette to Adrienne de Noailles de Lafayette, January 6, 1778, in *Lafayette in the Age of the American Revolution: Selected Letters and Papers, 1776–1790*, ed. Stanley J. Idzerda (Ithaca: Cornell University Press, 1977), 1:225.
46. Nathanael Greene to Catharine Greene, April 8, 1777, in *Greene Papers*, 2:54.

CHAPTER 3: MARTHA WASHINGTON AT THE OTHER ENCAMPMENTS

1. George Washington to Martha Washington, June 18, 1775, in *Worthy Partner*, 159–60.
2. George Washington to Martha Washington, June 23, 1775, in ibid., 161.
3. George Washington to John A. Washington, October 13, 1775, *Writings of George Washington, Washington Papers*, LOC, http://memory.loc.gov/cgi-bin/query/r?ammem/mgw:@field(DOCID+@lit(gw040029)).
4. Lund Washington to George Washington, October 29, 1775, in *Papers of George Washington, Revolutionary War Series*, 2:256.
5. Lund Washington to George Washington, November 5, 1775, in ibid., 2:304.
6. Fielding Lewis to George Washington, November 14, 1775, in *The Papers of George Washington, Digital Edition*, ed. Theodore J. Crackel, 2007, http://rotunda.upress.virginia.edu:8080/pgwde/dflt.xqy?keys=search-Rev02d321&hi=Fielding+Lewis+to+George+Washington.
7. Fitzpatrick, "When Mrs. Washington Went to Camp," 136.
8. James Thomas Flexner, *George Washington in the American Revolution, 1775–1783* (Boston: Little, Brown, 1968), 59.
9. Fitzpatrick, "When Mrs. Washington Went to Camp," 136.

10. Martha Washington to Elizabeth Ramsay, December 30, 1775, in *Worthy Partner*, 164.

11. George Washington to Capt. George Baylor, November 28, 1775, *Papers of George Washington, Revolutionary War Series*, 2:444.

12. Washington to Ramsay, December 30, 1775, 164.

13. Martha Washington to Anna Maria Bassett, January 31, 1776, in *Worthy Partner*, 166–67.

14. Martha Washington to Mercy Otis Warren, January 8, 1776, in *Worthy Partner*, 166.

15. Patricia Brady, *Martha Washington: An American Life* (New York: Viking, 2005), 108.

16. Fitzpatrick, "When Mrs. Washington Went to Camp," 138.

17. George Washington to John Augustine Washington, April 29, 1776, *Writings of George Washington, Washington Papers*, LOC, http://memory.loc.gov/cgi-bin/query/r?ammem/mgw:@field(DOCID+@lit(gw040434)).

18. George Washington to John Augustine Washington, May 31, 1776, *Writings of George Washington, Washington Papers*, LOC, http://memory.loc.gov/cgi-bin/query/r?ammem/mgw:@field(DOCID+@lit(gw050090)). See also George Washington to Burwell Bassett, June 4, 1776, in *Papers of George Washington, Revolutionary War Series*, 4:435.

19. Martha Washington to Anna Maria Dandridge Bassett, August 28, 1776, in *Worthy Partner*, 172.

20. Martha Daingerfield Bland, "Life in Morristown in 1777," letter to Frances Bland Randolph, May 12, 1777, *Proceedings of the New Jersey Historical Society* 51:3 (July 1933): 150–53.

21. Frank Moore, *The Diary of the Revolution* (Hartford, CT: J. B. Burr, 1875), 446.

22. Martha Washington to Bartholomew Dandridge, November 2, 1778, in *Worthy Partner*, 180.

23. George Washington to John Mitchell, November 11, 1778, *Writings of George Washington, Washington Papers*, LOC, http://memory.loc.gov/cgi-bin/query/r?ammem/mgw:@field(DOCID+@lit(gw130213)).

24. Moore, *Diary of the Revolution* (1875), 636.

25. Nathanael Greene to Lord Stirling, December 27, 1788, in *Greene Papers*, 3:126.

26. George Washington to the Marquis de Lafayette, March 8, 1779, *Writings of George Washington, Washington Papers*, LOC, http://memory.loc.gov/cgi-bin/query/r?ammem/mgw:@field(DOCID+@lit(gw140219)).

27. Martha Washington to John Parke and Eleanor Custis, March 19, 1779, in *Worthy Partner*, 181.

28. Frank Moore, comp., *The Diary of the American Revolution, 1775–1781*, ed. John Anthony Scott (New York: Washington Square Press, 1967), 346–47.

29. Moore, *Diary of the Revolution* (1875), 659.

30. Nathanael Greene to Col. Jeremiah Wadsworth, March 19, 1779, *Greene Papers*, 3:354.

31. Thacher, *Military Journal of the American Revolution*, 162–63.

32. Benson J. Lossing, *Mary and Martha: The Mother and the Wife of George Washington* (New York: Harper & Brothers, 1886), 185.

33. George Washington to William Gordon, August 2, 1779, *Writings of George Washington, Washington Papers*, LOC, http://memory.loc.gov/cgi-bin/query/r?ammem/mgw:@field(DOCID+@lit(gw160043)).

34. "Lady Washington at Bethlehem, 1779," *The Pennsylvania Magazine of History and Biography* 38 (1914): 250.

35. Nathanael Greene to Catharine Greene, July 8, 1779, in *Greene Papers*, 4:212.

36. George Washington to John Mitchell, October 17, 1779, *Writings of George Washington, Washington Papers*, LOC, http://memory.loc.gov/cgi-bin/query/r?ammem/mgw:@field(DOCID+@lit(gw160499)).

37. John Mitchell to George Washington, October 30, 1779, Image 186, Series 4: General Correspondence, October 21–December 8, 1779, *Washington Papers*, LOC, http://memory.loc.gov/cgi-bin/ampage?collId=mgw4&fileName=gwpage062.db&recNum=185. Mitchell had some problems securing the tea, for on November 27, 1779, he wrote to Nathanael Greene asking him to return tea that Mrs. Greene had been sent by error: General "Washington will want the tea for Mrs. Washington that was mistakenly sent Mrs. Greene." Col. John Mitchell to Nathanael Greene, November 27, 1779, in *Greene Papers*, 5:121.

38. George Washington to John Mitchell, November 6, 1779, *Writings of George Washington, Washington Papers*, LOC, http://memory.loc.gov/cgi-bin/query/r?ammem/mgw:@field(DOCID+@lit(gw170111)).

39. George Washington to Nathanael Greene, January 22, 1780, ibid., http://memory.loc.gov/cgi-bin/query/r?ammem/mgw:@field(DOCID+@lit(gw170488)).

40. Martha Washington to Elizabeth Schuyler, 1780, in *Worthy Partner*, 182.

41. Andrew M. Sherman, *Historic Morristown, New Jersey: The Story of Its First Century* (Morristown, NJ: Howard Publishing Company, 1905), 367.

42. John Mitchell to George Washington, June 26, 1780, Image 636, Series 4: General Correspondence, June 7–July 10, 1780, *Washington Papers*, LOC, http://memory.loc.gov/cgi-bin/ampage?collId=mgw4&fileName=gwpage067.db&recNum=635.

43. Joseph Reed to George Washington, July 15, 1780, Image 190, Series 4: General Correspondence, July 6–September 23, 1780, *Washington Papers*, LOC, http://memory.loc.gov/cgi-bin/ampage?collId=mgw4&fileName=gwpage068.db&recNum=189&tempFile=./temp/~ammem_T33Y&filecode=mgw&next_filecode=mgw&itemnum=1&ndocs=12.

44. Evans, *Weathering the Storm*, 289.

45. George Washington to Esther Reed, August 10, 1780, *Writings of George Washington, Washington Papers*, LOC, http://memory.loc.gov/cgi-bin/query/r?ammem/mgw:@field(DOCID+@lit(gw190421)).

46. George Washington to Sarah F. Bache, January 15, 1781, *Writings of George Washington, Washington Papers*, LOC, http://memory.loc.gov/cgi-bin/query/r?ammem/mgw:@field(DOCID+@lit(gw210118)).

47. George Washington to Mrs. Francis, Hillegas, Clarkson, Bache, and Blair, February 13, 1781, *Writings of George Washington, Washington Papers*, LOC, http://memory.loc.gov/cgi-bin/query/r?ammem/mgw:@field(DOCID+@lit(gw210243)).

48. Martha Washington to Burwell Bassett, July 18, 1780, in *Worthy Partner*, 183.

49. Nathanael Greene to Catharine Greene, September 29, 1780, in *Greene Papers*, 6:321.

50. John Smith Hanna, *A History of the Life and Services of Captain Samuel Dewees, a Native of Pennsylvania, and Soldier of the Revolutionary and Last Wars* (Baltimore: Robert Neilson, 1844), 210.

51. Marquis de Chastellux, *Travels in North America in the Years 1780, 1781 and 1782*, trans. Howard C. Rice Jr. (Chapel Hill: University of North Carolina Press, 1963), 1:134.

52. George Washington to the Marquis de Lafayette, December 14, 1780, *Writings of George Washington, Washington Papers*, LOC, http://memory.loc.gov/cgi-bin/query/r?ammem/mgw:@field(DOCID+@lit(gw200520)).

53. Chastellux, *Travels in North America*, 1:190.

54. Martha Washington to Charles Willson Peale, December 26, 1780, in *Worthy Partner*, 185. Also, Charles Willson Peale to Martha Washington, January 16, 1781, in ibid., 185.

55. George Washington to Lund Washington, April 30, 1781, *Writings of George Washington, Washington Papers*, LOC, http://memory.loc.gov/cgi-bin/query/r?ammem/mgw:@field(DOCID+@lit(gw220025)).

56. Elias Boudinot to George Washington, June 28, 1781, Image 90, Series 4: General Correspondence, June 25–July 30, 1781, *Washington Papers*, LOC, http://memory.loc.gov/cgi-bin/ampage?collId=mgw4&fileName=gwpage079.db&recNum=89&tempFile=./temp/~ammem_mxQj&filecode=mgw&next_file code=mgw&itemnum=1&ndocs=5.

57. Mrs. Abraham Mortier to Martha Washington, June 15, 1781, in *Worthy Partner*, 186.

58. George Washington to Mrs. Abraham Mortier, June 21, 1781, *Writings of George Washington, Washington Papers*, LOC, http://memory.loc.gov/cgi-bin/query/r?ammem/mgw:@field(DOCID+@lit(gw220268)). The curative powers of citrus fruit were well recognized, and a year later Washington sent a dozen lemons to Lord Stirling when Stirling became seriously ill.

59. John Parke Custis to Martha Washington, October 12, 1781, in *Worthy Partner*, 187.

60. Gen. George Weedon to Nathanael Greene, November 11, 1781, in *Greene Papers*, 9:566.

61. George Washington to Nathanael Greene, December 15, 1781, Image 452, Series 4: General Correspondence, November 5, 1781–January 27, 1782, *Washington Papers*, LOC, http://memory.loc.gov/cgi-bin/ampage?collId=mgw4&fileName=gwpage082.db&recNum=451.

62. Chastellux, *Travels in North America*, 1:299.

63. George Washington to Archibald Cary, June 15, 1782, *Writings of George Washington, Washington Papers*, LOC, http://memory.loc.gov/cgi-bin/query/r?ammem/mgw:@field(DOCID+@lit(gw240380)).

64. George Washington to Martha Washington, October 1, 1782, in *Worthy Partner*, 188–89. See these pages for the text of Brown's letter.

65. George Washington to Nathanael Greene, October 17, 1782, *Writings of George Washington, Washington Papers*, LOC, http://memory.loc.gov/cgi-bin/query/r?ammem/mgw:@field(DOCID+@lit(gw250302)).

66. Chastellux, *Travels in North America*, 2:513–14.

67. Lossing, *Mary and Martha*, 220.

68. General Orders, Newburgh, NY (comments in transcription), April 15, 1783, *Writings of George Washington, Washington Papers*, LOC, http://memory.loc.gov/cgi-bin/query/r?ammem/mgw:@field(DOCID+@lit(gw260371)).

69. George Washington to Elias Boudinot, June 18, 1783, ibid., http://memory.loc.gov/cgi-bin/query/r?ammem/mgw:@field(DOCID+@lit(gw270030)).

70. George Washington to Clement Biddle, October 2, 1783, ibid., http://memory.loc.gov/cgi-bin/query/r?ammem/mgw:@field(DOCID+@lit(gw270200)).

71. George Washington to Clement Biddle, August 13, 1783, ibid., http://memory.loc.gov/cgi-bin/query/r?ammem/mgw:@field(DOCID+@lit(gw270123)).

72. George Washington to George Clinton, September 11, 1783, ibid., http://memory.loc.gov/cgi-bin/query/r?ammem/mgw:@field(DOCID+@lit(gw270170)). On August 30, 1783, one of Washington's aides wrote this from Rocky Hill: "We are situated here agreeable enough and all cleverly; except Mrs. Washington whose health is not so good as when she left Newburgh." "Some Unpublished Revolutionary Manuscripts," *Proceedings of the New Jersey Historical Society* 2:13 (May 1894): 81–82.

73. Stanley Weintraub, *General Washington's Christmas Farewell: A Mount Vernon Homecoming, 1783* (New York: Free Press, 2003), 125.

74. George Washington to Henry Knox, September 23, 1783, *Writings of George Washington, Washington Papers*, LOC, http://memory.loc.gov/cgi-bin/query/r?ammem/mgw:@field(DOCID+@lit(gw270185)).

75. John Parke Custis to Martha Washington, August 21, 1776, in *Worthy Partner*, 170–71.

76. Weintraub, *General Washington's Christmas Farewell*, 86.

77. "Explanation Note to Revolutionary War Expense Account," Series 5: Financial Papers, 1750–1796, *Washington Papers*, LOC, http://memory.loc.gov/ammem/gwhtml/gwseries5.html.

78. Weintraub, *General Washington's Christmas Farewell*, 129.

79. George Washington to Friedrich Wilhelm, Baron von Steuben, December 23, 1783, *Writings of George Washington, Washington Papers*, LOC, http://memory.loc.gov/cgi-bin/query/r?ammem/mgw:@field(DOCID+@lit(gw270327)).

80. George Washington's Resignation Address, December 23, 1783, *Writings of George Washington, Washington Papers*, LOC, http://memory.loc.gov/cgi-bin/query/r?ammem/mgw:@field(DOCID+@lit(gw270328)).

81. Benson J. Lossing, *The Pictorial Field-Book of the Revolution* (New York: Harper & Brothers, 1860), 2:635.

CHAPTER 4: CATHARINE GREENE AND LUCY KNOX

1. Johann de Kalb to Madame de Kalb, May 12, 1778, in Boyle, *Writings from the Valley Forge Encampment*, 6:133.

2. William Bradford Jr. to Rachel Bradford Boudinot, May 14, 1778, in Boyle, *Writings from the Valley Forge Encampment*, 2:125.

3. *Peale Papers*, 1:271.

4. DuPonceau, "Autobiographical Letters of Peter S. DuPonceau," 181.

5. Israel Shreve to Mary Shreve, March 3, 1778, in Boyle, *Writings from the Valley Forge Encampment*, 2:64.

6. Elias Boudinot to Hannah Boudinot, April 17, 1778, in ibid., 1:110.

7. William Bradford Jr. to Rachel Bradford Boudinot, May 14, 1778, in ibid., 2:125.
8. Rankin, *Narratives of the American Revolution*, 193.
9. David Perry to George Washington, September 6, 1775, Image 110, Series 4: General Correspondence, November 12, 1773–September 6, 1775, *Washington Papers*, LOC, http://memory.loc.gov/cgi-bin/ampage?collId=mgw4&fileName =gwpage033.db&recNum=1109.
10. Elizabeth Ellet, *Revolutionary Women in the War for American Independence*, ed. Lincoln Diamant (Westport, CT: Praeger, 1998), 112.
11. George Washington to Nathanael Greene, December 15, 1781, *Writings of George Washington, Washington Papers*, LOC, http://memory.loc.gov/cgi-bin/ query/r?ammem/mgw:@field(DOCID+@lit(gw230433)).
12. Martha Littlefield Phillips, "Recollections of Washington and His Friends," *Century Magazine* 55 (January 1898): 363–74.
13. Elizabeth Ellet, *The Women of the American Revolution*, 2nd ed. (New York: Baker and Scribner, 1848), 1:64.
14. Nathanael Greene to Catharine Greene, July 12, 1777, in *Greene Papers*, 2:121.
15. Nathanael Greene to Catharine Greene, November 2, 1777, in ibid., 2:190.
16. Nathanael Greene to Jacob Greene, January 3, 1778, in ibid., 2:245.
17. Nathanael Greene to William Greene, March 7, 1778, in ibid., 2:304.
18. DuPonceau, "Autobiographical Letters of Peter S. DuPonceau," 181.
19. Nathanael Greene to Col. Clement Biddle, March 30, 1778, in *Greene Papers*, 2:328.
20. *Peale Papers*, 1:271.
21. Nathanael Greene to Col. James Abeel, March 16, 1778, in *Greene Papers*, 2:315.
22. Moore, *Diary of the American Revolution* (1967), 304.
23. Elihue Greene to Nathanael Greene, April 13, 1778, in *Greene Papers*, 2:337.
24. Griffin Greene to Nathanael Greene, April 12, 1778, in ibid., 2:338.
25. Samuel Ward to Phoebe Ward, April 28, 1778, in Boyle, *Writings from the Valley Forge Encampment*, 1:123.
26. Nathanael Greene to Governor William Greene, May 25, 1778, in *Greene Papers*, 2:408.
27. Nathanael Greene to Griffin Greene, May 25, 1778, in ibid., 2:406.
28. Nathanael Greene to Catharine Greene, December 16, 1776, in ibid., 1:368.
29. Nathanael Greene to Catharine Greene, June 4, 1778, in ibid., 2:425–426. There is some controversy as to the warmth between Catharine Greene and Lucy Knox. Both had husbands in Washington's inner circle. Both were young, intelligent, willful women. Both ladies were also likely vying for Martha Washington's attention and friendship.
   Nathanael Greene makes several references to Lucy Knox in letters to his wife. Consider, for example, his letter to Caty in May 1777, written soon after Caty left Valley Forge—a letter that could not have endeared Lucy Knox to Caty Greene. "If you are in want of anything from Boston," Greene wrote, "write to Mrs. Knox. She will furnish you and I'll pay the General here. But remember when you write to Mrs. Knox you write to a good scholar, there mind and spell well. You are defective in this matter, my love, a little attention

will soon correct it. Bad writing is nothing if the spelling is but good. People are often laughed at for not spelling well but never for not writing well. It is said it is ungenteel for Gentlemen to make observations upon Ladies writing. I hope you wont [*sic*] think it unkind in me. Nothing but the affection and regard I feel for you makes me wish to have you appear an accomplished Lady in every point of view. PS This is the last letter I'll write until I receive one." (Nathanael Greene to Catharine Greene, May 20, 1777, in *Greene Papers*, 2:84.)

There was, however, nothing but warm regard and friendship between General Knox and General Greene. In 1781, when Greene was engaged in the southern campaign, Knox wrote to Greene: "I would be extremely happy were circumstances to happen, which would bring us together again. . . . You will always command separately whilst there shall remain any separate command, and I am so linked in with the cursed cannon that I know not how to tear myself from them. [If I could] I would fly to you, with much more rapidity than most fat men." (Henry Knox to Nathanael Greene, November 1, 1781, in *Greene Papers*, 9:508.)

30. Catharine Greene to Dr. Peter Turner, June 9, 1778, in John F. Stegeman and Janet A. Stegeman, *Caty: A Biography of Catharine Littlefield Greene* (Athens: University of Georgia Press, 1977), 61–62.

31. Nathanael Greene to Catharine Greene, August 16, 1778, in *Greene Papers*, 2:480.

32. Nathanael Greene to George Washington, September 16, 1778, Image 124, Series 4: General Correspondence, September 13–October 10, 1778, *Washington Papers*, LOC, http://memory.loc.gov/cgi-bin/ampage?collId=mg w4&fileName=gwpage052.db&recNum=123&tempFile=./temp/~ammem_ WbBw&filecode=mgw&next_filecode=mgw&itemnum=1&ndocs=10.

33. Nathanael Greene to Gen. John Hancock, September 30, 1778, in *Greene Papers*, 2:528.

34. Gen. George Weedon to Nathanael Greene, November 9, 1778, in ibid., 3:54–55.

35. Gen. James Varnum to Nathanael Greene, October 3, 1778, in ibid., 2:538.

36. William Moore to Nathanael Greene, November 10, 1778, in ibid., 3:61.

37. Nathanael Greene to Catharine Greene, November 13, 1778, in ibid., 3:67.

38. Nathanael Greene to Griffin Greene, December 21, 1778, in ibid., 3:122.

39. Nathanael Greene to Col. James Abeel, February 28, 1779, in ibid., 3:321.

40. Col. James Abeel to Nathanael Greene, February 28, 1779, in ibid., 3:320.

41. Col. James Abeel to Nathanael Greene, March 2, 1779, in ibid., 3:328.

42. Joseph Webb to Nathanael Greene, November 1, 1779, in ibid., 5:3.

43. Nathanael Greene to Gov. William Greene, December 3, 1779, in ibid., 5:143.

44. Nathanael Greene to Moore Furman, February 14, 1780, in ibid., 5:378.

45. Nathanael Greene to Nehemiah Hubbard, December 16, 1779, in ibid., 5:180.

46. Samuel Ogden to Nathanael Greene, June 15, 1780, in ibid., 6:7–8.

47. Nathanael Greene to Catharine Greene, June 9, 1780, in ibid., 6:9.

48. Nathanael Greene to Catharine Greene, July 11, 1780, in ibid., 6:85–86.

49. Nathanael Greene to Catharine Greene, September 28, 1780, in ibid., 6:319.

50. Nathanael Greene to Catharine Greene, October 7, 1780, in ibid., 6:350–51.

51. Jacob Greene to Nathanael Greene, October 1, 1780, in ibid., 6:326.
52. Nathanael Greene to Catharine Greene, October 15 or 16, 1780, in ibid., 6:397–98.
53. Ibid., 398.
54. Nathanael Greene to Catharine Greene, October 21, 1780, in *Greene Papers*, 6:415.
55. Claude Blanchard, *The Journal of Claude Blanchard*, ed. Thomas Balch (Albany: J. Munsell, 1876), 11.
56. Nathanael Greene to Catharine Greene, January 12, 1781, in *Greene Papers*, 7:102.
57. Nathanael Greene to Catharine Greene, December 29, 1780, in ibid., 7:16.
58. Extract of a letter from Fredericksburg, Virginia, dated February 15, 1782, as reported in the *Maryland Gazette*, March 14, 1782.
59. Maj. Ichabod Burnet to Nathanael Greene, March 21, 1782, in Stegeman and Stegeman, *Caty*, 94.
60. Nathanael Greene to Catharine Greene, September 22, 1780, in *Greene Papers*, 6:305.
61. Nathanael Greene to Gen. Lewis Morris, August 26, 1782, in ibid., 6:506.
62. Lewis Morris to Ann Elliott, in two letters dated October 29, 1782, and November 19, 1782, in Stegeman and Stegeman, *Caty*, 99.
63. Nathanael Greene to Samuel Ward Jr., December 21, 1782, in "Nathanael Greene's Letters to 'Friend Sammy Ward,'" ed. Clifford P. Monahan and Clarkson A. Collins III, *Rhode Island History* 17:1 (January 1958): 19.
64. Nathanael Greene to Catharine Greene, September 8, 1784, in Stegeman and Stegeman, *Caty*, 112.
65. Greene to Ward, April 4, 1786, 21.
66. *Journal of the House of Representatives of the United States, 1789–1793*, April 27, 1792, LOC, http://memory.loc.gov/cgi-bin/ampage?collId=llhj@fileName=001/llhj001.db&recNum=583.
67. Catharine Greene to Nat Pendleton, May 25, 1782, in Stegeman and Stegeman, *Caty*, 155.
68. Phillips, "Recollections of Washington and His Friends," 372.
69. Rev. John Murray to Nathanael Greene, January 21, 1780, in *Greene Papers*, 5:299.
70. Ibid., 2:319n.
71. Isaac Briggs to Joseph Thomas, November 23, 1785, in Stegeman and Stegeman, *Caty*, 121.
72. Nathanael Greene to Christopher Greene, April 22, 1778, in *Greene Papers*, 2:350.
73. Nathanael Greene to Catharine Greene, July 20, 1779, in ibid., 4:244.
74. Jacob Greene to Nathanael Greene, March 23, 1780, in ibid., 5:475.
75. Phillips, "Recollections of Washington and His Friends," 368.
76. Ibid., 369.
77. Ibid., 372.
78. Ibid., 364.
79. Ibid., 364, 366.
80. Ibid., 365.

81. Catharine Greene to Eli Whitney, October 12–19, 1810, in Stegeman and Stegeman, *Caty*, 202.
82. Eli Whitney to Dr. Lemuel Kollack, December 17, 1810, in ibid., 203.
83. George Washington to Nathanael Greene, October 17, 1782, *Writings of George Washington, Washington Papers*, LOC, http://memory.loc.gov/cgi-bin/query/r?ammem/mgw:@field(DOCID+@lit(gw250302)).
84. Stegeman and Stegeman, *Caty*, 203, 207.
85. George Washington to Catharine Greene, December 15, 1780, Image 495, Series 4: General Correspondence, November 27, 1780–January 6, 1781, *Washington Papers*, LOC, http://memory.loc.gov/cgi-bin/ampage?collId=mgw4&fileName=gwpage073.db&recNum=494&tempFile=./temp/~ammem_jX8O&filecode=mgw&next_filecode=mgw&itemnum=1&ndocs=11.
86. Catharine Greene to Nathaniel Pendleton Jr., November 22, 1789, in Stegeman and Stegeman, *Caty*, 144.
87. Daniel Turner to his parents, April 20, 1805, in ibid., 187.
88. Catharine Greene to Eli Whitney, December 31, 1808, in ibid., 195.
89. Catharine Greene to Eli Whitney, April 16, and July 5, 1814, in ibid., 208.
90. Lucy Knox to Henry Knox, August 23, 1777, Gilder Lehrman Institute of American History, New York, http://www.gilderlehrman.org/collection/trans_knox_knox.html.
91. Diana Forbes-Robertson, "Lady Knox," *American History* 17:3 (April 1966): 47.
92. Ibid.
93. Thomas Morgan Griffiths, *Major General Henry Knox and the Last Heirs to Montpelier* (Monmouth, ME: Monmouth Press, 1991), 42.
94. Forbes-Robertson, "Lady Knox," 74.
95. Lucy Knox to Henry Knox, August 23, 1777, Gilder Lehrman Institute of American History, www.gilderlehrman.org/search/display_results.php?id=GLC02437.04.43.
96. Ibid.
97. Mark M. Boatner III, *Encyclopedia of the American Revolution*, 3rd ed. (Mechanicsburg, PA: Stackpole Books, 1994), 588.
98. Forbes-Robertson, "Lady Knox," 74.
99. Nathanael Greene to Catharine Greene, June 23, 1778, in *Greene Papers*, 2:444.
100. North Callahan, *Henry Knox: General Washington's General* (n.p.: Friends of Montpelier, 1989), 272.
101. Griffiths, *Major General Henry Knox*, 50.
102. Ibid., 47.
103. Chastellux, *Travels in North America*, 1:282.
104. Griffiths, *Major General Henry Knox*, 47.
105. Nathanael Greene to Catharine Greene, June 23, 1778, in *Greene Papers*, 2:444.
106. Lucy Knox to Henry Knox, August 23, 1777, Gilder Lehrman Institute of American History, www.gilderlehrman.org/search/display_results.php?id=GLC02437.04.43.
107. Henry Knox to Lucy Knox, December 27, 1777 in Boyle, *Writings from the Valley Forge Encampment*, 5:10.
108. Henry Knox to William Knox, May 27, 1778, in ibid., 6:146.
109. Callahan, *Henry Knox*, 129.

110. Joseph Reed to Esther Reed, June 9, 1778, in *Letters of Delegates to Congress 1774–1789*, ed. Paul H. Smith (Washington, DC: Library of Congress, 1977), 10:62.
111. Callahan, *Henry Knox*, 143. Pierre S. DuPonceau, who accompanied Baron von Steuben into Philadelphia after the British occupation, also wrote about the filthy conditions of the city. "Such was the filth of the city," DuPonceau recalled in 1836, "that it was impossible for us to drink a comfortable dish of tea that evening. As fast as our cups were filled, myriads of flies took possession of them." Friedrich Kapp, *The Life of Frederick William von Steuben: Major General in the Revolutionary Army* (New York: Mason Brothers, 1859), 156.
112. *New Jersey Gazette*, March 3, 1779, in *Greene Papers*, 3:268.
113. John Lewis Seidel, "The Archaeology of the American Revolution: A Reappraisal and Case Study at the Continental Artillery Cantonment of 1778–1779, Pluckemin, New Jersey" (dissertation, University of Pennsylvania, 1987), 1:215–219.
114. Callahan, *Henry Knox*, 156.
115. Nathanael Greene to Catharine Greene, July 8, 1779, in *Greene Papers*, 4:212.
116. Nathanael Greene to Catharine Greene, July 20, 1779, in ibid., 4:244.
117. Chastellux, *Travels in North America*, 1:112.
118. Ibid., 1:191.
119. Callahan, *Henry Knox*, 189.
120. Ibid., 271.
121. Forbes-Robertson, "Lady Knox," 76.
122. Ibid., 77.
123. Callahan, *Henry Knox*, 383.
124. Forbes-Robertson, "Lady Knox," 78.
125. Callahan, *Henry Knox*, 383.
126. Ibid., 356.
127. Ibid., 380.
128. Ibid., 381–82.
129. Ibid., 382.
130. Forbes-Robertson, "Lady Knox," 78.
131. Lucy Knox to Henry Knox, August 23, 1777, Gilder Lehrman Institute of American History, www.gilderlehrman.org/search/display_results.php?id=GLC02437.04.43.
132. Griffiths, *Major General Henry Knox*, 72.
133. Caroline Swan to John Holmes, March 15, 1837, in ibid., 72.
134. Lucy F. K. Thatcher to Henry Knox Thatcher, January 11, 1845, in ibid., 75–76.
135. Lucy F. K. Thatcher to Caroline F. Smith, July 29, 1845, in ibid., 79.
136. Griffiths, *Major General Henry Knox*, 90.
137. Callahan, *Henry Knox*, 294.
138. Lucy F. K. Thatcher to Henry Knox Thatcher, June 23, 1828, in Griffiths, *Major General Henry Knox*, 56.
139. Callahan, *Henry Knox*, 291.
140. Griffiths, *Major General Henry Knox*, 66.
141. Caroline Swan to John Holmes, April 8, 1837, in ibid., 58.
142. Caroline Swan to John Holmes, no date, in ibid., 60.

143. Callahan, *Henry Knox*, 190.
144. Ibid., 262.
145. Ibid., 266.
146. Ibid., 360.
147. Ibid., 363.
148. Henry Knox to Clement Biddle, March 3, 1798, in Griffiths, *Major General Henry Knox*, 48.

CHAPTER 5: REBEKAH BIDDLE, LADY STIRLING, AND ALICE SHIPPEN AT VALLEY FORGE

1. Nathanael Greene to Col. Jeremiah Wadsworth, April 14, 1779, in *Greene Papers*, 3:405.
2. Ellet, *Women of the American Revolution*, 2:235–36.
3. "The First Marshal of Pennsylvania: Clement Biddle," *The First Generation of United States Marshals*, http://www.usdoj.gov/marshals/history/firstmarshals/biddle.htm. Information on Biddle's occupations after the war from John F. Reed, "Clement Biddle at Moore Hall," *The Bulletin of the Historical Society of Montgomery County* 22:3 (Fall 1980): 250.
4. Martha Washington to Col. Clement Biddle, July 1790, in *Worthy Partner*, 228.
5. Tobias Lear to Clement Biddle, February 10, 1790, *Writings of George Washington*, *Washington Papers*, LOC, http://memory.loc.gov/cgi-bin/query/r?ammem/mgw:@field(DOCID+@lit(gw310020)).
6. DuPonceau, "Autobiographical Letters of Peter S. DuPonceau," 181.
7. Catherine Alexander to Kitty Livingston, May 3, 1778, typed manuscript, John F. Reed Collection, Valley Forge National Historical Park, PA. See also Ellet, *Women of the American Revolution*, 2:117.
8. Alan Valentine, *Lord Stirling* (New York: Oxford University Press, 1969), 272.
9. Ibid., 96.
10. Ibid., 116, 130, 272.
11. George Washington to William Alexander, Lord Stirling, May 6, 1777, *Writings of George Washington*, *Washington Papers*, LOC, http://memory.loc.gov/cgi-bin/query/r?ammem/mgw:@field(DOCID+@lit(gw080029)).
12. William Alexander, Lord Stirling, to George Washington, May 6, 1777, Image 765, Series 4: General Correspondence, April 6, 1777–April 12, 1778, *Washington Papers*, LOC, http://memory.loc.gov/cgi-bin/ampage?collId=mgw4&fileName=gwpage041.db&recNum=764.
13. Valentine, *Lord Stirling*, 236.
14. Lafayette, *Lafayette in the Age of the American Revolution*, 1:286.
15. Valentine, *Lord Stirling*, 241.
16. Paul David Nelson, *William Alexander, Lord Stirling* (University: University of Alabama Press, 1987), 164.
17. Valentine, *Lord Stirling*, 279.
18. Ibid., 279.
19. Ibid., 280.
20. Ibid., 203.
21. William Alexander Duer, *The Life of William Alexander, Earl of Stirling, Major-General in the Army of the United States during the Revolution* (New York: Wiley & Putnam, 1847), 2:201.

22. Nelson, *William Alexander*, 133.
23. George Washington to Lady Sarah L. Stirling, January 20, 1783, *Writings of George Washington, Washington Papers*, LOC, http://memory.loc.gov/cgi-bin/query/r?ammem/mgw:@field(DOCID+@lit(gw260072)).
24. Valentine, *Lord Stirling*, 272.
25. Nelson, *William Alexander*, 140.
26. Douglas Southall Freeman, *George Washington: A Biography* (New York: Scribner, 1951), 4:241A.
27. Valentine, *Lord Stirling*, 217.
28. Ibid., 115.
29. Anne Home Shippen Livingston, *Nancy Shippen: Her Journal Book*, ed. Ethel Armes (Philadelphia: Lippincott, 1935), 52.
30. Ibid., 56.
31. Sarah Wister, *Sally Wister's Journal, a True Narrative*, ed. Albert Cook Myers (Philadelphia: Ferris & Leach, 1902), 190.
32. William Shippen Jr. to Nancy Shippen, June 7, 1778, in Boyle, *Writings from the Valley Forge Encampment*, 1:153–54.
33. Paul C. Nagel, *The Lees of Virginia: Seven Generations of an American Family* (New York: Oxford University Press, 1990), 117.
34. Nathanael Greene to Colonel Jeremiah Wadsworth, April 14, 1779, in *Greene Papers*, 3:405.
35. John Adams' diary, September 3, 1774, in Livingston, *Nancy Shippen*, 57.
36. Alice Shippen to Nancy Shippen, September 22, 1777, in ibid., 40–41.
37. William Shippen Jr. to Nancy Shippen, February 9, 1778, in ibid., 62.
38. Alice Shippen to Nancy Shippen, November 8, 1777, in ibid., 41.
39. Livingston, *Nancy Shippen*, 72.
40. Ibid., 117.
41. Pierre Regnier de Roussi to George Washington, March 24, 1778, in Boyle, *Writings from the Valley Forge Encampment*, 4:97.
42. Livingston, *Nancy Shippen*, 146.
43. William Shippen Jr. to Mrs. Henry B. Livingston, July 25, 1781, in ibid., 120.
44. Livingston, *Nancy Shippen*, 179.
45. Ibid., 249.
46. Nagel, *Lees of Virginia*, 155.
47. Alice Shippen to Nancy Shippen, September 22, 1777, in Livingston, *Nancy Shippen*, 40.
48. Ibid., 250.
49. Nagel, *Lees of Virginia*, 156.

CHAPTER 6: THE WOMEN WITH WASHINGTON'S "FAMILY"

1. Martha Bland, a friend of Martha Washington's, wrote from the Morristown encampment that the general's aides were "all polite sociable gentlemen who make the day pass with a great deal of satisfaction to the Visitors." Robert Hanson Harrison, who served as Washington's military secretary at Valley Forge, was described by Mrs. Bland as a "worthy man." Both Harrison and Alexander Hamilton ("a sensible Genteel polite young fellow a West Indian") participated in formal negotiations for an exchange of prisoners with the British

during the Valley Forge period. As did the other aides, Hamilton worked exceedingly hard and had little time for recreation; one officer observed at Valley Forge, "He looks like Death!!!" Arthur S. Lefkowitz, *George Washington's Indispensable Men: The 32 Aides-de-Camp Who Helped Win American Independence* (Mechanicsburg, PA: Stackpole Books, 2003), 145.

Washington also depended on, among others, John Laurens, described by Mrs. Bland as a gentleman of "wealth, education, polished manners, and European travels." (All observations by Mrs. Bland about Washington's military family are from Bland, "Life in Morristown in 1777," 152.)

See chapter 2 of this book for Martha Bland's comments on Captain Gibbs and Col. Tench Tilghman, two other gentlemen who served in Washington's military family at Valley Forge.

2. George Washington to Clement Biddle, July 28, 1784, *Writings of George Washington, Washington Papers,* LOC, http://memory.loc.gov/cgi-bin/query/r?ammem/mgw:@field(DOCID+@lit(gw270472)).
3. Lefkowitz, *George Washington's Indispensable Men,* 134.
4. Ibid., 145.
5. Martha Washington to Mercy Otis Warren, March 7, 1778, in *Worthy Partner,* 178.
6. George Washington to Col. James Clinton, June 28, 1776, in *Papers of George Washington, Revolutionary War Series,* 5:132.
7. Washington to Biddle, July 28, 1784.
8. John F. Watson, *The Annals of Philadelphia* (Philadelphia: E. L. Carey and A. Hart, 1830), 552–53.
9. Caleb Gibbs and Mary Smith, 1776–80, Revolutionary War Household Expenses, Image 25, Series 5: Financial Papers, *Washington Papers,* LOC, http://memory.loc.gov/cgi-bin/ampage?collId=mgw5&fileName=gwpage028.db&recNum=124.
10. Ibid., Image 112.
11. Watson, *Annals of Philadelphia,* 552–53.
12. Israel Trask, "Revolutionary War Pension and Bounty-Lane Warrant Application Files," Massachusetts, Publication # M804. S. 30171, NARA. See http://www.footnote.com/image/19356582/Revolutionary%7cIsrael%20Trask%7cWar%7crevolutionaries%7cwars/#19356568.
13. Margaret Thomas to Caleb Gibbs, April 4, 1778, Revolutionary War Accounts, Vouchers, and Receipted Accounts 1, 1776–1780, Image 235, Series 5: Financial Papers, *Washington Papers,* LOC, http://memory.loc.gov/cgi-bin/ampage?collId=mgw5&fileName=gwpage029.db&recNum=234.
14. Washington to Biddle, July 28, 1784.
15. Washington to Clinton, June 28, 1776.
16. Col. James Clinton to George Washington, July 4, 1776, in *Papers of George Washington, Revolutionary War Series,* 5:197.
17. George Washington to Caleb Gibbs, May 1, 1777, in ibid., 8:321.
18. Katherine B. Menz, *Washington's Headquarters, Valley Forge National Historical Park* (Harpers Ferry, WV: Harpers Ferry Center, National Park Service, 1988), 27–28.
19. Revolutionary War Household Expenses, 1776–1780, Image 74, Series 5:

Financial Papers, *Washington Papers*, LOC, http://memory.loc.gov/cgi-bin/am page?collId=mgw5&fileName=gwpage028.db&recNum=73.

20. Elizabeth Thompson to George Washington, October 10, 1783, Image 374, Series 4: General Correspondence, September 2–December 28, 1783, *Washington Papers*, LOC, http://memory.loc.gov/cgi-bin/ampage?collId=mgw4&file Name=gwpage093.db&recNum=373&tempFile=./temp/~ammem_Ej6w &filecode=mgw&next_filecode=mgw&itemnum=1&ndocs=100.

21. George Washington to Daniel Parker, September 18, 1783, *Writings of George Washington*, *Washington Papers*, LOC, http://memory.loc.gov/cgi-bin/query/ r?ammem/mgw:@field(DOCID+@lit(gw270176)).

22. Thompson to Washington, October 10, 1783.

23. Elizabeth Thompson to George Washington, December 3, 1783, Revolutionary War Accounts, Vouchers, and Receipted Accounts 2, 1775–1783, Image 427, Series 5: Financial Papers, *Washington Papers*, LOC, http://memory.loc.gov/cgi-bin/ampage?collId=mgw5&fileName=gwpage024.db&recNum=426.

24. Elizabeth Thompson to Congress, February 17, 1785, in *Papers of George Washington, Revolutionary War Series*, 5:132.

25. George Washington to Alexander Spotswood, April 30, 1777, *Writings of George Washington*, *Washington Papers*, LOC, http://memory.loc.gov/cgi-bin/query/ r?ammem/mgw:@field(DOCID+@lit(gw070481)).

26. "A List of Shoes Deliver'd to the Men Belonging to Major General Lord Stirlings Guard Feby 4. 1778," in Boyle, *Writings from the Valley Forge Encampment*, 6:53.

27. "The Commander in Chief's Guard," 84.

28. Ibid., 83.

CHAPTER 7: CAMP WOMEN AT VALLEY FORGE

1. Israel Angell, *Diary of Israel Angell: Commanding the Second Rhode Island Continental Regiment during the American Revolution, 1778–1781*, transcribed by Edward Field and Norman Desmarias (Providence, RI: Preston and Rounds Company, 1899), 13. Also available at http://digitalcommons.providence.edu/ cgi/viewcontent.cgi?article=1000&context=primary.

2. For the number of camp women at Valley Forge, see "Quartermaster's Dept Letters — Account of Rations Drawn by the Infantry of the Ye Standing Army," item #192, M 247, Roll 199, Letters and Papers Relative to the Quartermaster's Department, 1777–84, Papers of the Continental Congress, NARA, http://www. footnote.com/viewer.php?image=435216&query=account+of+rations+1777&w ords=accounts%7Caccount%7C1777%7Crations. This report enumerates the rations drawn by commissioned officers, noncommissioned officers, privates fit for duty, and privates unfit for duty at the Valley Forge encampment. The return has a column entitled, surprisingly, "Died, Discharged, and Deserted," and, finally, tacked on at the end, a column entitled "Woman" (*sic*). Although the return is undated, evidence shows it was drawn in late December 1777 or early January 1778. Assuming that women received a ration each, we know that about four hundred women trudged along with the baggage to Valley Forge on December 19, 1777.

3. Martin, *Private Yankee Doodle*, 197–98.

4. General Orders, Germantown, PA, August 23, 1777, *Writings of George*

Washington, Washington Papers, LOC, http://memory.loc.gov/cgi-bin/query/ r?ammem/mgw:@field(DOCID+@lit(gw090125)).

5. Blumenthal, *Women Camp Followers,* 65–66.

6. Raphael, *People's History of the American Revolution,* 157.

7. Martin, *Private Yankee Doodle,* 132–33.

8. Henry Steele Commanger and Robert B. Morris, eds., *The Spirit of 'Seventy-Six: The Story of the American Revolution as Told by Participants* (Indianapolis: Bobbs Merrill, 1958), 1:152.

9. Ibid., 153–54.

10. Samuel Hay to Col. William Irvine, Camp White Marsh, November 11, 1777, Drape Manuscripts, Series AA, Irvine Papers, Historical Society of Pennsylvania, Philadelphia.

11. Harry Emerson Wildes, *Valley Forge* (New York: Macmillan Co., 1938), 232. Also see Trussell, *Birthplace of an Army,* 84–85. See also Muster Roll, Valley Forge National Historical Park, http://valleyforgemusterroll.org/.

12. E. B. Hillard, *The Last Men of the Revolution* (Hartford, CT: N. A. and R. A. Moore, 1864). Also available at http://www.americanrevolution.org/lastmen. html.

13. Maria Cronkite, deposition, Greene County, NY, May 17, 1839, Pension #W16932. Pub. #M804, Revolutionary War Pension and Bounty Land Warrant Application Files, New York, NARA, http://www.footnote.com/search.php?q uery%5B0%5D=Cronkite&query%5B1%5D=maria.

14. Herbert T. Wade and Robert A. Lively, *This Glorious Cause: The Adventures of Two Company Officers in Washington's Army* (Princeton, NJ: Princeton University, 1958), 235.

15. John Blair Linn and William H. Egle, eds., *Pennsylvania in the War of the Revolution, Battalions and Line: 1775–1783* (Harrisburg: L. S. Hart, 1880), 2:465.

16. Regimental Orders, Fredricksburg, VA, 1778, *Journal of the First Continental Regiment of Foot,* no. 4 (October–November 1990): 8, in Holly A. Mayer, *Belonging to the Army: Camp Followers and Community during the American Revolution* (Columbia: University of South Carolina Press, 1996), 141.

17. Janet Dempsey, *Washington's Last Cantonment: "High Time for a Peace"* (Monroe, NY: Library Research Associates, 1987), 113.

18. Blumenthal, *Women Camp Followers,* 63.

19. General Orders, Valley Forge, May 14, 1778, *Writings of George Washington, Washington Papers,* LOC, http://memory.loc.gov/cgi-bin/query/r?ammem/ mgw:@field(DOCID+@lit(gw110379)). See also General Orders, Brunswick, NJ, July 2, 1778, ibid., http://memory.loc.gov/cgi-bin/query/r?ammem/mgw:@ field(DOCID+@lit(gw120177)). Orders were also given for the soldiers to wash their own linen. September 28, 1780: "Should the day Cleare up, the soldiers will wash their linen in ye Creek . . . as this may be the most favorable opportunity that ye will Present for two or three days to come." Linn and Egle, *Pennsylvania in the War of the Revolution,* 2:599.

20. William Shainline Middleton, "Medicine at Valley Forge," *The Picket Post: A Record of Patriotism* 38:77 (July 1962): 24. October 14, 1777: "Orders were received for the collection of clothing for the soldiers in the army. . . . We made several collections of blankets for the destitute soldiers, also shoes, stockings,

and breeches for the convalescents in the Hospital, many of whom had come here attired in rags swarming with vermin, while others during their stay had been deprived of their all by their comrades." John W. Jordan, "Bethlehem during the Revolution," *The Pennsylvania Magazine of History and Biography* 13 (1889): 75.

21. Jedediah Huntington to Jabez Huntington, January 16, 1778, in Boyle, *Writings from the Valley Forge Encampment*, 4:33.

22. Enoch Poor to Meshech Weare, March 4, 1778, in ibid., 2:68.

23. Elias Boudinot to Elisha Boudinot, March 15, 1778, in ibid., 2:79.

24. Thacher, *Military Journal of the American Revolution*, 257.

25. George Washington to John Stark, August 5, 1778, *Writings of George Washington, Washington Papers*, LOC, http://memory.loc.gov/cgi-bin/query/r?ammem/mgw:@field(DOCID+@lit(gw120314)).

26. George Washington to Continental Congress, September 14, 1776, *Writings of George Washington, Washington Papers*, LOC, http://memory.loc.gov/cgi-bin/query/r?ammem/mgw:@field(DOCID+@lit(gw060057)).

27. Linda K. Kerber, *Women of the Republic: Intellect and Ideology in Revolutionary America* (Chapel Hill: University of North Carolina Press, 1980), 59

28. Edward C. Papenfuse, *The Pursuit of Profit: The Annapolis Merchants in the Era of the American Revolution, 1763–1805* (Baltimore: Johns Hopkins Press, 1975), 85.

29. Middleton, "Medicine at Valley Forge," 23.

30. Commager and Morris, *Spirit of 'Seventy-Six*, 1:647.

31. "A List of the Soldiers in the Court House Hospital at Reading November 17, 1777"; "A List of the Soldiers in the Brick House Hospital at Reading November 17, 1777"; "A List of the Sick in the Potters Shop at Reading," John F. Reed Collection, Horace Willcox Memorial Library, Valley Forge National Historical Park.

32. Middleton, "Medicine at Valley Forge," 25.

33. Elijah Fisher's Journal, 1775–1784, ibid., 7.

34. John W. Jordan, ed., "Extracts from the Journals of Rev. James Sprout, Hospital Chaplain of the Middle Department, 1778," *The Pennsylvania Magazine of History and Biography* 27 (October 1903): 442.

35. Middleton, "Medicine at Valley Forge," 15.

36. James McHenry to Barnabas Binney, May 21, 1778, in Boyle, *Writings from the Valley Forge Encampment*, 4:152.

37. General Orders, Valley Forge, May 31, 1778, *Writings of George Washington, Washington Papers*, LOC, http://memory.loc.gov/cgi-bin/query/r?ammem/mgw:@field(DOCID+@lit(gw110484)).

38. Stoudt, *Ordeal at Valley Forge*, 237.

39. Trussell, *Birthplace of an Army*, 84. Trussell states the poem was written by a regimental surgeon (perhaps Albigence Waldo) on April 26, 1778, at Valley Forge.

40. George Washington to John A. Washington, March 31, 1776, *Writings of George Washington, Washington Papers*, LOC, http://memory.loc.gov/cgi-bin/query/r?ammem/mgw:@field(DOCID+@lit(gw040371)).

41. Boudinot, *Journal or Historical Recollections*, 77–78. The incident, however, may

be in question, as Douglas Southall Freeman writes that Boudinot "wrote late and included some incidents that are rendered dubious by the tests of internal evidence." Freeman, *George Washington*, 4:624.

42. General Orders, Valley Forge, June 6, 1778, *Writings of George Washington, Washington Papers*, LOC, http://memory.loc.gov/cgi-bin/query/r?ammem/ mgw:@field(DOCID+@lit(gw120035)).

43. Weedon, *Valley Forge Orderly Book*, 215–16.

44. Ibid., 215.

45. Ibid., 216.

46. Joseph Lee Boyle, "From Saratoga to Valley Forge: The Diary of Lt. Samuel Armstrong," *The Pennsylvania Magazine of History and Biography* 121:3 (July 1997): 262.

47. Mordecai Gist, Runaway Advertisement, in John U. Rees, " . . . The Number of Rations Issued to Women in the Camp: New Material Concerning Female Followers with Continental Regiments," *The Brigade Dispatch: Journal of the Brigade of the American Revolution* 28:1 (Spring 1998): 4.

48. Martin, *Private Yankee Doodle*, 103.

49. Ibid., 197.

CHAPTER 8: CAMP WOMEN WITH THE CONTINENTAL ARMY

1. Bland, "Life in Morristown in 1777," 150–53.

2. Sarah Osborn Benjamin Revolutionary War Pension and Bounty-Land Warrant Application File, Publication #M804, W 4558, NARA, http://www.footnote. com/image/25753131/Pension%7cRevolutionary%7csarahs%7cosborn%7cWa r%7crevolutionaries%7cwars%7cpensions%7csarah/#25753137.

3. John U. Rees, " . . . The Multitude of Women: An Examination of the Numbers of Female Camp Followers with the Continental Army," *The Brigade Dispatch: Journal of the Brigade of the American Revolution* 23:4 (Fall 1992): 6.

4. Mayer, *Belonging to the Army*, 1.

5. General Orders, Roxboro, PA, August 4, 1777, *Writings of George Washington, Washington Papers*, LOC, http://memory.loc.gov/cgi-bin/query/r?ammem/ mgw:@field(DOCID+@lit(gw090027)).

6. General Orders, Wilmington, DE, August 27, 1777, *Writings of George Washington, Washington Papers*, LOC, http://memory.loc.gov/cgi-bin/query/ r?ammem/mgw:@field(DOCID+@lit(gw090141)).

7. Information on the number of women with the Continental Army, British Army, and Hessian forces is from John U. Rees's excellent articles: " . . . The Multitude of Women," Fall 1992; " . . . The Multitude of Women," *The Brigade Dispatch* 24:1 (Winter 1993) and 24:2 (Spring 1993).

8. Rees, " . . . The Multitude of Women," Spring 1993, 3–4.

9. This figure is an estimate. Because of lost records, inaccuracies, multiple enlistments, and military practices of the time, among other things, it is impossible to give an accurate, unduplicated count of the number of soldiers with the Continental Army who fought in the American Revolution. Boatner, for example, in *Encyclopedia of the American Revolution*, writes that 231,771 Continental Army soldiers (and 145,000 militia) fought in the war and the total "should be reduced to not more than 250,000 in view of multiple enlistments"

(p. 264). Gordan S. Wood in *The American Revolution: A History* (New York: Modern Library, 2002) states, "Perhaps as many as 200,000 men bore arms at one time or another in the Continental Army and state militias" (p. 115). Henry Knox's return of May 10, 1780, lists 46,891 "Men in Continental Pay" in 1776. (Cornelius C. Vermuele, "Numbers of Soldiers in the Revolution," *Proceedings of the New Jersey Historical Society* 7:3 (July 1922): 224.)

10. Robert Kirkwood, *The Journal and Order Book of Captain Robert Kirkwood of the Delaware Regiment of the Continental Line*, ed. Joseph Brown Turner (Wilmington: Historical Society of Delaware, 1910), 94, 105.

11. General Orders, Morristown, July 4, 1777, *Writings of George Washington*, Washington Papers, LOC, http://memory.loc.gov/cgi-bin/query/r?ammem/mgw:@field(DOCID+@lit(gw080299)).

12. General Orders, Wilmington, August 27, 1777, *Writings of George Washington*, Washington Papers, LOC, http://memory.loc.gov/cgi-bin/query/r?ammem/mgw:@field(DOCID+@lit(gw090141)).

13. General Orders, Valley Forge, May 31, 1778, *Writings of George Washington*, Washington Papers, LOC, http://memory.loc.gov/cgi-bin/query/r?ammem/mgw:@field(DOCID+@lit(gw110484)).

14. General Orders, near Valley Forge, June 19, 1778, *Writings of George Washington*, Washington Papers, LOC, http://memory.loc.gov/cgi-bin/query/r?ammem/mgw:@field(DOCID+@lit(gw120115)).

15. General Orders, Smith's Tavern, June 7, 1779, *Writings of George Washington*, Washington Papers, LOC, http://memory.loc.gov/cgi-bin/query/r?ammem/mgw:@field(DOCID+@lit(gw150239)).

16. General Orders, Steenrapia, September 19, 1780, *Writings of George Washington*, Washington Papers, LOC, http://memory.loc.gov/cgi-bin/query/r?ammem/mgw:@field(DOCID+@lit(gw200085)).

17. General Orders, Morristown, July 10, 1777, *Writings of George Washington*, Washington Papers, LOC, http://memory.loc.gov/cgi-bin/query/r?ammem/mgw:@field(DOCID+@lit(gw080324)).

18. General Orders, Ramapough, July 23, 1777, *Writings of George Washington*, Washington Papers, LOC, http://memory.loc.gov/cgi-bin/query/r?ammem/mgw:@field(DOCID+@lit(gw080393)).

19. General Orders, near Germantown, September 13, 1777, *Writings of George Washington*, Washington Papers, LOC, http://memory.loc.gov/cgi-bin/query/r?ammem/mgw:@field(DOCID+@lit(gw090216)).

20. General Orders, Smith's Tavern, June 7, 1779.

21. Kirkwood, *Journal and Order Book of Captain Robert Kirkwood*, 86.

22. Jordan, "Bethlehem during the Revolution," 74.

23. John W. Jordan, "Nazareth, Pennsylvania, during the Revolution, 1775–1779," *The Pennsylvania Magazine of History and Biography* 38 (1914): 307.

24. General Orders, King's Ferry, August 22, 1781, *Writings of George Washington*, Washington Papers, LOC, http://memory.loc.gov/cgi-bin/query/r?ammem/mgw:@field(DOCID+@lit(gw230043)).

25. Rees, " . . . The Multitude of Women," Winter 1993, 7.

26. Rees, " . . . The Multitude of Women," Fall 1992, 15.

27. See John U. Rees's articles titled " . . . The Number of Rations Issued to Women in the Camp," 4–8.

28. Mayer, *Belonging to the Army*, 223.

29. General Orders, Valley Forge, April 16, 1778, *Writings of George Washington, Washington Papers*, LOC, http://memory.loc.gov/cgi-bin/query/r?ammem/mgw:@field(DOCID+@lit(gw110264)).

30. Martin, *Private Yankee Doodle*, 103.

31. Rankin, *Narratives of the American Revolution*, 185–86.

32. Johann de Kalb to the Comte de Broglie, December 25, 1777, in Boyle, *Writings from the Valley Forge Encampment*, 4:8.

33. John W. Jackson, *With the British Army in Philadelphia, 1777–1778* (San Raphael, CA: Presidio Press, 1979), 92.

34. General Orders, Newburgh, December 28, 1782, *Writings of George Washington, Washington Papers*, LOC, http://memory.loc.gov/cgi-bin/query/r?ammem/mgw:@field(DOCID+@lit(gw250555)).

35. George Washington to Robert Morris, January 29, 1783, Image 25, Series 3h: Varick Transcripts, *Washington Papers*, LOC, http://memory.loc.gov/cgi-bin/ampage?collId=mgw3&fileName=mgw3h/gwpage003.db&recNum=36&tempFile=./temp/~ammem_U3nQ&filecode=mgw&next_filecode=mgw&prev_filecode=mgw&itemnum=3&ndocs=11. For examples of military wages, consider these examples from the Valley Forge encampment: "We now have Six Months wages due to us" (Archeleus Lewis to Jesse Partridge, February 1, 1778, in Boyle, *Writings from the Valley Forge Encampment*, 1:40); "I have received November's Pay [in February] & paid the Officers & Men" (George Fleming to Sebastian Bauman, February 12, 1778, in ibid., 52); "Our regiment has never received but two months pay for twelve months past" (John Brooks to Unidentified, January 5, 1778, in ibid., 17).

36. Kirkwood, *Journal and Order Book of Captain Robert Kirkwood*, 147.

37. On January 2, 1778, John Buss wrote his father one of the few surviving letters from an enlisted soldier at Valley Forge. The men, he wrote, "were building huts very fast," four inches of snow arrived on December 28, and the provisions at camp were "much Short." Private Buss closed with this charming ditty: "My ink is poor/My pen is bad/If you can read this/I shall be glad." John Buss to Stephen Buss, January 2, 1778, in Boyle, *Writings from the Valley Forge Encampment*, 3:23–24.

38. Jacob Nagle, *The Nagle Journal: A Diary of the Life of Jacob Nagle, Sailor, from the Year 1775 to 1841*, ed. John C. Dann (New York: Weidenfeld & Nicolson, 1988), 7, in Mayer, *Belonging to the Army*, 140.

39. Thomas Anburey, *Travels through the Interior Parts of America* (New York: New York Times, 1969), 1:258.

40. John U. Rees, "The Proportion of Women which ought to be allowed . . . : An Overview of Continental Army Female Camp Followers," *The Continental Soldier (Journal of the Continental Line)* 8:3 (Spring 1995): 9, http://www.revwar75.com/library/rees/proportion.htm.

41. Blumenthal, *Women Camp Followers*, 85.

42. Anburey, *Travels Through the Interior Parts of America*, 2:24–25.

43. "Proceedings of July 25, 1780," *Journals of the Continental Congress* 17, image 664, in Law Library of Congress, *A Century of Lawmaking for a New Nation: U.S. Congressional Documents and Debates, 1774–1875*, http://memory.loc.gov/

cgi-bin/ampage?collId=lljc&fileName=017/lljc017.db&recNum=251&itemLin
k=?%230170252&linkText=1.

44. Alfred F. Young, *Masquerade: The Life and Times of Deborah Sampson, Continental Soldier* (New York: Vintage Books, 2004), 80.

45. Herman Mann, *The Female Review: Life of Deborah Sampson, the Female Soldier in the War of Revolution* (1866; reprint, North Stratford, NH: Ayer, 2000), xxix.

46. Young, *Masquerade*, 151.

47. Ibid., 228.

48. "Proceedings, November 28, 1797," *Journals of the House of Representatives of the United States, 1797–1801* 3, image 90, in Law Library of Congress, *Century of Lawmaking for a New Nation*, http://memory.loc.gov/cgi-bin/ampage?collId=llh j&fileName=003/llhj003.db&recNum=87&itemLink=D%3Fhlaw%3A2%3A.%2 Ftemp%2F%7Eammem_ZHNh%3A%3A%230030076&linkText=1.

49. "Proceedings, July 7, 1838, H. R. 184," *Journal of the House of Representatives of the United States* 32, image 1287, in Law Library of Congress, *Century of Lawmaking for a New Nation*, http://memory.loc.gov/cgi-bin/ampage?collId=llhj&fileName =032/llhj032.db&recNum=1286&itemLink=D?hlaw:19:./temp/~ammem_Qmq m::%230321302&linkText=1.

50. Mann, *Female Review*, xxii.

51. Ibid., 229.

52. Young, *Masquerade*, 210.

53. Sandra Gioia Treadway, "Anna Maria Lane: An Uncommon Soldier of the American Revolution," *Virginia Cavalcade* 37:3 (Winter 1988), 134.

CHAPTER 9: THE GENERAL RETURNS TO VALLEY FORGE

1. Henry Woodman, *History of Valley Forge* (Oaks, PA: J. U. Francis Sr., 1922), 126–27. Woodman writes that he is retelling the encounter between his father and George Washington at Valley Forge in late summer, 1796. Although there is no record of Washington revisiting Valley Forge at that time, Washington did record in his diary that he fished in the Valley Forge area on July 30, 1787. Washington also visited the Valley Forge encampment area on July 31, 1787, for on that day he wrote, "Before breakfast I rid [sic] to the Valley Forge and over the whole Cantonment & works of the American Army in the Winter of 1777–8." See George Washington, *The Diaries of George Washington*, ed. Donald Jackson and Dorothy Twohig (Charlottesville: University Press of Virginia, 1979), 5:178–79, 243.

2. George Washington to John Banister, April 21, 1778, *Writings of George Washington, Washington Papers*, LOC, http://memory.loc.gov/cgi-bin/query/ r?ammem/mgw:@field(DOCID+@lit(gw110283)). Washington's words to Banister: "To see men, without clothes to cover their nakedness, without blankets to lie on, without shoes (for the want of which their marches might be traced by the blood from their feet) and almost as often without provisions as with them, marching through the frost and snow, and, at Christmas taking up their winter-quarters within a day's march of the enemy, without a house or hut to cover them; and submitting without a murmur, is a proof of patience and obedience which in my opinion can scarce be paralleled."

3. George Washington to Continental Congress, December 23, 1777, *Writings of*

George Washington, Washington Papers, LOC, http://memory.loc.gov/cgi-bin/query/r?ammem/mgw:@field(DOCID+@lit(gw100200)).

4. Martha Washington to Hannah Stockton Boudinot, January 15, 1784, in *Worthy Partner,* 193.

Appendix: Making the Myth of Martha Washington

1. Mercy Otis Warren, *History of the Rise, Progress, and Termination of the American Revolution: Interspersed with Biographical, Political, and Moral Observations* (Indianapolis: Liberty Classics, 1988), 1:211.

2. Ibid., 2:638.

3. David Humphreys, *Life of General Washington: With George Washington's "Remarks,"* ed. Rosemarie Zagarri (Athens: University of Georgia Press, 1991), 24.

4. John Marshall, *The Life of George Washington* (Fredericksburg, VA: Citizens' Guild of Washington's Boyhood Home, 1926), 2:52.

5. DuPonceau, "Harvest Home Oration," 2.

6. Bland, "Letter from Morristown 1777," 152.

7. Sherman, *Historic Morristown, New Jersey,* 366.

8. Elizabeth Schuyler's impressions of Mrs. Washington at Morristown: "She received [my aunt and me] so kindly, kissing us both, for the general and papa were very warm friends. She was then nearly fifty years old, but was still handsome. She was quite short; a plump little woman with dark brown eyes, her hair a little frosty, and very plainly dressed for such a grand lady as I considered her. She wore a plain, brown gown of homespun stuff, a large white handkerchief, a neat cap, and her plain gold wedding ring, which she had worn for more than twenty years. She was always my ideal of a true woman." Hugh Howard, *Houses of the Founding Fathers* (New York: Artisan, 2007), 147.

9. Chastellux, *Travels in North America,* 1:298.

10. Julian Ursyn Niemcewicz, *Under Their Vine and Fig Tree: Travels through America in 1797–1799, 1805, with Some Further Account of Life in New Jersey,* trans. and ed. Metchie J. E. Budka (Elizabeth, NJ: Grassmann Publishing Co., 1965), 102.

11. Mason L. Weems, *The Life of Washington,* ed. Marcus Cunliffe (Cambridge, MA: Belknap Press, 1962), 53.

12. Sparks, *Life of George Washington,* 96.

13. James Herring and James B. Longacre, *The National Portrait Gallery of Distinguished Americans* (New York: Monson Bancroft, 1834), vol. 1.

14. George Washington Parke Custis, "The Birth-Date of Washington," *The Daily National Intelligencer,* February 22, 1847.

15. October 3, 1797, entry, in *The Diaries of George Washington, Vol. 6, January 1790–December 1799,* ed. Donald Jackson and Dorothy Twohig, Image 280, *Washington Papers,* LOC, http://memory.loc.gov/cgi-bin/ampage?collId=mgwd&fileName=mgwd/gwpagewd06.db&recNum=279&itemLink=P?mgw:1:./temp/~ammem_I0DX::%23wd060280&linkText=1.

16. George Washington, *The Papers of George Washington, Retirement Series,* ed. Dorothy Twohig (Charlottesville: University Press of Virginia, 1999), 3:339.

17. George Washington Parke Custis to John Pickett, April 17, 1857, Collection

of the Mount Vernon Ladies Association of the Union, *The George Washington Papers: Provenance and Publication History*, LOC, http://memory.loc.gov/ammem/gwhtml/gwabout.html.

18. Franklin Steiner, "George Washington, the Vestryman Who Was Not a Communicant," in *The Religious Beliefs of our Presidents: From Washington to F. D. R.* (Amherst, NY: Prometheus Books, 1995).

19. David M. Matteson, "The Fredericksburg Peace Ball," *The Virginia Magazine of History and Biography* 49 (1941): 152–56, in *The Rappahannock Gazette* 3:1 (January–February 2000): 4, http://www.rchsinc.org/newsletter/2000.001.pdf.

20. Nagel, *Lees of Virginia*, 235.

21. Weems, *The Life of Washington*, xvii.

22. Ellet, *Women of the American Revolution*, 1:xi.

23. Linda K. Kerber, "History Will Do It No Justice: Women's Lives in Revolutionary America" (lecture, University of Iowa, 1987), 12, http://sdrc.lib.uiowa/preslectures/kerber87/index.html.

24. Michael J. Kiskis, review of *Constructing American Lives: Biography and Culture in Nineteenth-Century America* by Scott E. Caspar (Chapel Hill: University of North Carolina, 1999), 5, http://facstaff.uww.edu/hoganj/Kiskis162.html.

25. Drew Gilpin Faust, *Mothers of Invention: Women of the Slaveholding South in the American Civil War* (New York: Vintage Books, 1997), 160.

26. Michael A. Capps and Steven A. Davis, *Moores Creek National Battlefield: An Administrative History* (Atlanta, GA: Cultural Resources Stewardship, Southeast Regional Office, National Park Service, 1999).

27. "Story of Emily Geiger's Ride Refuted," *South Carolina Historical and Genealogical Magazine* 1:1 (January 1900): 91.

28. Griffiths, *Major General Henry Knox*, 90.

29. Ellet, *Women of the American Revolution*, 2:13.

30. Herring and Longacre, *National Portrait Gallery of Distinguished Americans*, vol.1.

31. Ellet, *Women of the American Revolution*, 2:13.

32. Warren, *History of the Rise, Progress, and Termination*, 2:638.

33. Ellet, *Women of the American Revolution*, 2:13.

34. Ibid., 2:13. See Ellet's footnote.

35. Thacher, *Military Journal of the American Revolution* (1862), 192. See also Thacher, *Military Journal of the American Revolution* (1998), 160–61.

36. Thacher, *Military Journal of the American Revolution* (1862), 507.

37. Martha Washington to Mr. Devenport, November 5, 1775, in *Worthy Partner*, 163.

38. Anonymous to Martha Washington, February 2, 1792, in *Worthy Partner*, 235.

39. Sister St. Mary to Martha Washington, December 18, 1796, in *Worthy Partner*, 295.

40. At least one author suggests that Mary Custis Lee, Gen. Robert E. Lee's wife, did knit for the Civil War soldiers. "Mary and her daughters began a useful project in Richmond. They joined in knitting socks for the woefully bedraggled Confederate troops. It was a task they carried out with astonishing zeal, shipping stockings in enormous numbers to [General Lee's] attention." Nagel, *Lees of Virginia*, 280.

41. Margaret C. Conkling, *Memoirs of the Mother and Wife of Washington* (Auburn, NY: Derby, Miller and Co., 1850), 149.

42. Ibid., 153–54.

43. Lewis L. Gould, *American First Ladies: Their Lives and Their Legacy* (New York: Routledge, 2001), 10.

44. Nathaniel Hervey, *The Memory of Washington: With Biographical Sketches of His Mother and Wife* (Boston: J. Munroe, 1852), 41.

45. Washington, *Worthy Partner*, 478.

46. Gould, *American First Ladies*, 10.

47. Benson J. Lossing, *The Home of Washington: Or, Mount Vernon and Its Associations, Historical, Biographical, and Pictorial* (Hartford, CT: A. S. Hale & Co., 1870), 114.

48. Custis, *Recollections and Private Memoirs*, 403.

49. Benson J. Lossing, *Martha Washington* (New York: J. C. Buttre, 1865), 18–19.

50. Lossing, *Mary and Martha*, 168–71.

51. Ibid., 165.

52. Ibid., 171.

53. Ibid., 165.

54. Ibid., 171–72.

55. Editorial note in George Washington to George William Fairfax, June 30, 1785, Writings of George Washington, *Washington Papers*, LOC, http://memory.loc.gov/cgi-bin/query/r?ammem/mgw:@field(DOCID+@lit(gw280139)).

56. Lossing, *Mary and Martha*, 160.

57. Ibid., 185.

58. Ibid., 220.

59. Martha Washington to Mercy Otis Warren, March 7, 1778, in *Worthy Partner*, 178.

60. For examples, see Martha Washington to Anna Maria Bassett, January 7, 1776, in ibid., 167 ("A few days a goe [sic] Gen. Clinton, with several companies Sailed out of Boston harbor to what place for, we cannot find out"); see also Washington to Warren, March 7, 1778, 177 ("It has given me unspeakable pleasure to hear that Genl Burgoyne and his army air [sic] in safe quarters in your state"); see also Martha Washington to John Parke and Eleanor Custis March 19, 1779 in *Worthy Partner*, 181 ("It is from the south ward that we expect to hear news, —we are very anxious to know how our affairs are going in that quarters [sic]").

61. DuPonceau, "Harvest Home Oration," 2.

62. Hillard, *Last Men of the Revolution*.

63. John D. Born Jr., review of *The Last Men of the Revolution* by E. B. Hillard, *Military Affairs* 32:4 (February 1969): 209.

Bibliography

Anburey, Thomas. *Travels through the Interior Parts of America*. 2 vols. New York: New York Times, 1969.

Angell, Israel. *Diary of Israel Angell: Commanding the Second Rhode Island Continental Regiment during the American Revolution, 1778–1781*. Transcribed by Edward Field and Norman Desmarais. Providence, RI: Preston and Rounds Company, 1899.

Blanchard, Claude. *The Journal of Claude Blanchard*. Edited by Thomas Balch. Albany: J. Munsell, 1876.

Bland, Martha Daingerfield. "Life in Morristown in 1777." Letter to Frances Bland Randolph, May 12, 1777. *Proceedings of the New Jersey Historical Society* 51:3 (July 1933): 150–53.

Bloomfield, Joseph. *Citizen Soldier: The Revolutionary War Journal of Joseph Bloomfield*. Edited by Mark E. Lender and James Kirby Martin. Newark: New Jersey Historical Society, 1982.

Blumenthal, Walter. *Women Camp Followers of the American Revolution*. Philadelphia: G. S. MacManus Co., 1952.

Boatner, Mark M., III. *Encyclopedia of the American Revolution*. 3rd ed. Mechanicsburg, PA: Stackpole Books, 1994.

Bodle, Wayne K., and Jacqueline Thibaut. *Valley Forge Historical Research Report*. 3 vols. Valley Forge, PA: Valley Forge National Historical Park, 1980.

Born, John D., Jr. Review of *The Last Men of the Revolution*, by E. B. Hillard. *Military Affairs* 32:4 (February 1969): 209.

Boudinot, Elias. *Journal or Historical Recollections of American Events during the Revolutionary War*. Philadelphia: F. Bourquin, 1894.

Boyle, Joseph Lee. "From Saratoga to Valley Forge: The Diary of Lt. Samuel Armstrong." *The Pennsylvania Magazine of History and Biography* 121:3 (July 1997): 237–70.

———. *Writings from the Valley Forge Encampment of the Continental Army, December 19, 1777–June 19, 1778*. 6 vols. Bowie, MD: Heritage Books, 2000–2007.

Brady, Patricia. *Martha Washington: An American Life*. New York: Viking, 2005.

Brigham, Paul. "A Revolutionary Diary of Captain Paul Brigham, November 19, 1777–September 4, 1778." Edited by Edward A. Hoyt. *Vermont History* 34:1 (January 1966): 3–30.

Brucksch, John P. *Historic Furnishings Report: Varnum's Quarters, Valley Forge National Historical Park.* Harpers Ferry, WV: Division of Historic Furnishings, Harpers Ferry National Park, 1993.

Cadwalader Papers. Historical Society of Pennsylvania, Philadelphia.

Callahan, North. *Henry Knox: General Washington's General.* N.p.: Friends of Montpelier, 1989.

Capps, Michael A., and Steven A. Davis. *Moores Creek National Battlefield: An Administrative History.* Atlanta, GA: Cultural Resources Stewardship, Southeast Regional Office, National Park Service, 1999.

Chastellux, Marquis de. *Travels in North America in the Years 1780, 1781, and 1782.* Translated by Howard C. Rice Jr. 2 vols. Chapel Hill: University of North Carolina Press, 1963.

Chaloner, John, to Robert Dodd. Undated (March 3, 1778). Mss. 17137, Series 8D, #12, container 6, Ephraim Blaine Letterbook, Roll 75, Frame 1217. Peter Force Collection. Library of Congress, Washington, DC.

"The Commander in Chief's Guard." *The Pennsylvania Magazine of History and Biography* 38 (1914): 83–88.

Commanger, Henry Steele, and Robert B. Morris, eds. *The Spirit of 'Seventy-Six: The Story of the American Revolution as Told by Participants.* Vol. 1. Indianapolis: Bobbs Merrill, 1958.

Conkling, Margaret C. *Memoirs of the Mother and Wife of Washington.* Auburn, NY: Derby, Miller and Co., 1850.

Cronkite, Maria. Deposition, Greene County, NY. May 17, 1839. Pension #W16932, Pub. #M804. Revolutionary War Pension and Bounty Land Warrant Application Files, New York. NARA, Washington, DC.

Custis, George Washington Parke. "The Birth-Date of Washington." *The Daily National Intelligencer,* February 22, 1847.

———. *Recollections and Private Memoirs of Washington.* New York: Derby & Jackson, 1860. Reprint, Bridgewater, VA: American Foundation Publications, 1999.

Currie, William. "An Account of Damages Sustained by Ye Subscriber from Ye British Army September 19, 1777." November 15, 1782. Chester County Historical Society, West Chester, PA.

Dann, John D., ed. *The Revolution Remembered: Eyewitness Accounts of the War for Independence.* Chicago: University of Chicago Press, 1980.

Dempsey, Janet. *Washington's Last Cantonment: "High Time for a Peace."* Monroe, NY: Library Research Associates, 1987.

Drape Manuscripts, Series AA. Irvine Papers. Historical Society of Pennsylvania, Philadelphia.

Drinker, Elizabeth Sandwith. *The Diary of Elizabeth Drinker.* Edited by Elaine Forman Crane. 3 vols. Boston: Northeastern University Press, 1991.

Duer, William Alexander. *The Life of William Alexander, Earl of Stirling, Major-General in the Army of the United States during the Revolution.* Vol. 2. New York: Wiley & Putnam, 1847.

DuPonceau, Peter S. "Autobiographical Letters of Peter S. DuPonceau." *The Pennsylvania Magazine of History and Biography* 40 (1916): 172–86.

———. "Harvest Home Oration." *Republican Star and General Advertiser* 29:51 (August 19, 1828): 2.

Ellet, Elizabeth F. *Revolutionary Women in the War for American Independence: A One-Volume Revised Edition of Elizabeth Ellet's 1848 Landmark Series.* Edited by Lincoln Diamant. Westport, CT: Praeger, 1998.

————. *The Women of the American Revolution.* 2nd ed. 2 vols. New York: Baker and Scribner, 1848–50.

Evans, Elizabeth. *Weathering the Storm: Women of the American Revolution.* New York: Scribner, 1975.

Faust, Drew Gilpin. *Mothers of Invention: Women of the Slaveholding South in the American Civil War.* New York: Vintage Books, 1997.

"The First Marshal of Pennsylvania: Clement Biddle." *The First Generation of United States Marshals.* http://www.usdoj.gov/marshals/history/firstmarshals/biddle.htm.

Fish, Richard. "Master Report of Washington's Headquarters." Unpublished manuscript, Horace Willcox Memorial Library, Valley Forge National Historical Park, PA, February 9, 1976.

Fisher, Elijah. *Elijah Fisher's Journal, 1775–1784.* John F. Reed Collection, Horace Willcox Memorial Library, Valley Forge National Historical Park, PA.

Fitzpatrick, John C. "When Mrs. Washington Went to Camp." *Daughters of the American Revolution Magazine* 59:3 (March 1925): 135–47.

Flexner, James Thomas. *George Washington in the American Revolution, 1775–1783.* Boston: Little, Brown, 1968.

Forbes-Robertson, Diana. "Lady Knox." *American History* 17:3 (April 1966): 46–47, 74–79.

Freeman, Douglas Southall. *George Washington: A Biography.* 7 vols. New York: Scribner, 1948–57.

Gilder Lehrman Institute of American History, New York. http://www.gilderlehrman.org.

Greene, Nathanael. *The Papers of General Nathanael Greene.* Edited by Richard K. Showman. Vols. 1–7, 9. Chapel Hill: University of North Carolina Press, 1976, 1980, 1983, 1986, 1989, 1991, 1994, 1996.

Griffiths, Thomas Morgan. *Major General Henry Knox and the Last Heirs to Montpelier.* Monmouth, ME: Monmouth Press, 1991.

Gould, Lewis L., ed. *American First Ladies: Their Lives and Their Legacy.* New York: Routledge, 2001.

Hanna, John Smith. *A History of the Life and Services of Captain Samuel Dewees, a Native of Pennsylvania, and Soldier of the Revolutionary and Last Wars.* Baltimore: Robert Neilson, 1844.

Havard, John. "An Inventory of Ye Goods & Chattels Taken from Ye Subscriber . . . by Ye Hessians & Others of Ye British Army during Their Encampment Here upon the Eighteenth, Nineteenth and Twentieth Days of September AD 1777 upon Command of General Howe." November 18, 1782. Unpublished manuscript, Chester County Historical Society, West Chester, PA.

Herring, James, and James B. Longacre. *The National Portrait Gallery of Distinguished Americans.* Vol. 1. New York: Monson Bancroft, 1834.

Hervey, Nathaniel. *The Memory of Washington: With Biographical Sketches of His Mother and Wife.* Boston: J. Munroe, 1852.

Hillard, E. B. *The Last Men of the Revolution*. Hartford, CT: N. A. and R. A. Moore, 1864.

Hoffman, Ronald, and Peter J. Albert, eds. *Women in the Age of the American Revolution*. Charlottesville: University Press of Virginia, 1989.

Howard, Hugh. *Houses of the Founding Fathers*. New York: Artisan, 2007.

Howel, Mary. "An Estimate of Damages Sustained by the British Army under the Command of General Howe and His Army on Their March through the Great Valley Tredyffrin Township, Chester County, on the 17th of September 1777 by Me, Mary Howel." November 17, 1782. Chester County Historical Society, West Chester, PA.

Humphreys, David. *Life of George Washington: With George Washington's "Remarks."* Edited by Rosemarie Zagarri. Athens: University of Georgia Press, 1991.

Jackson, John W. *With the British Army in Philadelphia, 1777–1778*. San Raphael, CA: Presidio Press, 1979.

John F. Reed Collection. Horace Willcox Memorial Library, Valley Forge National Historical Park, PA.

Jordan, John W. "Bethlehem during the Revolution." *The Pennsylvania Magazine of History and Biography* 13 (1889): 71–89.

———, ed. "Extracts from the Journals of Rev. James Sprout, Hospital Chaplain of the Middle Department, 1778." *The Pennsylvania Magazine of History and Biography* 27 (1903): 441–45.

———. "Nazareth, Pennsylvania, during the Revolution, 1775–1779." *The Pennsylvania Magazine of History and Biography* 38 (1914): 302–10.

Journals of the Continental Congress. Library of Congress, Washington, DC. http://memory.loc.gov/ammem/collections/continental/index.html.

Journal of the House of Representatives of the United States, 1789–1793. Library of Congress, Washington, DC. http://www.memory.loc.gov/ammem/amlaw/lwhj.html.

Kapp, Friedrich. *The Life of Frederick William von Steuben: Major General in the Revolutionary Army*. New York: Mason Brothers, 1859.

———. *The Life of John Kalb: Major-General in the Revolutionary Army*. New York: H. Holt and Co., 1884.

Kerber, Linda K. "History Will Do It No Justice: Women's Lives in Revolutionary America." Lecture, University of Iowa, 1987. http://sdrc.lib.uiowa/preslectures/kerber87/index.html.

———. *Women of the Republic: Intellect and Ideology in Revolutionary America*. Chapel Hill: University of North Carolina Press, 1980.

Kirkwood, Robert. *The Journal and Order Book of Captain Robert Kirkwood of the Delaware Regiment of the Continental Line*. Edited by Joseph Brown Turner. Wilmington: Historical Society of Delaware, 1910.

Kiskis, Michael J. Review of *Constructing American Lives: Biography and Culture in Nineteenth-Century America*, by Scott E. Caspar. Chapel Hill: University of North Carolina, 1999. http://facstaff.uww.edu/hoganj/Kiskis162.html.

"Lady Washington at Bethlehem, 1779." *The Pennsylvania Magazine of History and Biography* 38 (1914): 250.

Lafayette, Marquis de. *Lafayette in the Age of the American Revolution: Selected Letters and Papers, 1776–1790.* Edited by Stanley J. Idzerda. Vol. 1. Ithaca: Cornell University Press, 1977.

Laurens, John. *The Army Correspondence of Colonel John Laurens in the Years 1777–8.* New York: New York Times, 1969.

Lefkowitz, Arthur S. *George Washington's Indispensable Men: The 32 Aides-de-camp Who Helped Win American Independence.* Mechanicsburg, PA: Stackpole Books, 2003.

Linn, John Blair, and William H. Egle, eds. *Pennsylvania in the War of the Revolution, Battalions and Line: 1775–1783.* Vol. 2. Harrisburg: L. S. Hart, 1880.

Livingston, Anne Home Shippen. *Nancy Shippen: Her Journal Book.* Edited by Ethel Armes. Philadelphia: Lippincott, 1935.

Lossing, Benson J. *The Home of Washington: Or, Mount Vernon and Its Associations, Historical, Biographical, and Pictorial.* Hartford, CT: A. S. Hale & Co., 1870.

———. *Martha Washington.* New York: J. C. Buttre, 1865.

———. *Mary and Martha: The Mother and Wife of George Washington.* New York: Harper & Brothers, 1886.

———. *The Pictorial Field-Book of the Revolution.* New York: Harper & Brothers, 1860.

Mann, Herman. *The Female Review: Life of Deborah Sampson, the Female Soldier in the War of Revolution.* 1866. Reprint, North Stratford, NH: Ayer, 2000.

Marshall, Christopher. *Extracts from the Diary of Christopher Marshall, 1774–1781.* Edited by William Duane. New York: New York Times, 1969.

Marshall, John. *The Life of George Washington.* Vol. 2. Fredericksburg, VA: Citizen's Guild of Washington's Boyhood Home, 1926.

———. *The Papers of John Marshall.* Edited by Herbert A. Johnson. Vol. 1. Chapel Hill: University of North Carolina Press, 1974.

Martin, Joseph Plumb. *Private Yankee Doodle: Being a Narrative of Some of the Adventures, Dangers and Sufferings of a Revolutionary Soldier.* Edited by George E. Scheer. Fort Washington, PA: Eastern National, 1998.

Matteson, David M. "The Fredericksburg Peace Ball." *The Virginia Magazine of History and Biography* 49 (1941): 152–56. In *The Rappahannock Gazette* 3:1 (January–February 2000). http://www.rchsinc.org/Newsletter/2000.001.pdf.

Mayer, Holly A. *Belonging to the Army: Camp Followers and Community during the American Revolution.* Columbia: University of South Carolina Press, 1996.

Menz, Katherine B. *Washington's Headquarters, Valley Forge National Historical Park.* Harpers Ferry, WV: Harpers Ferry Center, National Park Service, 1988.

Middleton, William Shainline. "Medicine at Valley Forge." *The Picket Post: A Record of Patriotism* 38:77 (July 1962): 15–26.

Monahan, Clifford P., and Clarkson A. Collins, eds. "Nathanael Greene's Letters to 'Friend Sammy' Ward." *Rhode Island History* 17:1 (January 1958): 14–21.

Moore, Frank, comp. *The Diary of the American Revolution, 1775–1781.* Abridged and edited by John Anthony Scott. New York: Washington Square Press, 1967.

———. *The Diary of the Revolution.* Hartford, CT: J. B. Burr, 1875.

Muster Roll. Valley Forge National Historical Park. http://valleyforgemuster roll.org/.

Nagel, Paul C. *The Lees of Virginia: Seven Generations of an American Family.* New York: Oxford University Press, 1990.

Niemcewicz, Julian Ursyn. *Under Their Vine and Fig Tree: Travels through America in 1797–1799, 1805, with Some Further Account of Life in New Jersey.* Translated and edited by Metchie J. E. Budka. Elizabeth, NJ: Grassmann Publishing Co., 1965.

Nelson, Paul David. *William Alexander, Lord Stirling.* University: University of Alabama Press, 1987.

Papenfuse, Edward C. *The Pursuit of Profit: The Annapolis Merchants in the Era of the American Revolution, 1763–1805.* Baltimore: Johns Hopkins Press, 1975.

Papers of the Continental Congress. NARA, Washington, DC.

Peale, Charles Willson. *The Selected Papers of Charles Willson Peale and His Family.* Edited by Lillian B. Miller. Vol. 1. New Haven, CT: Yale University Press, 1983.

Phillips, Martha Littlefield. "Recollections of Washington and His Friends." *Century Magazine* 55 (January 1898): 363–74.

"Quartermaster's Dept Letters—Account of Rations Drawn by the Infantry of the Ye Standing Army." Item #192, M 247, Roll 199. Letters and Papers relative to the Quartermaster's Department, 1777–84. Papers of the Continental Congress. National Archives.

Rankin, Hugh F., ed. *Narratives of the American Revolution as Told by a Young Sailor, a Home-Sick Surgeon, a French Volunteer, and a German General's Wife.* Chicago: Lakeside Press, 1976.

Raphael, Ray. *A People's History of the American Revolution: How Common People Shaped the Fight for Independence.* New York: Perennial, 2002.

Reed, John F. "The British at Valley Forge and Norriton." *The Bulletin of the Historical Society of Montgomery County* 22:1 (Fall 1979): 68–86.

———. "Clement Biddle at Moore Hall." *The Bulletin of the Historical Society of Montgomery County* 22:3 (Fall 1980): 247–73.

———. *Valley Forge: Crucible of Victory.* Monmouth Beach, NJ: Philip Freneau Press, 1969.

Rees, John U. " . . . The Multitude of Women: An Examination of the Numbers of Female Camp Followers with the Continental Army." *The Brigade Dispatch: Journal of the Brigade of the American Revolution* 23:4 (Fall 1992): 5–17; 24:1 (Winter 1993): 6–16; 24:2 (Spring 1993): 2–6.

———. " . . . The Number of Rations Issued to Women in the Camp: New Material Concerning Female Followers with Continental Regiments." *The Brigade Dispatch: Journal of the Brigade of the American Revolution* 28:1 (Spring 1998): 2–10; and 28:2 (Summer 1998): 2–14.

———. "The Proportion of Women Which Ought to Be Allowed . . . :An Overview of Continental Army Female Camp Followers." *The Continental Soldier (Journal of the Continental Line)* 8:3 (Spring 1995): 51–58. http://www.revwar75.com/library/rees/proportion.htm.

Saffell, W. R. T. *Records of the Revolutionary War: Containing the Military and Financial Correspondence of Distinguished Officers.* 3rd ed. Baltimore: C. C. Saffell, 1894. Facsimile reprint, Bowie, MD: Heritage Books, 1999.

Sarah Osborn Benjamin Revolutionary War Pension and Bounty-Land Warrant Application File. Publication #M804, W 4558, National Archives. http://www.

footnote.com/image/25753131/Pension%7cRevolutionary%7csarahs%7ccosbor
n%7cWar%7crevolutionaries%7cwars%7cpensions%7csarah/#25753137.

Seidel, John Lewis. "The Archaeology of the American Revolution: A Reappraisal and Case Study at the Continental Artillery Cantonment of 1778–1779, Pluckemin, New Jersey." Vol. 1. Dissertation, University of Pennsylvania, 1987.

Sherman, Andrew M. *Historic Morristown, New Jersey: The Story of Its First Century.* Morristown, NJ: Howard Publishing Company, 1905.

Smith, Paul H., ed. *Letters of Delegates to Congress, 1774–1789.* Vol. 10. Washington, DC: Library of Congress, 1977.

Sobol, Donald J., ed. *An American Revolutionary War Reader.* New York: F. Watts, 1964.

Sparks, Jared. *The Life of George Washington.* New York: Perkins Book Company, 1902.

Stegeman, John F., and Janet A. Stegeman. *Caty: A Biography of Catharine Littlefield Greene.* Athens: University of Georgia Press, 1977.

Steiner, Franklin. "George Washington, the Vestryman Who Was Not a Communicant." In *The Religious Beliefs of Our Presidents: From Washington to F.D.R.* Amherst, NY: Prometheus Books, 1995.

"Story of Emily Geiger's Ride Refuted." *South Carolina Historical and Genealogical Magazine* 1:1 (January 1900): 90–91.

Stoudt, John Joseph. *Ordeal at Valley Forge: A Day-by-Day Chronicle from December 17, 1777, to June 18, 1778.* Philadelphia: University of Pennsylvania Press, 1963.

Svejda, George J. *Quartering, Disciplining, and Supplying the Army at Morristown, 1779–1780.* Washington, DC: Division of History, Office of Archeology and Historic Preservation, 1970.

Thacher, James. *Military Journal of the American Revolution, from the Commencement to the Disbanding of the American Army.* Hartford, CT: Hurlbut, Williams & Co, 1823, 1861, 1862.

———. *Military Journal of the American Revolution, 1775–1783.* Gansevoort, NY: Corner House Historical Publications, 1998.

Trask, Israel. "Revolutionary War Pension and Bounty-Lane Warrant Application Files." Massachusetts, Publication # M804. S. 30171, National Archives. http://www.footnote.com/image/19356582/Revolutionary%7cIsrael%20Trask%7cWar%7crevolutionaries%7cwars/#19356568.

Treadway, Sandra Gioia. "Anna Maria Lane: An Uncommon Soldier of the American Revolution." *Virginia Cavalcade* 37:3 (Winter 1988): 134–41.

Trussell, John B. B., Jr. *Birthplace of an Army: A Study of the Valley Forge Encampment.* Harrisburg: Pennsylvania Historical and Museum Commission, 1998.

"Some Unpublished Revolutionary Manuscripts." *Proceedings of the New Jersey Historical Society* 2:13 (May 1894): 79–88.

U.S. Continental Army, Second New Jersey Regiment. *Parole: Quebec — Countersign, Ticonderoga: Second New Jersey Regimental Orderly Book, 1776.* Edited by Doyen Salsig. Rutherford, NJ: Fairleigh Dickinson Press, 1980.

Valentine, Alan. *Lord Stirling.* New York: Oxford University Press, 1969.

Vermeule, Cornelius C. "Numbers of Soldiers in the Revolution." *Proceedings of the New Jersey Historical Society* 7:3 (July 1922): 223–27.

Wade, Herbert T., and Robert A. Lively. *This Glorious Cause: The Adventures of Two Company Officers in Washington's Army.* Princeton, NJ: Princeton University, 1958.

Walker, Paul K. *Engineers of Independence: A Documentary History of the Army Engineers in the American Revolution, 1775–1783.* Washington, DC: Historical Division, Office of the Chief of Engineers, 1981.

Warren, Mercy Otis. *History of the Rise, Progress, and Termination of the American Revolution: Interspersed with Biographical, Political, and Moral Observations.* 2 vols. Indianapolis: Liberty Classics, 1988.

Washington, George. *The Diaries of George Washington.* Edited by Donald Jackson and Dorothy Twohig. Vol. 5. Charlottesville: University Press of Virginia, 1979.

———. *The George Washington Papers at the Library of Congress, 1741–1799.* Library of Congress, Washington, DC. http://memory.loc.gov/ammem/gwhtml/gw home.html.

———. *The Papers of George Washington, Digital Edition.* Edited by Theodore J. Crackel. 2007. http://rotunda.upress.virginia.edu:8080/pgwde/dflt.xqy?mode= menu&keys=menu-info-home-public.

———. *The Papers of George Washington, Retirement Series.* Edited by Dorothy Twohig. Vol. 3. Charlottesville: University Press of Virginia, 1999.

———. *The Papers of George Washington, Revolutionary War Series.* Edited by Philander D. Chase. Vols. 2, 5. Charlottesville: University Press of Virginia, 1987, 1993.

———. *The Writings of George Washington from the Original Manuscript Sources, 1745–1799.* Edited by John C. Fitzpatrick. Vols. 1–10. Washington, DC: U.S. Government Printing Office, 1931–33.

Washington, Martha. *Worthy Partner: The Papers of Martha Washington.* Compiled by Joseph E. Fields. Westport, CT: Greenwood Press, 1994.

Watson, John F. *The Annals of Philadelphia.* Philadelphia: E. L. Carey & A. Hart, 1830.

Weedon, George. *Valley Forge Orderly Book of General George Weedon of the Continental Army under Command of General George Washington, in the Campaign of 1777–8.* New York: Dodd, Mead, 1902.

Weems, Mason L. *The Life of Washington.* Edited by Marcus Cunliffe. Cambridge, MA: Belknap Press, 1962.

Weintraub, Stanley. *General Washington's Christmas Farewell: A Mount Vernon Homecoming, 1783.* New York: Free Press, 2003.

Wildes, Harry Emerson. *Valley Forge.* New York: Macmillan Co., 1938.

Wister, Sally. *Sally Wister's Journal, a True Narrative.* Edited by Albert Cook Myers. Philadelphia: Ferris & Leach, 1902.

Wood, Gordon S. *The American Revolution: A History.* New York: Modern Library, 2002.

Woodman, Henry. *History of Valley Forge.* Oaks, PA: J. U. Francis Sr., 1921.

Young, Alfred F. *Masquerade: The Life and Times of Deborah Sampson, Continental Soldier.* New York: Vintage Books, 2004.

Index

About the Author

Nancy K. Loane, Ed.D., researches, writes, and speaks on the women—and the very special ladies—who came to the famous 1777–78 Valley Forge encampment. A former seasonal park ranger at Valley Forge National Historical Park, she currently serves as a volunteer costumed interpreter at the park. She is a founding member of the American Revolution Round Table of Philadelphia, an honorary lifetime member of the Society of the Descendents of Washington's Army at Valley Forge, and an officer in the Friends of Valley Forge Park. A former Pennsylvania Commonwealth speaker, she has appeared in documentaries about Valley Forge and commentaries about the encampment.

Dr. Loane has combed hundreds of primary documents and visited numerous libraries and historic sites to gather material for *Following the Drum: Women at the Valley Forge Encampment.* She and her husband live in Valley Forge.